סדר תפלות ישראל

The Union Prayer=Book

for

Jewish Worship.

PART II

EDITED AND PUBLISHED

BY

THE CENTRAL CONFERENCE OF AMERICAN RABBIS

NEW YORK
BLOCH PUBLISHING CO., Sole Agents
1918

COPYRIGHT 1894
BY
THE CENTRAL CONFERENCE OF AMERICAN RABBIS

PART II

NEW YEAR'S DAY
DAY OF ATONEMENT.

CONTENTS

Scriptural Selections for Silent Devotion....... 5
Evening Service for the New Year............ 11
Morning Service for the New Year............ 37
Evening Service for the Day of Atonement..... 87
Morning Service for the Day of Atonement.... 123
Afternoon Service for the Day of Atonement.... 205
Memorial Service........................... 291
Concluding Service for the Day of Atonement.. 309

SCRIPTURAL SELECTIONS.

For Silent Reading.

THE Lord is nigh unto all that call upon Him, to all that call upon Him in truth.

[Psalm cxlv, 18.]

The Lord is full of compassion and mercy; long-suffering, and of great goodness. For as the heaven is high above the earth, so great is His kindness toward them that fear Him.

[Psalm ciii, 8, 11.]

Yet now saith the Lord: turn ye unto me with all your heart; rend your hearts, and not your garments, and turn unto the Lord, your God, for He is gracious and merciful, slow to anger, and of great kindness.

[Joel II, 12-13.]

For this commandment which I command thee this day, is not hidden from thee, neither is it far off. It is not in heaven, that thou shouldst say, who shall go up for us to heaven, and bring it unto us, that we may hear it, and do it? Neither is it beyond the sea, that thou shouldst say, who shall go over the sea for us, and bring it unto us, that we may hear it, and do it? But the word is very nigh unto thee, in thy mouth, and in thy heart, that thou mayest do it.

See, I have set before thee this day life and good, and death and evil; in that I command thee this day, to love the Lord thy God, to walk in His ways, and to keep His commandments, and His statutes, and His judgments, that thou mayest live, and the Lord thy God shall bless thee.

[Deuteronomy xxx, 11-16.]

Lead me in Thy truth, and teach me; for Thou art the God of my help. Cause me to know Thy ways, O Lord; teach me Thy paths!

[Psalm xxv, 4-5.]

Teach me to do Thy will; for Thou art my God! Let Thy good spirit lead me in a plain path. Quicken me, O Lord, for Thy name's sake! In Thy righteousness bring my soul out of distress.

[Psalm cxliii, 10-11.]

Search me, O God! and know my heart; try me, and know my thoughts; and see if there be any wicked way in me, and lead me in the way everlasting.

[Psalm cxxxix, 23-24.]

Send out Thy light and Thy truth; let them lead me; let them bring me to Thy holy mountain, and to Thy habitation.

[Psalm xliii, 3.]

He that planted the ear, shall He not hear? He that formed the eye, shall He not see? He that chastiseth nations, shall He not correct? He that teacheth man knowledge, shall He not know? The Lord knoweth the thoughts of men, that they are vanity. Blessed is the man, whom Thou chastisest, O Lord, and teachest him out of Thy law; that Thou mayest give him rest in the days of adversity.

[Psalm xciv, 9-12.]

He healeth the broken in heart, and bindeth up their wounds. He counteth the number of the stars; He calleth them all by their names. The Lord lifteth up the meek. He casteth the wicked down to the ground.

[Psalm cxlvii, 3-6.]

Blessed is he that considereth the poor; the Lord will uphold him in the time of trouble. The Lord will preserve him, and keep him alive; and he shall be blessed upon the earth.

[Psalm xli, 2-3.]

Thus saith the Lord: Keep ye judgment and do justice, for my salvation is near to come, and my righteousness to be revealed. Blessed is the man that doeth this, and the son of man that layeth hold of it; that keepeth the Sabbath and profaneth it not, and keepeth his hand from doing evil. The strangers, also, that join themselves to the Lord to serve Him, to love the name of the Lord, and to be His servants, them will I bring to my holy mountain, and I will make them rejoice in my house of prayer: for my house shall be called a house of prayer for all nations.

[Isaiah lvi, 1-2, 6-7.]

Return unto the Lord and forsake thy sins; make thy prayer before His face. Turn again to the Most High, and turn away from iniquity, for He will lead thee out of darkness into the way of light. As a drop of water unto the sea, and as a grain of sand, so are a thousand years to the days of eternity. Therefore is God patient with men and poureth forth His mercy

upon them. The mercy of man is toward his neighbor; but the mercy of the Lord is upon all flesh. He reproveth, and chasteneth, and teacheth, and bringeth again as a shepherd his flock.

[Ben Sirach.]

Prayer is the purest service which the heart can offer unto God. The gates of repentance are always open.

When thou prayest lift up not alone thy voice but also thy heart unto God. Before thou prayest, examine thy heart, whether a devout spirit animate thee.

Prayer without devotion is a body without a soul. When thou prayest turn thine eyes toward the earth, but let thy heart be turned toward heaven.

God will surely hear the prayer of him who prayeth for others, though he himself may stand in need of divine mercy.

Though all other prayers should cease, the prayer of thanksgiving shall never cease.

Be thou as God-fearing in secret as thou seemest in public, always acknowledging the truth and harboring the truth in thy heart. Say every morning: Lord of the world, not in reliance upon mine own righteousness, but trusting in Thine infinite mercy do I make supplication unto Thee.

"Kind and just is the Lord, therefore showeth He to sinners the way;" He is kind because He is just— He is just because He is kind.

"Thou shalt love thy neighbor as thyself;" this is the chief commandment of the Torah.

[Talmud.]

New Year's Day.

Evening Service for the New Year.

Choir:

[Psalm cxxi.]

I lift mine eyes unto the hills; whence cometh my help? My help cometh from the Lord, who made heaven and earth. He will not suffer thy foot to stumble; thy guardian doth not slumber. Behold, the guardian of Israel, He slumbereth not, and He sleepeth not. The Lord is thy guardian; the Lord is thy shade at thy right hand. The sun shall not smite thee by day, nor the moon by night. The Lord shall preserve thee from all evil; He will preserve thy soul. The Lord will watch over thy going out, and thy coming in, from this time forth and for evermore.

אֶשָּׂא עֵינַי אֶל הֶהָרִים. מֵאַיִן יָבֹא עֶזְרִי: עֶזְרִי מֵעִם יְיָ. עֹשֵׂה שָׁמַיִם וָאָרֶץ: אַל־יִתֵּן לַמּוֹט רַגְלֶךָ. אַל־יָנוּם שֹׁמְרֶךָ: הִנֵּה לֹא־יָנוּם וְלֹא יִישָׁן שׁוֹמֵר יִשְׂרָאֵל: יְיָ שֹׁמְרֶךָ. יְיָ צִלְּךָ עַל יַד יְמִינֶךָ: יוֹמָם הַשֶּׁמֶשׁ לֹא יַכֶּכָּה. וְיָרֵחַ בַּלָּיְלָה: יְיָ יִשְׁמָרְךָ מִכָּל רָע. יִשְׁמֹר אֶת נַפְשֶׁךָ: יְיָ יִשְׁמָר־צֵאתְךָ וּבוֹאֶךָ. מֵעַתָּה וְעַד עוֹלָם:

11

EVENING SERVICE FOR THE NEW YEAR.

Minister:

HEAVENLY Father! In the twilight of the vanishing year we lift up our hearts to Thee to thank Thee for all the benefits which we have received at Thy hand in the past, and to implore Thy guidance and Thy blessing for the future. Thy providence has watched over our lives and over the lives of those dear to us. In affliction Thou hast strengthened us, and in sorrow Thou hast comforted us. Thou hast brightened our lives with the joys of home and of friendship. Thy loving-kindness has provided abundantly for our wants, and has enabled us to give of our bounty to the poor.

And as we thank Thee for the joys of life, even so do we praise Thee for its sorrows. Many a tear has furrowed our cheeks; many a tender tie has been severed by the hand of death; but Thou dost not willingly afflict Thy children. With a father's love hast Thou disciplined us, that we might turn unto Thee.

May we listen to the solemn admonition of this hour. May we, as we grow older in years, grow stronger in wisdom, broader in charity and truer to the noblest aspirations of heart and mind.

Hidden from our gaze, O God, are the events of the future. But we trust in Thee and fear not. Open unto us in mercy the portals of the new year, and grant us life and health, prosperity and joy, knowledge and peace. Amen.

Alternate Reading for Minister and Congregation

(Psalm xci.)

HE who dwelleth under the shelter of the Most High will abide in the shadow of the Almighty.

I say to the Lord, Thou art my refuge and my fortress; my God, in whom I trust.

Surely He will deliver thee from the snare of the fowler, and from the wasting pestilence;

He will cover thee with His pinions, and under His wings shalt thou find refuge; His faithfulness shall be thy shield and buckler.

Thou shalt not be afraid of the terror of the night, nor of the arrow that flieth by day;

Nor, the pestilence that walketh in darkness, nor of the plague that destroyeth at noonday.

Because thou hast made the Lord thy refuge, and the Most High thy habitation:

No evil shall befall thee, nor any plague come near thy dwelling.

For He will give His angels charge over thee, to guard thee in all thy ways.

Because he loveth me, I will deliver him; I will set him on high, because he knoweth my name.

When he calleth upon me, I will answer him; I will be with him in trouble;

I will deliver him, and bring him to honor.

With long life will I satisfy him, and show him my salvation.

EVENING SERVICE FOR THE NEW YEAR.

(Congregation standing.)

Minister:

Praise ye the Lord, to whom all praise is due!

Choir and Congregation:

Praised be the Lord from this time forth and forever.

(Congregation sitting.)

Minister:

PRAISE be unto Thee, O Eternal, Ruler of the world, at whose words the shades of evening fall, and by whose will the gates of morn are opened. Thy wisdom established the changes of times and seasons, and ordered the ways of the stars in their heavenly courses. Creator of day and night, Lord of hosts is Thy name. Thou, ever-living God, wilt rule over us forever. Praise be unto Thee, O God, for the day and its work and for the night and its rest.

Infinite as is Thy power, even so is Thy Love. Thou didst manifest it unto Israel, Thy servant. By laws and commandments, by statutes and ordinances hast Thou led us into the way of righteousness and brought us to the light of truth. Therefore, at our lying down and our rising up we meditate on Thy teachings and, at all times, rejoice in Thy laws. In them is true life and length of days. O, that Thy love may never depart from our hearts. Praise be to Thee, O God, who hast revealed Thy love unto Israel.

EVENING SERVICE FOR THE NEW YEAR.

(Congregation standing.)

Minister:

בָּרְכוּ אֶת יְיָ הַמְבֹרָךְ:

Choir and Congregation:

בָּרוּךְ יְיָ הַמְבֹרָךְ לְעוֹלָם וָעֶד:

(Congregation sitting.)

Minister:

בָּרוּךְ אַתָּה יְיָ אֱלֹהֵינוּ מֶלֶךְ הָעוֹלָם. אֲשֶׁר בִּדְבָרוֹ מַעֲרִיב עֲרָבִים. בְּחָכְמָה פּוֹתֵחַ שְׁעָרִים. וּבִתְבוּנָה מְשַׁנֶּה עִתִּים וּמַחֲלִיף אֶת הַזְמַנִּים. וּמְסַדֵּר אֶת הַכּוֹכָבִים בְּמִשְׁמְרוֹתֵיהֶם בָּרָקִיעַ כִּרְצוֹנוֹ. בּוֹרֵא יוֹם וָלָיְלָה. יְיָ צְבָאוֹת שְׁמוֹ. אֵל חַי וְקַיָּם תָּמִיד יִמְלֹךְ עָלֵינוּ לְעוֹלָם וָעֶד. בָּרוּךְ אַתָּה יְיָ הַמַּעֲרִיב עֲרָבִים:

אַהֲבַת עוֹלָם בֵּית יִשְׂרָאֵל עַמְּךָ אָהָבְתָּ. תּוֹרָה וּמִצְוֹת חֻקִּים וּמִשְׁפָּטִים אוֹתָנוּ לִמַּדְתָּ. עַל כֵּן יְיָ אֱלֹהֵינוּ בְּשָׁכְבֵּנוּ וּבְקוּמֵנוּ נָשִׂיחַ בְּחֻקֶּיךָ. וְנִשְׂמַח בְּדִבְרֵי תוֹרָתֶךָ וּבְמִצְוֹתֶיךָ לְעוֹלָם וָעֶד. כִּי הֵם חַיֵּינוּ וְאֹרֶךְ יָמֵינוּ. וּבָהֶם נֶהְגֶּה יוֹמָם וָלָיְלָה. וְאַהֲבָתְךָ אַל תָּסִיר מִמֶּנּוּ לְעוֹלָמִים בָּרוּךְ אַתָּה יְיָ אוֹהֵב עַמּוֹ יִשְׂרָאֵל:

(Congregation standing.)

Minister, then Choir and Congregation:

Hear, O Israel, the Lord our God, the Lord is One.
Praised be His glorious name forever and ever.

(Congregation sitting.)

Minister:

THOU shalt love the Lord, thy God, with all thy heart, with all thy soul, and with all thy might. And these words, which I command thee this day, shall be in thy heart. Thou shalt teach them diligently unto thy children, and shalt speak of them when thou sittest in thy house, when thou walkest by the way, when thou liest down, and when thou risest up. Bind them as a sign upon thy hand, and let them be as frontlets between thine eyes. Write them upon the doorposts of thy house and upon thy gates.

To the end that ye may remember to do according to all my commandments and your life shall be hallowed unto the Lord. I am the Lord your God.

For Alternate Reading or Chanting:

ETERNAL truth it is that Thou alone art God, and there is none besides;

And through Thy power alone has Israel been redeemed from the hands of oppressors.

Wonders without number hast Thou wrought for us, and hast protected us to this day.

Thou hast preserved our soul for life, and hast not suffered our foot to stumble.

EVENING SERVICE FOR THE NEW YEAR. 17

(Congregation standing.)

Minister, then Choir and Congregation:

שְׁמַע יִשְׂרָאֵל יְהוָֹה אֱלֹהֵינוּ יְהוָֹה אֶחָד:

בָּרוּךְ שֵׁם כְּבוֹד מַלְכוּתוֹ לְעוֹלָם וָעֶד:

(Congregation sitting.)

Minister:

וְאָהַבְתָּ אֵת יְיָ אֱלֹהֶיךָ בְּכָל־לְבָבְךָ וּבְכָל־נַפְשְׁךָ וּבְכָל־מְאֹדֶךָ: וְהָיוּ הַדְּבָרִים הָאֵלֶּה אֲשֶׁר אָנֹכִי מְצַוְּךָ הַיּוֹם עַל־לְבָבֶךָ: וְשִׁנַּנְתָּם לְבָנֶיךָ וְדִבַּרְתָּ בָּם. בְּשִׁבְתְּךָ בְּבֵיתֶךָ וּבְלֶכְתְּךָ בַדֶּרֶךְ וּבְשָׁכְבְּךָ וּבְקוּמֶךָ: וּקְשַׁרְתָּם לְאוֹת עַל־יָדֶךָ. וְהָיוּ לְטֹטָפֹת בֵּין עֵינֶיךָ: וּכְתַבְתָּם עַל־מְזֻזוֹת בֵּיתֶךָ וּבִשְׁעָרֶיךָ: לְמַעַן תִּזְכְּרוּ וַעֲשִׂיתֶם אֶת כָּל מִצְוֹתָי וִהְיִיתֶם קְדוֹשִׁים לֵאלֹהֵיכֶם: אֲנִי יְיָ אֱלֹהֵיכֶם:

For Alternate Reading or Chanting:

אֱמֶת וֶאֱמוּנָה כָּל זֹאת וְקַיָּם עָלֵינוּ. כִּי הוּא יְיָ אֱלֹהֵינוּ וְאֵין זוּלָתוֹ. וַאֲנַחְנוּ יִשְׂרָאֵל עַמּוֹ.

הַפּוֹדֵנוּ מִיַּד מְלָכִים. מַלְכֵּנוּ הַגּוֹאֲלֵנוּ מִכַּף כָּל־הֶעָרִיצִים.

Thy love has watched over us in the night of oppression; and Thy mercy has sustained us in the hour of trial.

And now that we live in a land of freedom, may we continue to be faithful to Thee and Thy word.

May Thy love rule in the hearts of all Thy children, and Thy truth unite them in the bonds of fellowship.

Let the righteous of all nations rejoice in Thy grace, and exult in Thy justice.

O God, Thou art our refuge and our hope; we glorify Thy name now, as did our fathers in the ancient days.

Choir and Congregation:

Who is like unto Thee, O God, among the mighty? Who is like unto Thee, glorious in holiness, extolled in praises, working wonders?

God reigneth forever and ever.

Minister:

As Thou hast redeemed Israel and saved him from arms stronger than his, so mayest Thou redeem all who are oppressed and persecuted. Blessed art Thou, O God, Redeemer of Israel.

Choir:

Sing joyfully to the Lord, our Strength! Rejoice before the God of Jacob! Sound the trumpet at the new moon, at the return of our solemn feast. For this is a statute unto Israel, a law of the God of Jacob.

EVENING SERVICE FOR THE NEW YEAR. 19

הָעוֹשֶׂה גְדֹלוֹת עַד אֵין חֵקֶר. וְנִפְלָאוֹת עַד אֵין מִסְפָּר.

הַשָּׂם נַפְשֵׁנוּ בַּחַיִּים. וְלֹא נָתַן לַמּוֹט רַגְלֵנוּ.

הָעוֹשֶׂה לָנוּ נִסִּים בְּמִצְרָיִם. אוֹתֹת וּמוֹפְתִים בְּאַדְמַת בְּנֵי חָם.

וְרָאוּ בָנָיו גְּבוּרָתוֹ. שִׁבְּחוּ וְהוֹדוּ לִשְׁמוֹ.

Choir and Congregation:

מִי־כָמֹכָה בָּאֵלִים יְיָ. מִי כָּמֹכָה נֶאְדָּר בַּקֹּדֶשׁ נוֹרָא תְהִלֹּת עֹשֵׂה פֶלֶא:

Minister:

מַלְכוּתְךָ רָאוּ בָנֶיךָ. זֶה אֵלִי עָנוּ וְאָמְרוּ.

Choir and Congregation:

יְיָ יִמְלֹךְ לְעֹלָם וָעֶד:

Minister:

וְנֶאֱמַר כִּי פָדָה יְהוָֹה אֶת יַעֲקֹב וּגְאָלוֹ מִיַּד חָזָק מִמֶּנּוּ בָּרוּךְ אַתָּה יְיָ גָּאַל יִשְׂרָאֵל:

Choir:

הַרְנִינוּ לֵאלֹהִים עוּזֵּנוּ הָרִיעוּ לֵאלֹהֵי יַעֲקֹב: תִּקְעוּ בַחֹדֶשׁ שׁוֹפָר בַּכֶּסֶה לְיוֹם חַגֵּנוּ: כִּי חֹק לְיִשְׂרָאֵל הוּא. מִשְׁפָּט לֵאלֹהֵי יַעֲקֹב:

EVENING SERVICE FOR THE NEW YEAR.

Minister:

PRAISE be unto Thee, O Eternal, our God, God of Abraham, Isaac and Jacob, our fathers; great, mighty, and Most High. Thou art He who bestowest loving-kindness upon all Thy creatures, who rememberest the merits of the fathers, and bringest redemption to their descendants, for the sake of Thy name.

Remember us unto life, O Sovereign who ordainest life, and inscribe us in the book of life, for Thy sake, O God of life. Thou art our helper, our redeemer, and protector. Praise be to Thee, O God, shield of Abraham.

Thou art omnipotent, O Lord, and mighty to save. In Thy kindness Thou sustainest the living, upholdest the falling, healest the sick, and settest the captives free. Thou wilt of a surety fulfill Thy promise of immortal life unto those who sleep in the dust. Who is like unto Thee, Almighty, Author of life and death, Thou who sendest salvation.

Who is like unto Thee, Father of mercies, who rememberest Thy children unto life eternal. Praise be to Thee, O God, who hast implanted within us immortal life.

Holy art Thou, awe-inspiring is Thy name; there is no God besides Thee. The Lord of Hosts is exalted in judgment, and the Holy One is sanctified through righteousness. Be praised, O God, who rulest in holiness.

Choir:—Amen.

EVENING SERVICE FOR THE NEW YEAR. 21

Minister:

בָּרוּךְ אַתָּה יְיָ אֱלֹהֵינוּ וֵאלֹהֵי אֲבוֹתֵינוּ. אֱלֹהֵי אַבְרָהָם אֱלֹהֵי יִצְחָק וֵאלֹהֵי יַעֲקֹב. הָאֵל הַגָּדוֹל הַגִּבּוֹר וְהַנּוֹרָא. אֵל עֶלְיוֹן. גּוֹמֵל חֲסָדִים טוֹבִים. וְקֹנֵה הַכֹּל וְזוֹכֵר חַסְדֵי אָבוֹת. וּמֵבִיא גְאֻלָּה לִבְנֵי בְנֵיהֶם. לְמַעַן שְׁמוֹ בְּאַהֲבָה:

זָכְרֵנוּ לַחַיִּים. מֶלֶךְ חָפֵץ בַּחַיִּים. וְכָתְבֵנוּ בְּסֵפֶר הַחַיִּים. לְמַעַנְךָ אֱלֹהִים חַיִּים:

מֶלֶךְ עוֹזֵר וּמוֹשִׁיעַ וּמָגֵן. בָּרוּךְ אַתָּה יְיָ מָגֵן אַבְרָהָם:

אַתָּה גִבּוֹר לְעוֹלָם אֲדֹנָי. רַב לְהוֹשִׁיעַ. מְכַלְכֵּל חַיִּים בְּחֶסֶד. מְחַיֵּה הַכֹּל בְּרַחֲמִים רַבִּים. סוֹמֵךְ נוֹפְלִים וְרוֹפֵא חוֹלִים וּמַתִּיר אֲסוּרִים. וּמְקַיֵּם אֱמוּנָתוֹ לִישֵׁנֵי עָפָר. מִי כָמוֹךָ בַּעַל גְּבוּרוֹת. וּמִי דּוֹמֶה לָּךְ. מֶלֶךְ מֵמִית וּמְחַיֶּה. וּמַצְמִיחַ יְשׁוּעָה:

מִי כָמוֹךָ אַב הָרַחֲמִים. זוֹכֵר יְצוּרָיו לַחַיִּים בְּרַחֲמִים: בָּרוּךְ אַתָּה יְיָ נֹטֵעַ בְּתוֹכֵנוּ חַיֵּי עוֹלָם:

קָדוֹשׁ אַתָּה וְנוֹרָא שְׁמֶךָ. וְאֵין אֱלוֹהַּ מִבַּלְעָדֶיךָ. כַּכָּתוּב. וַיִּגְבַּהּ יְיָ צְבָאוֹת בַּמִּשְׁפָּט. וְהָאֵל הַקָּדוֹשׁ נִקְדָּשׁ בִּצְדָקָה. בָּרוּךְ אַתָּה יְיָ הַמֶּלֶךְ הַקָּדוֹשׁ:

Choir—Amen.

Alternate Reading:

[Psalm xc.]

LORD, Thou hast been our refuge in all generations. Before the mountains were brought forth, or ever Thou hadst formed the earth and the world.

Even from everlasting to everlasting Thou art God.

Thou turnest man to dust, and sayest, return ye children of man.

A thousand years in Thy sight are as yesterday when it is past, and as a watch in the night.

Thou carriest men away as with a flood, they are as a sleep.

In the morning they are like grass which groweth up.

In the morning it groweth up and flourisheth, in the evening it is cut down and withereth.

The days of our years are threescore and ten, and if by reason of strength they be four score years;

Yet is their pride but labor and sorrow; for it is soon cut off, and we fly away.

Teach us so to number our days that we may apply our hearts to wisdom.

O, satisfy us early with Thy mercy, that we may rejoice and be glad all our days.

EVENING SERVICE FOR THE NEW YEAR.

Make us glad according to the days wherein we have been afflicted, and the years wherein we have seen evil.

Let Thy work appear unto Thy servants and Thy glory unto their children.

And let the favor of the Lord, our God, be upon us, and establish Thou the work of our hands.

Yea, the work of our hands, establish Thou it.

Minister:

SOVEREIGN of the world, great and holy God! In Thy hand are our lives and our destinies. Thine infinite wisdom ruleth the myriads of worlds. Thou encompassest all eternity. From Thee come life and health, riches and honor. Thou girdest the feeble with strength and endowest the despondent with new courage. We have assembled before Thee to thank Thee for the life which Thou hast vouchsafed unto us, and for the manifold gifts of Thy grace, with which Thou hast enriched us in the year that has passed; and standing now at the threshold of a new year, we beseech Thee to grant us life and sustenance, contentment and peace. In Thy fatherly love Thou hast sustained and shielded us in times of peril and trouble; blessings and joys, without number, didst Thou bestow upon us.

We extol Thy power, O God, when we look back to-night upon the ages during which Thou hast led Israel and hast ever been our guardian and shield.

Thy benign grace was our protection against every oppression; in whatever land we dwelt, Thy voice rebuked the mighty: Touch not mine anointed, and do my prophets no harm. For I am the Lord who changeth not, nor shall these my witnesses ever cease before me! We thank Thee, O Lord, that Thou hast sent deliverance unto the captives, and that a new light has dawned upon those that dwelt in darkness. Thy kindness has been exceedingly great unto us, whose lines have fallen in pleasant places. We thank Thee for the blessings of liberty and of justice that abound in our land. Thou hast knit our souls together by bonds of love, by zeal for Thy truth, and so we know that we have not toiled in vain. Grant Thy protection to our country and our nation in the year that now begins; enrich it with Thy goodness, so that it may be a year of life and health, of peace and concord, a year of contentment and plenty unto all Thy children. Create in us a pure heart, O God, and a right spirit renew Thou within us. Let the light of Thy truth shine upon us, that we may consecrate our lives to Thy service. Comfort those that are burdened with sorrow, and proclaim a year of peace and good-will to all the ends of the earth, that hatred and strife may forever cease. May justice be the fortress of every land, and righteousness the protecting wall of every city. Hear our prayer, O Father; in Thee alone we trust, for Thou art **our rock and our redeemer.** Amen.

EVENING SERVICE FOR THE NEW YEAR. 25

Choir:

The Lord is my light and my salvation, whom shall I fear? The Lord is the strength of my life, of whom shall I be afraid? Wait on the Lord! Be of good cheer; He shall strengthen your heart. Wait on the Lord!

Minister:

ובכן תן פחדך

OUR God, and God of our fathers! May Thy presence be manifest to us in all Thy works, and may reverence for Thee fill the hearts of all Thy creatures; may all the children of men bow before Thee in humility and unite to do Thy will with perfect hearts, and all acknowledge that Thine is the kingdom, the power and the majesty, and that Thy name is exalted above all.

Grant hope, O Lord, to them that seek Thee; inspire with courage all who wait for Thee, and be nigh unto all who trust in Thy name; that all men may walk in the light of Thy truth, and recognize that they are children of One Father, that One God has created them all. Then shall the just rejoice and the righteous be glad; then shall iniquity be no more and all men will render homage to Thee alone as their God and King.

Eternal, our God, may Thy kingdom come speedily, and the worship of Thy name and obedience to Thy law unite all men in the bonds of brotherhood and peace. that every creature may know that Thou hast created it, and every living being exclaim: The Eternal, the God of Israel, ruleth and His dominion endureth forever.

Choir:—Amen.

אתה בחרתנו

We render thanks unto Thee that Thou hast chosen our fathers from amongst all nations. Thou hast called us to Thy service, that through Israel Thy holy name may be known over all the earth. In Thy love hast Thou given us this Day of Memorial that we may remember that from day to day we are under Thy dispensation. Thou art our hope and our staff in times of trial, and trusting in Thy love, we shall resignedly accept whatever Thou mayest send unto us. May we ever remember the piety of our forefathers and the self-sacrifice with which they surrendered their possessions, yea, their very lives to the glory of Thy name. May we emulate their example in that we consecrate ourselves to Thy service and labor with all our powers for the welfare of our fellow-men. O sanctify us through Thy commandments, and enlighten us by Thy law. Satisfy us with Thy goodness and gladden us with Thy help. May we serve Thee in truth, for Thou, O God, art truth, and Thy word endureth forever. Blessed be Thou, O God, Ruler of the world, who sanctifiest Israel, and the Day of Memorial.

Choir:—Amen.

EVENING SERVICE FOR THE NEW YEAR.

Minister:

שים שלום

GRANT us peace, Thy most precious gift, O Thou eternal source of peace, and enable Israel to be a messenger of peace unto the peoples of the earth. Bless our country that it may ever be a stronghold of peace, and be its advocate in the councils of nations. May contentment reign within its borders, health and happiness within its homes. Strengthen the bonds of friendship and fellowship between all the inhabitants of our land. Plant virtue in every soul and may love of Thy name hallow every home and every heart.

Inscribe us in the book of life, and grant unto us a year of prosperity and joy. Blessed be Thou, O Lord, Giver of peace. Amen.

Silent Devotion:

אלהי נצור

O GOD, guard my tongue from evil and my lips from uttering deceit. Be my support when grief silences my voice, and my comfort when woe bends my spirit. Plant humility in my soul, and strengthen my heart with perfect faith in Thee. Help me to be strong when temptations and trials come, and to be meek when others wrong me, that I may readily forgive them. Guide me by the light of Thy counsel, and let me ever find rest in Thee, who art my Refuge and my Redeemer. Amen.

HYMN.

INTO the tomb of ages past
  Another year hath now been cast;
Shall time unheeded take its flight,
Nor leave one ray of higher light,
That on man's pilgrimage may shine,
And lead his soul to spheres divine?

With firm resolve your bosoms nerve.
The God of right alone to serve;
Speech, thought, and act to regulate,
By what His perfect laws dictate;
Nor from His holy precepts stray,
By worldly idols lured away.

Peace to the house of Israel!
May joy within it ever dwell!
May sorrow on the opening year,
Forgetting its accustomed tear,
With smiles again fond kindred meet,
With hopes revived the festal greet!

Minister, then Congregation.

OUR Father, our King, grant unto us a year of happiness.

    Choir:—Amen.

Our Father, our King, have mercy upon us and upon our children.

    Choir:—Amen.

Our Father, our King, keep far from our country, sickness, war and famine.

    Choir:—Amen.

Our Father, our King, help us to lead a life of purity and goodness.

    Choir:—Amen.

Our Father, our King, accept with mercy and with favor our supplications.

    Choir:—Amen.

ADORATION.

(Congregation standing.)

Minister:

LET us adore the ever-living God, and render praise unto Him who spread out the heavens and established the earth, whose glory is revealed in the heavens above and whose greatness is manifest throughout the world: He is our God, and there is none else.

We bow our head and bend our knee and magnify the King of kings, the Holy One, the Ever-blest.

Choir and Congregation:

וַאֲנַחְנוּ כֹּרְעִים וּמִשְׁתַּחֲוִים וּמוֹדִים לִפְנֵי מֶלֶךְ מַלְכֵי הַמְּלָכִים הַקָּדוֹשׁ בָּרוּךְ הוּא:

(Congregation sitting.)

Minister:

May the time not be far, O God, when Thy name shall be worshiped over all the earth, when unbelief shall disappear and error be no more. We fervently pray that the day may come upon which all men shall invoke Thy name, when corruption and evil shall give way to purity and goodness; when superstition shall no longer enslave the minds, nor idolatry blind the eyes, when all inhabitants of the earth shall perceive that to Thee alone every knee must bend and every tongue give homage. O may all, created in Thine image, recognize that they are brethren, so that they, one in spirit, and one in fellowship, may be forever united before Thee. Then shall Thy king-

EVENING SERVICE FOR THE NEW YEAR.

dom be established on earth, and the word of Thine ancient seer be fulfilled: The Eternal shall rule forever and aye.

Congregation:

On that day the Eternal shall be One, and His name shall be One.

Minister:

ALL you who mourn the loss of loved ones, and, at this hour, remember the goodness, the hope and the sweet companionship that have passed away with them, give ear to the word of comfort spoken to you in the ame of your God. Only the body has died and has been laid in the dust. The spirit lives and will live on forever in the land of undisturbed peace and perfect happiness. But in this life, also, the loved ones continue in the remembrance of those to whom they were precious. Every act of goodness they performed, every true and beautiful word they spoke, is treasured up as an incentive to walk in the path of goodness.

And when you ask in your grief: Whence shall come my help and my comfort? then, in the strength of faith, answer with the Psalmist: "My help cometh from God," who will not forsake me, nor leave me in my grief. Upon Him I cast my burden, and He will grant me strength according to the days He has apportioned to me. All souls are His, and no power can take them out of His hands. Come, then, and in the midst of sympathizing fellow-worshipers, rise, and hallow with me the name of God.

(The mourners standing and speaking with the Minister.)

EXTOLLED and hallowed be the name of God throughout the world which He has created, and which He governs according to His righteous will. Just is He in all His ways, and wise are all His decrees. May His Kingdom come, and His will be done in all the earth.

Congregation:

Blessed be the Lord of life and righteous Judge forever more.

Minister:

To the departed whom we now remember, may peace and bliss be granted in the world of eternal life. There may they find grace and mercy before the Lord of heaven and earth. May their souls rejoice in that ineffable good which God has laid up for those that fear Him, and may their memory be a blessing unto those that cherish it.

Congregation:

Amen.

Minister:

May the Father of peace send peace to all troubled souls, and comfort all the bereaved among us.

Congregation:

Amen.

EVENING SERVICE FOR THE NEW YEAR.

(The mourners standing and speaking with the Minister.)

יִתְגַּדַּל וְיִתְקַדַּשׁ שְׁמֵהּ רַבָּא. בְּעָלְמָא דִי־בְרָא כִרְעוּתֵהּ. וְיַמְלִיךְ מַלְכוּתֵהּ. בְּחַיֵּיכוֹן וּבְיוֹמֵיכוֹן וּבְחַיֵּי דְכָל בֵּית יִשְׂרָאֵל. בַּעֲגָלָא וּבִזְמַן קָרִיב. וְאִמְרוּ אָמֵן:

Congregation:

יְהֵא שְׁמֵהּ רַבָּא מְבָרַךְ. לְעָלַם וּלְעָלְמֵי עָלְמַיָּא.

Minister:

יִתְבָּרַךְ וְיִשְׁתַּבַּח וְיִתְפָּאַר וְיִתְרוֹמַם וְיִתְנַשֵּׂא וְיִתְהַדָּר וְיִתְעַלֶּה וְיִתְהַלָּל שְׁמֵהּ דְּקוּדְשָׁא. בְּרִיךְ הוּא. לְעֵלָּא מִן כָּל בִּרְכָתָא וְשִׁירָתָא. תֻּשְׁבְּחָתָא וְנֶחֱמָתָא. דַּאֲמִירָן בְּעָלְמָא. וְאִמְרוּ אָמֵן:

עַל יִשְׂרָאֵל וְעַל צַדִּיקַיָּא. וְעַל־כָּל־מַן דְּאִתְפְּטַר מִן עָלְמָא הָדֵין כִּרְעוּתֵהּ דֶּאֱלָהָא. יְהֵא לְהוֹן שְׁלָמָא רַבָּא וְחוּלָקָא טָבָא לְחַיֵּי עָלְמָא דְּאָתֵי. וְחִסְדָּא וְרַחֲמֵי מִן־קֳדָם מָרֵא שְׁמַיָּא וְאַרְעָא. וְאִמְרוּ אָמֵן:

יְהֵא שְׁלָמָא רַבָּא מִן־שְׁמַיָּא וְחַיִּים. עָלֵינוּ וְעַל־כָּל־יִשְׂרָאֵל. וְאִמְרוּ אָמֵן:

עֹשֶׂה שָׁלוֹם בִּמְרוֹמָיו. הוּא יַעֲשֶׂה שָׁלוֹם עָלֵינוּ וְעַל כָּל־יִשְׂרָאֵל. וְאִמְרוּ אָמֵן:

CLOSING HYMN.

THE Lord of all did reign supreme
  Ere yet this world was made and formed.
When all was finished by His will,
Then was His name as King proclaimed.

And should these forms no more exist,
He still will rule in majesty.
He was, He is, He shall remain;
His glory never shall decrease.

And one is He, and none there is
To be compared or joined to Him.
He ne'er began, and ne'er will end,
To Him belong dominion's power.

He is my God, my living God;
To Him I flee when tried in grief;
My banner high, my refuge strong,
Who hears and answers when I call.

My spirit I commit to Him,
My body, too, and all I prize,
Both, when I sleep and when I wake.
He is with me, I shall not fear.

BENEDICTION.

EVENING SERVICE FOR THE NEW YEAR.

CLOSING HYMN.

אֲדוֹן עוֹלָם אֲשֶׁר מָלַךְ. בְּטֶרֶם כָּל־יְצִיר נִבְרָא:

לְעֵת נַעֲשָׂה בְחֶפְצוֹ כֹּל. אֲזַי מֶלֶךְ שְׁמוֹ נִקְרָא:

וְאַחֲרֵי כִּכְלוֹת הַכֹּל. לְבַדּוֹ יִמְלוֹךְ נוֹרָא:

וְהוּא הָיָה וְהוּא הֹוֶה. וְהוּא יִהְיֶה בְּתִפְאָרָה:

וְהוּא אֶחָד וְאֵין שֵׁנִי. לְהַמְשִׁיל לוֹ לְהַחְבִּירָה:

בְּלִי רֵאשִׁית בְּלִי תַכְלִית. וְלוֹ הָעֹז וְהַמִּשְׂרָה:

וְהוּא אֵלִי וְחַי גֹּאֲלִי. וְצוּר חֶבְלִי בְּעֵת צָרָה:

וְהוּא נִסִּי וּמָנוֹס לִי. מְנָת כּוֹסִי בְּיוֹם אֶקְרָא:

בְּיָדוֹ אַפְקִיד רוּחִי. בְּעֵת אִישַׁן וְאָעִירָה:

וְעִם רוּחִי גְוִיָּתִי. יְיָ לִי וְלֹא אִירָא:

BENEDICTION.

PARTING BENEDICTIONS.

THE Lord our God be with us, and bless us with His peace. The favor of the Lord be upon this land from the beginning of the year even to the end thereof. Our help cometh from the Lord who made heaven and earth.

The Lord is our guardian; He will not leave us, nor forsake us. Preserve us, O God, from all evil; watch over our going out and our coming in; preserve our life and our peace, from this time forth and for ever more.

Lord, give strength unto Thy people, bless Thy people with peace. Thy peace be in our houses, that love may abound, and in this congregation, that no discord dwell among brethren. Thy peace be unto this city, unto our country, unto all men.

Praised be the Lord daily, for He hath shown us His wonderful kindness. Be of good courage; let your hearts be strong, all ye who trust in the Lord. Let all who seek Thee be glad and rejoice in Thee. Let those who love Thy protection ever rejoice in Thy help.

Morning Service for the New Year.

For Silent Devotion.

PRAISE the Lord, O my soul. I will praise the Lord as long as I live, I will sing praises to my God, while I have my being. He is God everlasting, Creator of all things in this vast universe which change according to His decrees. By His will all strength and power must some time come to naught. The mighty trees of the forest are uprooted, mountains crumble into dust. And amidst these changes ordained by Him, man does not abide. Even the strongest and wisest return unto the dust whence they came. Therefore, shall not the wise man glory in his wisdom, nor shall the mighty man glory in his might, nor shall the rich man glory in his riches; but let him that glories, glory in this, that he understands and knows God in that He is the Lord who exercises loving-kindness, judgment and righteousness. God is the giver of all good, and unto Him all praise is due. Surveying the endless ages and the countless worlds, He alone doth not change. Generation after generation shall pass away; even the sun, moon and stars shall disappear, but the Lord of hosts shall never change.

And merciful is He unto all His children. Therefore, do we turn to Him alone in our weakness, of which we become conscious when we see the heavens, the work of His hands. Then we ask: O God, what is man, that Thou rememberest him, and the son of man that Thou art mindful of him? And when our courage sinks and our own strength cannot sustain us, we look beseechingly to Thee, our Father, our help in time of need, our rock and our refuge.

As we witness changes in the world Thou hast created, even so do we experience changes in our own lives. We feel that day by day, and year by year, we are hastening ever nearer to our earthly goal. But we are sustained by the abiding hope Thou hast implanted within us, that our souls are immortal and that Thine image within us shall never die. O God, make us worthy of so great a gift; strengthen our faith in Thee and reveal Thyself to our hearts. Dispel the darkness which often hides Thy light, that we may ever know our Father in heaven. When our reason, struggling to overcome doubt and perplexity, is sorely troubled, O come Thou and help us. When, tried by sorrow, our hearts cannot feel Thy presence, O lift the clouds from us, and let us feel that Thou art nigh unto every soul that trusts in Thee.

Fervently do we supplicate Thee to strengthen and to guide us in the coming year. Vouchsafe unto us a continuance of Thy mercy. Bless the work of our hands. Sanctify the thoughts and aspirations of our minds. Surround us with Thy protection in our coming and our going, in our labor and our rest, even in the joys that gladden, and the sorrows that afflict us. Let the fulness of thy grace abide with us.

Our Father, bring nigh unto our minds the lessons of the flight of time. May this hour teach us to make good use of the days granted us here on earth. May we henceforth be stirred to greater earnestness, to greater zeal in the cause of truth, justice and charity. O God, we pray Thee, make us rich in virtue and holiness, and bring us nigh unto the fulfilment of our divine destiny. May it be Thy will to grant us life, and to help us to use it worthily. Support us through our allotted time on earth, strengthen us in our tasks and trials; sustain us amid the changing events of joy and sorrow, O Thou, who art our refuge and stay in time and eternity. May the words of our mouth and the meditations of our heart be acceptable before Thee, our rock and our redeemer. Amen.

MORNING SERVICE FOR THE NEW YEAR.

ANTHEM.

[Psalm c.]

Raise the voice of joy unto the Lord, all ye lands. Serve the Lord with gladness; come before His presence with singing. Know ye that the Eternal is God. It is He that hath made us, and we are His people, and the flock of His pasture. Enter His gates with thanksgiving, and His courts with praise; be thankful unto Him and bless His name. For the Lord is good, His mercy is everlasting; and His truth endureth to all generations.

הָרִיעוּ לַיְיָ כָּל־הָאָרֶץ: עִבְדוּ אֶת יְיָ בְּשִׂמְחָה. בֹּאוּ לְפָנָיו בִּרְנָנָה: דְעוּ כִּי יְיָ הוּא אֱלֹהִים. הוּא עָשָׂנוּ. וְלוֹ אֲנַחְנוּ. עַמּוֹ וְצֹאן מַרְעִיתוֹ: בֹּאוּ שְׁעָרָיו בְּתוֹדָה. חֲצֵרֹתָיו בִּתְהִלָּה. הוֹדוּ לוֹ בָּרְכוּ שְׁמוֹ: כִּי טוֹב יְיָ. לְעוֹלָם חַסְדּוֹ. וְעַד דֹּר וָדֹר אֱמוּנָתוֹ:

Minister:

מה טבו

HOW goodly are Thy tents, O Jacob, Thy tabernacles, O Israel. I rejoiced when they said unto me, Come, let us go unto the house of the Lord. O Lord, I love the habitation of Thy house, and the place where Thy glory dwelleth. I bend my knee before Thee, O King, and extol Thy name. Receive graciously my prayer on this Day of Remembrance.

O Thou, who weighest all the deeds of men and art acquainted with all their thoughts.

Be merciful to me, O Father, and hear my supplications, my Rock and my Redeemer.

Congregation:—Amen.

Minister:

אלהי נשמה

MY God, the soul which Thou hast given unto me came pure from Thy hands. Thou hast created it; Thou hast formed it; Thou hast breathed it into me; Thou hast preserved it in this body and, at the appointed time, Thou wilt take it from this earth that it may enter upon the life everlasting. While the soul animates my being I wil' worship Thee, Sovereign of the world and Lord of all souls. Blessed be Thou, O Lord, in whose hands are the souls of all the living and the spirits of all flesh.

אתה הוא

ALMIGHTY and merciful God, who hast called our Fathers to Thy service, and hast opened their eyes to behold Thy wondrous works and to proclaim Thy law unto all nations: Thou art the same to-day even as Thou wast at the beginning; Thou art our God in this life, and Thou art our hope and refuge in the life to come. Creator of heaven and earth, of the sea and all that is therein, Thine is all power in the heaven above and on the earth below, and none can say unto Thee: "What doest Thou?" Our heavenly Father, help us that by our lives we may sanctify Thy name before men, and testify of Thee and of Thy holy law. Praise be to Thee, who hast revealed to us Thy law of truth.

רבון כל העולמים

LORD of all the worlds! Not in reliance upon righteousness or merit in ourselves do we make our supplications to Thee, but trusting in Thine infinite mercy alone. For what are we, what is our life, what our goodness, what our power? What can we say in Thy presence? Are not all the mighty men as naught before Thee, and those of great renown as though they had never been; the wisest, as if without knowledge, and the men of understanding as if without discernment? Behold, nations are but as a drop of water, and accounted as a grain of dust in the balance. Many of our actions are vain; and our days pass away like shadows. Our life would be altogether vanity, were it not for the soul which, fashioned in Thine own image, gives us assurance of our higher destiny, and imparts to our fleeting days an abiding value.

We, therefore, beseech Thee, O our God! to help us banish from our hearts all pride and vain-glory, all confidence in worldly possessions, all self-sufficient leaning on our own reason. O give us the spirit of meekness and the grace of modesty, that we may become wise in Thy fear. May we never forget that all we have and prize is but lent to us, that we may use worthily every gift that cometh from Thee, to Thy honor, and the good of our fellow-men.

Congregation:—Amen.

נשמת כל חי

THINE alone, O Lord, is the greatness and the glory. Riches and honor come from Thee; in Thy hand are strength and power. Every living soul shall praise Thee; the spirit of all flesh shall glorify Thy name. Thou art God from everlasting to everlasting, and besides Thee there is no redeemer nor savior. Thou art the first and the last, the Lord of all generations. Thou rulest the world in kindness and all Thy creatures in mercy. Thou art our guardian who sleepeth not and slumbereth not. To Thee alone we give thanks. Yet, though our lips would overflow with song, and our tongues with joyous praise, we would still be unable to thank Thee even for a thousandth part of the bounties which Thou hast bestowed upon us and our fathers. Thou hast been our protector and our savior in every trial and peril. Thy mercy has watched over us and Thy loving-kindness has never failed us.

Praised be Thy holy name. Thou hast made Thine eternal law our portion, and hast given us a goodly heritage. Thou didst appoint us to proclaim Thy truth unto the nations and win them for Thy law of righteousness. Sanctify us for the service to which Thou hast called us, O Heavenly Father, that Thy name may be hallowed through us in all the world. Gather all Thy children around Thy banner of truth that Thy praise may resound from one end of the earth to the other, and that through Israel the entire human family may be blessed with truth and peace.

Choir:—Amen.

(Congregation standing.)

Minister:

Praise ye the Lord, to whom all praise is due!

Choir and Congregation:

Praised be the Lord from this time forth and forever.

(Congregation sitting.)

Minister:

PRAISE be to Thee, O Lord, our God, Ruler of the world, who in Thy mercy causest light to shine over the earth and all its inhabitants, and renewest daily in mercy the works of creation. How manifold are Thy works, O Eternal; in wisdom hast Thou made them all. The earth is full of Thy possessions. The heavens declare Thy glory and the firmament showeth Thy handiwork. Thou formest light and darkness, ordainest good and evil, bringest harmony into nature, and peace to the heart of man.

With love abounding hast Thou guided us, O our God, and with great compassion hast Thou borne with us. Because our fathers believed and trusted in Thee, therefore hast Thou taught them the laws of life, and shown them the way of wisdom. We beseech Thee, O merciful Father, to grant us discernment, that we may understand and fulfil all the teachings of Thy word. Make us gladly obedient to Thy commandments and fill our hearts with love and reverence for Thee. In Thee we put our trust; we rejoice and delight in Thy help; for with Thee alone is salvation. Thou hast appointed us as the teachers of

MORNING SERVICE FOR THE NEW YEAR. 45

(Congregation standing.)
Minister:

בָּרְכוּ אֶת יְיָ הַמְבֹרָךְ:

Choir and Congregation:

בָּרוּךְ יְיָ הַמְבֹרָךְ לְעוֹלָם וָעֶד:

(Congregation sitting.)
Minister:

בָּרוּךְ אַתָּה יְיָ אֱלֹהֵינוּ מֶלֶךְ הָעוֹלָם. יוֹצֵר אוֹר וּבוֹרֵא חֹשֶׁךְ. עֹשֶׂה שָׁלוֹם וּבוֹרֵא אֶת הַכֹּל:

הַמֵּאִיר לָאָרֶץ וְלַדָּרִים עָלֶיהָ בְּרַחֲמִים. וּבְטוּבוֹ מְחַדֵּשׁ בְּכָל־יוֹם תָּמִיד מַעֲשֵׂה־בְרֵאשִׁית: מָה־רַבּוּ מַעֲשֶׂיךָ יְיָ. כֻּלָּם בְּחָכְמָה עָשִׂיתָ. מָלְאָה הָאָרֶץ קִנְיָנֶךָ: תִּתְבָּרַךְ יְיָ אֱלֹהֵינוּ עַל־שֶׁבַח מַעֲשֵׂה יָדֶיךָ. וְעַל־מְאוֹרֵי־אוֹר שֶׁעָשִׂיתָ יְפָאֲרוּךָ סֶּלָה. בָּרוּךְ אַתָּה יְיָ יוֹצֵר הַמְּאוֹרוֹת:

אַהֲבָה רַבָּה אֲהַבְתָּנוּ יְיָ אֱלֹהֵינוּ. חֶמְלָה גְדוֹלָה וִיתֵרָה חָמַלְתָּ עָלֵינוּ. אָבִינוּ מַלְכֵּנוּ. בַּעֲבוּר אֲבוֹתֵינוּ שֶׁבָּטְחוּ בְךָ. וַתְּלַמְּדֵם חֻקֵּי חַיִּים. כֵּן תְּחָנֵּנוּ וּתְלַמְּדֵנוּ: הָאֵר עֵינֵינוּ בְּתוֹרָתֶךָ. וְדַבֵּק לִבֵּנוּ בְּמִצְוֹתֶיךָ. וְיַחֵד לְבָבֵנוּ לְאַהֲבָה וּלְיִרְאָה שְׁמֶךָ. וְלֹא נֵבוֹשׁ לְעוֹלָם וָעֶד: כִּי בְשֵׁם קָדְשְׁךָ בָּטָחְנוּ. נָגִילָה

Thy law; Thou hast chosen us for a holy mission unto mankind; therefore do we joyfully lift up our voices and proclaim Thy unity. Blessed be Thou, O God, who hast revealed Thy truth through Israel.

(Congregation standing.)

Minister, then Choir and Congregation:

Hear, O Israel, the Lord our God, the Lord is One.

Praised be His glorious name forever and ever.

(Congregation sitting.)

Minister:

THOU shalt love the Lord, thy God, with all thy heart, with all thy soul, and with all thy might. And these words, which I command thee this day, shall be in thy heart. Thou shalt teach them diligently unto thy children, and shalt speak of them when thou sittest in thy house, when thou walkest by the way, when thou liest down, and when thou risest up. Bind them as a sign upon thy hand, and let them be as frontlets between thine eyes. Write them upon the doorposts of thy house and upon thy gates. To the end that ye may remember and do all my commandments and be holy unto your God. I am the Lord your God.

TRUE it is that the God of all the world is our Ruler; He is the Rock of Israel, the Shield of our salvation. Unto all generations shall He alone endure, and His kingdom shall abide forever. His words are words of life and are established for all time. They are faithful and precious unto all generations.

MORNING SERVICE FOR THE NEW YEAR. 47

וְנִשְׂמְחָה בִּישׁוּעָתֶךָ. כִּי אֵל פּוֹעֵל יְשׁוּעוֹת אָתָּה.
וּבָנוּ בָחַרְתָּ וְקֵרַבְתָּנוּ לְשִׁמְךָ הַגָּדוֹל סֶלָה בֶּאֱמֶת.
לְהוֹדוֹת לְךָ וּלְיַחֶדְךָ בְּאַהֲבָה. בָּרוּךְ אַתָּה יְיָ
הַבּוֹחֵר בְּעַמּוֹ יִשְׂרָאֵל בְּאַהֲבָה:

(Congregation standing.)

Minister, then Choir and Congregation:

שְׁמַע יִשְׂרָאֵל יְהֹוָה אֱלֹהֵינוּ יְהֹוָה אֶחָד:

בָּרוּךְ שֵׁם כְּבוֹד מַלְכוּתוֹ לְעוֹלָם וָעֶד:

(Congregation sitting.)

Minister:

וְאָהַבְתָּ אֵת יְיָ אֱלֹהֶיךָ בְּכָל־לְבָבְךָ וּבְכָל־נַפְשְׁךָ
וּבְכָל־מְאֹדֶךָ: וְהָיוּ הַדְּבָרִים הָאֵלֶּה אֲשֶׁר אָנֹכִי
מְצַוְּךָ הַיּוֹם עַל־לְבָבֶךָ: וְשִׁנַּנְתָּם לְבָנֶיךָ וְדִבַּרְתָּ
בָּם. בְּשִׁבְתְּךָ בְּבֵיתֶךָ וּבְלֶכְתְּךָ בַדֶּרֶךְ וּבְשָׁכְבְּךָ
וּבְקוּמֶךָ: וּקְשַׁרְתָּם לְאוֹת עַל־יָדֶךָ. וְהָיוּ לְטֹטָפֹת
בֵּין עֵינֶיךָ: וּכְתַבְתָּם עַל־מְזֻזוֹת בֵּיתֶךָ וּבִשְׁעָרֶיךָ:
לְמַעַן תִּזְכְּרוּ וַעֲשִׂיתֶם אֶת־כָּל־מִצְוֹתָי וִהְיִיתֶם
קְדוֹשִׁים לֵאלֹהֵיכֶם: אֲנִי יְיָ אֱלֹהֵיכֶם:

אֱמֶת. אֱלֹהֵי עוֹלָם מַלְכֵּנוּ. צוּר יַעֲקֹב מָגֵן יִשְׁעֵנוּ.
לְדוֹר וָדוֹר הוּא קַיָּם וּשְׁמוֹ קַיָּם. וְכִסְאוֹ נָכוֹן
וּמַלְכוּתוֹ וֶאֱמוּנָתוֹ לָעַד קַיֶּמֶת. וּדְבָרָיו חָיִים

True it is that He is our God, our creator, and the rock of our salvation. Our redeemer and our savior is He forever, and there is no one besides, in whom we can put our trust. He is the first and the last. He has redeemed our fathers from the bondage of Egypt, and rescued them from the hand of their oppressor. Therefore did they praise and extol the Lord.

Choir and Congregation:

Who is like unto Thee, O God, among the mighty?
> Who is like unto Thee glorious in holiness, extolled in praises, working wonders?

God reigneth forever and ever.

Minister:

O Rock of Israel, be pleased to redeem them that are oppressed, and deliver them that are persecuted.

Praise be unto Thee, our redeemer, the Holy One of Israel.

Choir:—Amen.

Minister:

PRAISE be unto Thee, O Eternal, our God, God of our fathers, Abraham, Isaac and Jacob, the great, mighty, and most high God. Thou bestowest lovingkindness upon all Thy creatures; Thou rememberest the goodness of the fathers, and Thou sendest redemption to their descendants for the sake of Thy name.

Remember us unto life, O Sovereign, who ordainest life, and inscribe us in the book of life, for Thy sake,

MORNING SERVICE FOR THE NEW YEAR 49

וְקַיָּמִים. נֶאֱמָנִים וְנֶחֱמָדִים לָעַד וּלְעוֹלְמֵי עוֹלָמִים:
אֱמֶת אַתָּה הוּא רִאשׁוֹן וְאַתָּה הוּא אַחֲרוֹן.
וּמִבַּלְעָדֶיךָ אֵין לָנוּ מֶלֶךְ גּוֹאֵל וּמוֹשִׁיעַ. מִמִּצְרַיִם
גְּאַלְתָּנוּ יְיָ אֱלֹהֵינוּ. וּמִבֵּית עֲבָדִים פְּדִיתָנוּ.
עַל־זֹאת שִׁבְּחוּ אֲהוּבִים וְרוֹמְמוּ אֵל:

Choir and Congregation:

מִי־כָמֹכָה בָּאֵלִים יְיָ. מִי כָּמֹכָה נֶאְדָּר בַּקֹּדֶשׁ.
נוֹרָא תְהִלֹּת עֹשֵׂה־פֶלֶא:

Minister:

מַלְכוּתְךָ רָאוּ בָנֶיךָ. זֶה אֵלִי עָנוּ וְאָמְרוּ:

Choir and Congregation:

יְיָ יִמְלֹךְ לְעֹלָם וָעֶד:

Minister:

צוּר יִשְׂרָאֵל. קוּמָה בְּעֶזְרַת יִשְׂרָאֵל. גְּאָלֵנוּ יְיָ
צְבָאוֹת. שְׁמוֹ קְדוֹשׁ יִשְׂרָאֵל. בָּרוּךְ אַתָּה יְיָ גָּאַל
יִשְׂרָאֵל:

בָּרוּךְ אַתָּה יְיָ אֱלֹהֵינוּ וֵאלֹהֵי אֲבוֹתֵינוּ. אֱלֹהֵי
אַבְרָהָם אֱלֹהֵי יִצְחָק וֵאלֹהֵי יַעֲקֹב. הָאֵל הַגָּדוֹל
הַגִּבּוֹר וְהַנּוֹרָא. אֵל עֶלְיוֹן. גּוֹמֵל חֲסָדִים טוֹבִים.
יִקְנֶה הַכֹּל וְזוֹכֵר חַסְדֵי אָבוֹת. וּמֵבִיא גְאֻלָּה לִבְנֵי
בְנֵיהֶם. לְמַעַן שְׁמוֹ בְּאַהֲבָה:

O God of life. Thou art our helper, our redeemer and protector; praise be to Thee, O God, Shield of Abraham.

Thou art omnipotent, O Lord, and mighty to save. In Thy kindness Thou sustainest the living, upholdest the falling, healest the sick, and settest the captives free. Thou wilt of a surety fulfil Thy promise of immortal life unto those who sleep in the dust. Who is like unto Thee, Almighty, Author of life and death, Thou who sendest salvation.

Who is like unto Thee, Father of mercies, who rememberest Thy children unto life eternal. Praise be to Thee, O God, who hast implanted within us immortal life.

SANCTIFICATION.

(Congregation standing.)

We hallow Thy name on earth, even as it is hallowed in heaven; and with the prophet say in humble adoration:

Choir and Congregation:

Holy, holy, holy is the Lord of hosts, the whole earth is full of His glory.

Minister:

God our strength, God our Lord, how excellent is Thy name in all the earth.

MORNING SERVICE FOR THE NEW YEAR. 51

זָכְרֵנוּ לַחַיִּים. מֶלֶךְ חָפֵץ בַּחַיִּים. וְכָתְבֵנוּ בְּסֵפֶר הַחַיִּים. לְמַעֲנָךְ אֱלֹהִים חַיִּים:

מֶלֶךְ עוֹזֵר וּמוֹשִׁיעַ וּמָגֵן. בָּרוּךְ אַתָּה יְיָ מָגֵן אַבְרָהָם:

אַתָּה גִבּוֹר לְעוֹלָם אֲדֹנָי. רַב לְהוֹשִׁיעַ. מְכַלְכֵּל חַיִּים בְּחֶסֶד. מְחַיֶּה הַכֹּל בְּרַחֲמִים רַבִּים. סוֹמֵךְ נוֹפְלִים וְרוֹפֵא חוֹלִים וּמַתִּיר אֲסוּרִים. וּמְקַיֵּם אֱמוּנָתוֹ לִישֵׁנֵי עָפָר. מִי כָמוֹךָ בַּעַל גְּבוּרוֹת. וּמִי דּוֹמֶה־לָּךְ. מֶלֶךְ מֵמִית וּמְחַיֶּה. וּמַצְמִיחַ יְשׁוּעָה:

מִי כָמוֹךָ אַב הָרַחֲמִים. זוֹכֵר יְצוּרָיו לְחַיִּים בְּרַחֲמִים: בָּרוּךְ אַתָּה יְיָ נֹטֵעַ בְּתוֹכֵנוּ חַיֵּי עוֹלָם:

(Congregation standing.)

נְקַדֵּשׁ אֶת שִׁמְךָ בָּעוֹלָם. כְּשֵׁם שֶׁמַּקְדִּישִׁים אוֹתוֹ בִּשְׁמֵי מָרוֹם. כַּכָּתוּב עַל־יַד נְבִיאֶךָ. וְקָרָא זֶה אֶל־זֶה וְאָמַר:

Choir and Congregation.

קָדוֹשׁ קָדוֹשׁ קָדוֹשׁ יְיָ צְבָאוֹת. מְלֹא כָל־הָאָרֶץ כְּבוֹדוֹ:

Minister:

אַדִּיר אַדִּירֵנוּ יְיָ אֲדוֹנֵנוּ מָה־אַדִּיר שִׁמְךָ בְּכָל הָאָרֶץ:

Choir and Congregation:

In all places of Thy dominion Thy name is praised and glorified.

Minister:

Our God is one; He is our Father; He is our King; He is our Helper; and in His mercy He will answer our petition in the sight of all the living.

Choir and Congregation:

God will reign forever, thy God, O Zion, from generation to generation.—Hallelujah!

(Congregation sitting.)

Minister:

Holy art Thou and awe-inspiring is Thy name. There is no God beside Thee. The Lord of hosts is exalted in judgment and the Holy One is sanctified through righteousness. Praise be to Thee, O God, who rulest in holiness.

Choir:—Amen.

Minister:

SANCTIFY us, O God, through Thy commandments, and let us share the blessings of Thy law. Satisfy us with Thy goodness and gladden us with Thy help. May we serve Thee in truth; for Thou, O God, art truth, and Thy word endureth forever. Blessed be Thou, O God, Ruler of the world who sanctifiest Israel, and the Day of Memorial.

MORNING SERVICE FOR THE NEW YEAR.

Choir and Congregation:

בָּרוּךְ כְּבוֹד יְיָ מִמְּקוֹמוֹ:

Minister:

אֶחָד הוּא אֱלֹהֵינוּ. הוּא אָבִינוּ. הוּא מַלְכֵּנוּ. וְהוּא מוֹשִׁיעֵנוּ: וְהוּא יַשְׁמִיעֵנוּ בְּרַחֲמָיו לְעֵינֵי כָּל חָי:

Choir and Congregation:

יִמְלֹךְ יְיָ לְעוֹלָם אֱלֹהַיִךְ צִיּוֹן לְדֹר וָדֹר הַלְלוּיָהּ:

(Congregation sitting.)

Minister:

קָדוֹשׁ אַתָּה וְנוֹרָא שְׁמֶךָ. וְאֵין אֱלוֹהַּ מִבַּלְעָדֶיךָ. כַּכָּתוּב. וַיִּגְבַּהּ יְיָ צְבָאוֹת יְ . . . ט. וְהָאֵל הַקָּדוֹשׁ נִקְדַּשׁ בִּצְדָקָה. בָּרוּךְ אַתָּה יְיָ הַמֶּלֶךְ הַקָּדוֹשׁ:

Choir:—Amen.

Minister:

אֱלֹהֵינוּ וֵאלֹהֵי אֲבוֹתֵינוּ. קַדְּשֵׁנוּ בְּמִצְוֹתֶיךָ· וְתֵן חֶלְקֵנוּ בְּתוֹרָתֶךָ. שַׂבְּעֵנוּ מִטּוּבֶךָ. וְשַׂמְּחֵנוּ בִּישׁוּעָתֶךָ. וְטַהֵר לִבֵּנוּ לְעָבְדְּךָ בֶּאֱמֶת. כִּי אַתָּה אֱלֹהִים אֱמֶת. וּדְבָרְךָ אֱמֶת וְקַיָּם לָעַד. בָּרוּךְ אַתָּה יְיָ מֶלֶךְ עַל כָּל הָאָרֶץ. מְקַדֵּשׁ יִשְׂרָאֵל וְיוֹם הַזִּכָּרוֹן:

LOOK down with compassion, O Lord, upon Israel, Thy servant, and in Thy love accept his worship offered Thee at all times. Praise be to Thee, O Lord, whom alone we will serve in reverence.

We gratefully acknowledge, O Lord, our God, that Thou art our Creator and Preserver, the Rock of our life and the Shield of our help. We render thanks unto Thee for our lives which are in Thy hands, for our souls which are ever in Thy keeping, for Thy wondrous providence and for Thy continuous goodness, which Thou bestowest upon us day by day. Truly, Thy mercies never fail and Thy loving-kindness never ceases. Therefore in Thee do we forever put our trust.

OUR God, and God of our fathers, O may Thy blessing rest upon us, according to the gracious promise of Thy word, spoken through the priests of yore, ministering at Thy holy altar saying:

May the Lord bless thee and keep thee.

Choir:—Amen.

May the Lord let his countenance shine upon thee and be gracious unto thee.

Choir:—Amen.

May the Lord lift up His countenance upon thee and give thee peace.

Choir:—Amen.

MORNING SERVICE FOR THE NEW YEAR. 55

רְצֵה יְיָ אֱלֹהֵינוּ בְּעַמְּךָ יִשְׂרָאֵל. וְתִפְלָתָם בְּאַהֲבָה תְקַבֵּל. וּתְהִי לְרָצוֹן תָּמִיד עֲבוֹדַת יִשְׂרָאֵל עַמֶּךָ. בָּרוּךְ אַתָּה יְיָ שֶׁאוֹתְךָ לְבַדְּךָ בְּיִרְאָה נַעֲבוֹד:

מוֹדִים אֲנַחְנוּ לָךְ. שָׁאַתָּה הוּא יְיָ אֱלֹהֵינוּ וֵאלֹהֵי אֲבוֹתֵינוּ לְעוֹלָם וָעֶד. צוּר חַיֵּינוּ מָגֵן יִשְׁעֵנוּ. אַתָּה הוּא לְדוֹר וָדוֹר. נוֹדֶה לְךָ וּנְסַפֵּר תְּהִלָּתֶךָ. עַל חַיֵּינוּ הַמְּסוּרִים בְּיָדֶךָ. וְעַל נִשְׁמוֹתֵינוּ הַפְּקוּדוֹת לָךְ. וְעַל נִסֶּיךָ שֶׁבְּכָל יוֹם עִמָּנוּ. וְעַל נִפְלְאוֹתֶיךָ שֶׁבְּכָל עֵת. עֶרֶב וָבֹקֶר וְצָהֳרָיִם. הַטּוֹב כִּי לֹא כָלוּ רַחֲמֶיךָ. וְהַמְרַחֵם כִּי לֹא תַמּוּ חֲסָדֶיךָ. מֵעוֹלָם קִוִּינוּ לָךְ:

אֱלֹהֵינוּ וֵאלֹהֵי אֲבוֹתֵינוּ. בָּרְכֵנוּ בַּבְּרָכָה הַמְשֻׁלֶּשֶׁת הַכְּתוּבָה בַּתּוֹרָה:

יְבָרֶכְךָ יְיָ וְיִשְׁמְרֶךָ:

Choir:—Amen.

יָאֵר יְיָ פָּנָיו אֵלֶיךָ וִיחֻנֶּךָּ:

Choir:—Amen.

יִשָּׂא יְיָ פָּנָיו אֵלֶיךָ וְיָשֵׂם לְךָ שָׁלוֹם:

Choir:—Amen.

MORNING SERVICE FOR THE NEW YEAR.

Minister:

וּבְכֵן תֵּן פַּחְדְּךָ

OUR God, and God of our fathers! May Thy presence be manifest to us in all Thy works, and may reverence for Thee fill the hearts of all Thy creatures; may all the children of men bow before Thee in humility and unite to do Thy will with perfect hearts, and all acknowledge that Thine is the kingdom, the power and the majesty, and that Thy name is exalted above all.

Grant hope, O Lord, to them that seek Thee; inspire with courage all who wait for Thee, and be nigh unto all who trust in Thy name; that all men may walk in the light of Thy truth, and recognize that they are children of One Father, that One God has created them all. Then shall the just rejoice and the righteous be glad; then shall iniquity be no more and all men will render homage to Thee alone as their God and King.

Eternal, our God, may Thy kingdom come speedily, and the worship of Thy name and obedience to Thy law unite all men in the bonds of brotherhood and peace, that every creature may know that Thou hast created it, and every living being exclaim: The Eternal, the God of Israel, ruleth and His dominion endureth forever.

Choir:—Amen.

אתה בחרתנו

We render thanks unto Thee that Thou hast chosen our fathers from amongst all nations. Thou hast called us to Thy service, that through Israel, Thy holy name may be known over all the earth. In Thy love hast Thou given us this Day of Memorial that we may remember that from day to day we are under Thy dispensation. Thou art our hope and our staff in times of trial, and trusting in Thy love, we shall resignedly accept whatever Thou mayest send unto us. May we ever remember the piety of our forefathers and the self-sacrifice with which they surrendered their possessions, yea, their very lives to the glory of Thy name. May we emulate their example in that we consecrate ourselves to Thy service, and labor with all our powers for the welfare of our fellow-men.

Lord our God, let the whole world be enlightened by Thy law, and Thy kingdom of righteousness be established all over the earth, that all Thy creatures may serve Thee in truth, and all living beings praise Thy name forever.

Choir:—Amen.

Minister:

שים שלום

GRANT us peace, Thy most precious gift, O Thou eternal source of peace, and enable Israel to be a messenger of peace unto the peoples of the earth. Bless our country that it may ever be a stronghold of peace, and be its advocate in the councils of nations. May contentment reign within its borders, health and happiness within its homes. Strengthen the bonds of friendship and fellowship between all the inhabitants of our land. Plant virtue in every soul and may love of Thy name hallow every home and every heart.

Inscribe us in the book of life, and grant unto us a year of prosperity and joy. Blessed be Thou, O Lord, Giver of peace. Amen.

Silent Devotion:

אלהי נצור

O GOD, guard my tongue from evil and my lips from uttering deceit. Be my support when grief silences my voice, and my comfort when woe bends my spirit. Plant humility in my soul, and strengthen my heart with perfect faith in Thee. Help me to be strong when temptations and trials come, and to be meek when others wrong me, that I may readily forgive them. Guide me by the light of Thy counsel, and let me ever find rest in Thee, who art my Refuge and my Redeemer. Amen.

MORNING SERVICE FOR THE NEW YEAR.

READING OF THE SCRIPTURE.

Minister:

WHO shall ascend the hill of the Lord? and who shall stand in His holy place? He that hath clean hands and a pure heart; who hath not inclined his soul to falsehood, nor sworn deceitfully. He shall receive a blessing from the Lord, and favor from the God of his salvation. This is the generation of those that seek Thee; those that seek Thy face, O God of Israel.

[Psalm xxiv.]

Choir:

Lift up your heads, O ye gates, and be ye lifted up, ye everlasting doors, for the King of glory shall enter. Who is the King of glory? The Lord of hosts —He is the King of glory.

שְׂאוּ שְׁעָרִים רָאשֵׁיכֶם.
וּשְׂאוּ פִּתְחֵי עוֹלָם. וְיָבֹא
מֶלֶךְ הַכָּבוֹד: מִי הוּא
זֶה מֶלֶךְ הַכָּבוֹד. יְיָ
צְבָאוֹת. הוּא מֶלֶךְ
הַכָּבוֹד סֶלָה:

(Congregation standing.)

Minister, then Choir:

The Lord, the Lord God, merciful and gracious, long-suffering and abundant in goodness and ever-true; keeping mercy for thousands, forgiving iniquity, transgression and sin.

יְהֹוָה יְהֹוָה אֵל רַחוּם
יְחַנּוּן אֶרֶךְ אַפַּיִם וְרַב־
חֶסֶד וֶאֱמֶת. נֹצֵר חֶסֶד
לָאֲלָפִים נֹשֵׂא עָוֹן וָפֶשַׁע
וְחַטָּאָה:

Minister, then Congregation:

Our Father, our King, we have sinned before Thee.

Our Father, our King, none is our Lord but Thee.

Our Father, our King, renew the year unto us for good.

Our Father, our King, keep far from our country sickness, war and famine.

Our Father, our King, help us to lead a good and pure life.

Our Father, our King, O pardon and blot out our sins.

Our Father, our King, accept graciously our petitions.

Our Father, our King, O be merciful and answer us; and though we can plead no merit, deal with us according to Thy loving kindness and help us.

Choir: Amen.

(Minister takes the Scroll from the Ark, and turning to the congregation says:)

The Torah which God gave through Moses is the heritage of the house of Israel. Come ye and let us walk in the light of the Lord, that we may receive the spirit of wisdom and understanding, the spirit of counsel and strength, the spirit of knowledge and the fear of God.

Minister and Congregation:

Hear, O Israel, the Lord, our God, the Lord is One.

(Congregation sitting.)

MORNING SERVICE FOR THE NEW YEAR. 61

Minister, then Congregation.

אָבִינוּ מַלְכֵּנוּ חָטָאנוּ לְפָנֶיךָ:

אָבִינוּ מַלְכֵּנוּ אֵין לָנוּ מֶלֶךְ אֶלָּא אָתָּה:

אָבִינוּ מַלְכֵּנוּ חַדֵּשׁ עָלֵינוּ שָׁנָה טוֹבָה:

אָבִינוּ מַלְכֵּנוּ כַּלֵּה דֶּבֶר וְחֶרֶב וְרָעָב וּמַשְׁחִית מֵעָלֵינוּ:

אָבִינוּ מַלְכֵּנוּ כָּתְבֵנוּ בְּסֵפֶר חַיִּים טוֹבִים:

אָבִינוּ מַלְכֵּנוּ זָכְרֵנוּ לִגְאֻלָּה וְלִישׁוּעָה:

אָבִינוּ מַלְכֵּנוּ סְלַח וּמְחַל לְכָל עֲוֹנוֹתֵינוּ:

אָבִינוּ מַלְכֵּנוּ קַבֵּל בְּרַחֲמִים וּבְרָצוֹן אֶת תְּפִלָּתֵנוּ:

אָבִינוּ מַלְכֵּנוּ חָנֵּנוּ וַעֲנֵנוּ כִּי אֵין בָּנוּ מַעֲשִׂים עֲשֵׂה עִמָּנוּ צְדָקָה וָחֶסֶד וְהוֹשִׁיעֵנוּ:

Choir:—Amen.

(Minister takes the Scroll from the Ark, and turning to the congregation says:)

תּוֹרָה צִוָּה לָנוּ מֹשֶׁה . מוֹרָשָׁה קְהִלַּת יַעֲקֹב:

בֵּית יַעֲקֹב לְכוּ וְנֵלְכָה בְּאוֹר יְהוָה:

Minister and Congregation:

שְׁמַע יִשְׂרָאֵל יְהוָה אֱלֹהֵינוּ יְהוָה אֶחָד:

(Congregation sitting.)

Choir:

Thine, O Lord, is the greatness and the power, the glory, and the victory, and the majesty; for all that is in the heavens and in the earth is Thine, Thine is dominion, and Thou art exalted above all.

(Before reading from the Torah.)

Minister:

Blessed be Thou, O Lord, our God, Ruler of the world, who hast called Israel from amongst the nations and given him Thy Law. Praise be to Thee, O God, Giver of the Law.

[Genesis, Chapt. xxii.]

AND it came to pass after these things, that God did prove Abraham, and said unto him, Abraham! and he said, Behold, here am I. And he said, Take now thy son, thy only son Isaac, whom thou lovest, and get thee into the land of Moriah, and offer him there for a burnt-offering, upon one of the mountains which I will tell thee of. And Abraham rose up early in the morning, saddled his ass, and took two of his young men with him, and Isaac, his son; and he clave the wood for a burnt-offering, and rose up, and went unto the place of which God had told him. On the third day, Abraham lifted up his eyes, and saw the place afar off. And Abraham said unto his young men, Abide you here with the ass, and I and the lad will go yonder, and we will worship, and return again to you. And Abraham took the wood of the burnt-offering, and laid it upon

MORNING SERVICE FOR THE NEW YEAR.

Choir:

לְךָ יְיָ הַגְּדֻלָּה וְהַגְּבוּרָה ׳ וְהַתִּפְאֶרֶת וְהַנֵּצַח וְהַהוֹד כִּי כֹל בַּשָּׁמַיִם וּבָאָרֶץ ׳ לְךָ יְיָ הַמַּמְלָכָה ׳ וְהַמִּתְנַשֵּׂא לְכֹל לְרֹאשׁ:

(Before reading from the Torah.)

בָּרוּךְ אַתָּה יְיָ אֱלֹהֵינוּ מֶלֶךְ הָעוֹלָם אֲשֶׁר בָּחַר בָּנוּ מִכָּל־הָעַמִּים וְנָתַן לָנוּ אֶת־תּוֹרָתוֹ ׳ בָּרוּךְ אַתָּה יְיָ נוֹתֵן הַתּוֹרָה:

בראשית כ״ב

וַיְהִי אַחַר הַדְּבָרִים הָאֵלֶּה וְהָאֱלֹהִים נִסָּה אֶת־אַבְרָהָם וַיֹּאמֶר אֵלָיו אַבְרָהָם וַיֹּאמֶר הִנֵּנִי: וַיֹּאמֶר קַח־נָא אֶת־בִּנְךָ אֶת־יְחִידְךָ אֲשֶׁר־אָהַבְתָּ אֶת־יִצְחָק וְלֶךְ־לְךָ אֶל־אֶרֶץ הַמֹּרִיָּה וְהַעֲלֵהוּ שָׁם לְעֹלָה עַל אַחַד הֶהָרִים אֲשֶׁר אֹמַר אֵלֶיךָ: וַיַּשְׁכֵּם אַבְרָהָם בַּבֹּקֶר וַיַּחֲבֹשׁ אֶת־חֲמֹרוֹ וַיִּקַּח אֶת־שְׁנֵי נְעָרָיו אִתּוֹ וְאֵת יִצְחָק בְּנוֹ וַיְבַקַּע עֲצֵי עֹלָה וַיָּקָם וַיֵּלֶךְ אֶל־הַמָּקוֹם אֲשֶׁר־אָמַר־לוֹ הָאֱלֹהִים: בַּיּוֹם

Isaac, his son; and he took the fire in his hand, and the knife, and they went both of them together. And Isaac spoke unto Abraham, his father, and said, My father: and he said, Here am I, my son. And he said, Behold the fire and the wood; but where is the lamb for a burnt-offering? And Abraham said, God will provide himself a lamb for a burnt-offering, my son: so they went both of them together. And they came to the place which God had told him of; and Abraham built an altar there, and laid the wood in order, and bound Isaac his son, and placed him upon the altar, upon the wood. And Abraham stretched forth his hand, and took the knife to slay his son. And the angel of the Lord called unto him out of heaven, and said, Abraham, Abraham! and he said, Here am I. And he said, Lay not thy hand upon the lad, neither do thou any thing unto him; for now I know that thou fearest God, seeing thou hast not withheld thy son, thine only one, from me. And Abraham lifted up his eyes, and looked, and behold! behind him, a ram caught in a thicket by his horns; and Abraham went out and took the ram, and offered him up for a burnt-offering, in the stead of his son. And Abraham called the name of the place: "The Lord-Seeth;" as it is said to this day, "On the mount of the Lord shall it be seen." And the angel of the Lord called unto Abraham out of heaven, a second time, and said, By myself have I sworn, saith the Lord, because thou hast done this thing, and hast not withheld thy son, thine only one, that I will greatly bless thee, and exceedingly multi-

MORNING SERVICE FOR THE NEW YEAR.

הַשְּׁלִישִׁי וַיִּשָּׂא אַבְרָהָם אֶת־עֵינָיו וַיַּרְא אֶת־הַמָּקוֹם מֵרָחֹק: וַיֹּאמֶר אַבְרָהָם אֶל־נְעָרָיו שְׁבוּ־לָכֶם פֹּה עִם־הַחֲמוֹר וַאֲנִי וְהַנַּעַר נֵלְכָה עַד־כֹּה. וְנִשְׁתַּחֲוֶה וְנָשׁוּבָה אֲלֵיכֶם: וַיִּקַּח אַבְרָהָם אֶת־עֲצֵי הָעֹלָה וַיָּשֶׂם עַל־יִצְחָק בְּנוֹ וַיִּקַּח בְּיָדוֹ אֶת־הָאֵשׁ וְאֶת־הַמַּאֲכֶלֶת וַיֵּלְכוּ שְׁנֵיהֶם יַחְדָּו: וַיֹּאמֶר יִצְחָק אֶל־אַבְרָהָם אָבִיו וַיֹּאמֶר אָבִי וַיֹּאמֶר הִנֶּנִּי בְנִי. וַיֹּאמֶר הִנֵּה הָאֵשׁ וְהָעֵצִים וְאַיֵּה הַשֶּׂה לְעֹלָה: וַיֹּאמֶר אַבְרָהָם אֱלֹהִים יִרְאֶה־לּוֹ הַשֶּׂה לְעֹלָה בְּנִי וַיֵּלְכוּ שְׁנֵיהֶם יַחְדָּו: וַיָּבֹאוּ אֶל־הַמָּקוֹם אֲשֶׁר אָמַר־לוֹ הָאֱלֹהִים וַיִּבֶן שָׁם אַבְרָהָם אֶת־הַמִּזְבֵּחַ וַיַּעֲרֹךְ אֶת־הָעֵצִים וַיַּעֲקֹד אֶת־יִצְחָק בְּנוֹ וַיָּשֶׂם אֹתוֹ עַל־הַמִּזְבֵּחַ מִמַּעַל לָעֵצִים: וַיִּשְׁלַח אַבְרָהָם אֶת־יָדוֹ וַיִּקַּח אֶת־הַמַּאֲכֶלֶת לִשְׁחֹט אֶת־בְּנוֹ: וַיִּקְרָא אֵלָיו מַלְאַךְ יְהוָֹה מִן־הַשָּׁמַיִם וַיֹּאמֶר אַבְרָהָם אַבְרָהָם וַיֹּאמֶר הִנֵּנִי: וַיֹּאמֶר אַל־תִּשְׁלַח יָדְךָ אֶל־הַנַּעַר וְאַל־תַּעַשׂ לוֹ מְאוּמָה כִּי עַתָּה יָדַעְתִּי כִּי־יְרֵא אֱלֹהִים אַתָּה וְלֹא חָשַׂכְתָּ אֶת־בִּנְךָ אֶת־יְחִידְךָ מִמֶּנִּי: וַיִּשָּׂא

ply thy seed, as the stars of heaven, and as the sand which is upon the sea-shore; and thy seed shall possess the gates of their enemies; and in thy seed shall all the nations of the earth be blessed; because thou hast obeyed my voice. So Abraham returned to his young men, and they rose up, and went together to B'er-sheba: and Abraham dwelt at B'er-sheba.

(After Reading from the Torah.)

Praise be to Thee, O Eternal, our God, Ruler of the universe, who hast given us a law of truth and implanted eternal life within us. Praise be to Thee, O God, Giver of the Law. Amen.

(Before reading the Haphtarah.)

Blessed be the Lord our God, for the law of truth revealed in Israel and for the words of the prophets filled with His spirit and for the teachings of the masters and the preachers of righteousness, whom He raised up afore time and in these days. They made His word a light to our feet and a lamp on our paths. May we hear it reverently, read it understandingly, and follow willingly to the nurture and refreshment of the spiritual life which God has planted within us.

The Haphtarah.

(I Samuel, Chapter ii, 1-11.)

AND Hannah prayed and said, My heart rejoiceth in the Lord, mine horn is exalted in the Lord; my mouth is enlarged over mine enemies; because I

MORNING SERVICE FOR THE NEW YEAR. 67

אַבְרָהָם אֶת־עֵינָיו וַיַּרְא וְהִנֵּה־אַיִל אַחַר נֶאֱחַז בַּסְּבַךְ בְּקַרְנָיו וַיֵּלֶךְ אַבְרָהָם וַיִּקַּח אֶת־הָאַיִל וַיַּעֲלֵהוּ לְעֹלָה תַּחַת בְּנוֹ: וַיִּקְרָא אַבְרָהָם שֵׁם־הַמָּקוֹם הַהוּא יְהֹוָה יִרְאֶה אֲשֶׁר יֵאָמֵר הַיּוֹם בְּהַר יְהֹוָה יֵרָאֶה: וַיִּקְרָא מַלְאַךְ יְהֹוָה אֶל אַבְרָהָם שֵׁנִית מִן־הַשָּׁמָיִם: וַיֹּאמֶר בִּי נִשְׁבַּעְתִּי נְאֻם־יְהֹוָה כִּי יַעַן אֲשֶׁר עָשִׂיתָ אֶת־הַדָּבָר הַזֶּה וְלֹא חָשַׂכְתָּ אֶת־בִּנְךָ אֶת־יְחִידֶךָ: כִּי־בָרֵךְ אֲבָרֶכְךָ וְהַרְבָּה אַרְבֶּה אֶת־זַרְעֲךָ כְּכוֹכְבֵי הַשָּׁמַיִם וְכַחוֹל אֲשֶׁר עַל שְׂפַת הַיָּם וְיִרַשׁ זַרְעֲךָ אֵת שַׁעַר אֹיְבָיו: וְהִתְבָּרְכוּ בְזַרְעֲךָ כֹּל גּוֹיֵי הָאָרֶץ עֵקֶב אֲשֶׁר שָׁמַעְתָּ בְּקֹלִי: וַיָּשָׁב אַבְרָהָם אֶל־נְעָרָיו וַיָּקֻמוּ וַיֵּלְכוּ יַחְדָּו אֶל־בְּאֵר שָׁבַע וַיֵּשֶׁב אַבְרָהָם בִּבְאֵר שָׁבַע:

(After reading from the Torah.)

בָּרוּךְ אַתָּה יְיָ אֱלֹהֵינוּ מֶלֶךְ הָעוֹלָם . אֲשֶׁר נָתַן לָנוּ תּוֹרַת אֱמֶת וְחַיֵּי עוֹלָם נָטַע בְּתוֹכֵנוּ . בָּרוּךְ אַתָּה יְיָ נוֹתֵן הַתּוֹרָה:

rejoice in Thy salvation. There is none holy as the Lord: for there is none besides Thee; neither is there any rock like our God. Talk not exceeding proudly; let not arrogance come out of your mouth: for the Lord is a God of knowledge, and by Him actions are weighed. The bows of the mighty men are broken, and they that stumbled are girded with strength. They that were full have hired out themselves for bread; and they that were hungry ceased to want. The Lord ordereth death and giveth life; He bringeth down to the grave, and bringeth up again. The Lord maketh poor, and maketh rich; He bringeth low and lifteth up. He raiseth up the poor out of the dust, and lifteth up the beggar from his low estate, to set them among princes, and to make them inherit the throne of glory. For the pillars of the earth are the Lord's, and He hath set the world upon them. He will keep the feet of the righteous and the wicked shall be silent in darkness; for not by strength shall man prevail. The Lord shall judge the ends of the earth; and He shall give strength unto His king, and exalt the horn of His anointed.

Another Haphtarah.

(Nehemiah, Chapter viii.)

AND all the people gathered themselves together as one man into the street that was before the water-gate : and they spake unto Ezra, the scribe, to bring the book of the law of Moses, which the Lord had commanded to Israel. And Ezra, the priest, brought the law before the congregation, both men and women, and all that could hear with understanding, upon the first day of the month of Tishri. And Ezra, the scribe, stood upon a pulpit of wood, which they had made for the purpose. And Ezra opened the book in the sight of all the people; (for he was above all the people) and when he opened it, all the people stood up: And Ezra blessed the Lord, the great God. And all the people answered Amen, Amen, with lifting up their hands; and they bowed their heads and worshiped the Lord with their faces to the ground. Also Jeshua and the Levites caused the people to understand the law; and the people stood in their place. So they read in the book in the law of God distinctly, and gave the sense, and caused them to understand the reading. And Nehemiah, the cupbearer, and Ezra, the priest, the scribe, and the Levites that taught the people, said unto all the people, This day is holy unto the Lord your God; mourn not, nor weep. For all the people wept when they heard the words of the law. Then he said unto them, Go your way, eat the fat and drink the sweet, and send portions unto them for whom nothing is prepared: for this day is holy unto our Lord: neither be ye sorry; for the joy of the Lord is your strength. So the Levites stilled all the people, saying, Hold your peace, for the day is holy; neither be ye grieved. And all the people went their way to eat, and to drink, and to send portions, and to make great mirth, because they had understood the words that were declared unto them.

MORNING SERVICE FOR THE NEW YEAR.

THE SOUNDING OF THE SHOFAR.

מלכיות

Alternate Reading:

Come, let us worship and bow down, let us kneel before the Lord our Maker.

O worship the Lord in the beauty of holiness, fear before Him, all the earth.

The Lord reigneth, He shall judge the world with righteousness, and the people with His truth.

Who would not fear Thee, King of the nations, for to Thee alone reverence is due.

Thy kingdom is an everlasting kingdom, and Thy dominion endureth throughout all generations.

The Lord reigneth, let the earth rejoice; let the multitude of the islands break forth in joy.

With trumpet and the cornet, sound aloud the praises of the Lord, the King.

Minister:

OMNIPOTENT, who can encompass the greatness of Thy power! What are our works, measured by Thine, O Lord, who hast meted out the heaven with the span, and comprehended the dust of the earth in a measure, and weighed the mountains in scales and the hills in balances? What are our years measured by Thine, who endurest, though all else perish, and who art ever the same, though all things change. Thou hast laid the foundations of the earth. Thou spakest to the sea: Hitherto shalt thou come but no further, and here shall thy proud waves be stayed. When the morning stars sang together, and the heavenly hosts shouted for joy, then did Thy creative word bid the light break through darkness, and life issued forth from the treasure-houses of the depths and of the heights. And as Thou didst fashion all things from the beginning, so dost Thou sustain and rule them even unto the end. For Thou art the King of eternity, the immovable rock amidst the ebb and flow of the ages, and Thy throne is established forever.

Let this truth shine forth triumphantly among all mankind, that all may acknowledge Thee as their King and render homage to Thy holy name, for Thine is the kingdom and Thy dominion endureth forever.

The Shofar is sounded.

Choir:

The Lord reigneth, He is clothed with majesty; the Lord is girded with strength. Thy throne is established of old. Thou art from everlasting to everlasting.

זכרונות

Alternate Reading:

The Eternal is our Judge, the Eternal is our Lawgiver.

The Eternal is our King, He will save us.

Righteousness and judgment are the foundations of His throne, love and truth go before His countenance.

There is none holy like unto the Lord, and there is no rock like unto our God.

The Lord is a God of knowledge; and by Him all actions are weighed.

The Lord giveth life and death; the Lord maketh poor and maketh rich.

He raiseth up the poor man from the dust, He lifteth the lowly from their low estate.

For the pillars of the earth are the Lord's; He hath established the world upon justice.

The Lord will judge the ends of the earth.

He will give strength to His servants, and exalt the honor of His people.

Minister:

THOU, O God, knowest all the works of the past, before Thee all secrets are revealed. Naught is hidden from Thine eyes, nothing forgotten before Thy throne. Thou knowest the events of all times, the generations that were and those that shall be. All our deeds are remembered before Thee. Whether for correction or for mercy, Thou directest the destinies of men and nations according to Thy wisdom and justice. Happy the man who forgets Thee not, for they that seek Thee shall never stumble, and those that trust in Thee will never be put to shame.

Remember us, O Lord, in loving-kindness on this day, as we stand on the threshold of a new year, anxious to know what it will bring to us. But we have the assurance in Thy holy word, that Thy love will never forsake us. O remember us for good and grant us life and health. Aid us in every just undertaking and uphold us in all our trials that we may forever cling to Thee and hold fast to truth and righteousness.

The Shofar is sounded.

Choir:

For the mountains shall depart, and the hills be removed. But my kindness shall not depart from Thee, neither shall the covenant of peace be removed, saith the Lord that hath compassion upon Thee.

שופרות

Alternate Reading:

Blessed is the people that know the joyful sound; they walk in the light of Thy countenance, O Lord.

In Thy name shall they rejoice all the day,
In Thy righteousness are they exalted.

For Thou art the glory of their strength,
And in Thy favor our state is exalted.

For the Lord is our defence,
The Holy One of Israel is our King.

Minister:

O GOD, our Lord, the sounds of the Shofar remind us of that great moment when Thy truth was revealed to Israel on Sinai. Then didst Thou covenant with our fathers, that they become a nation sanctified by truth and righteousness. Then didst Thou send them forth to proclaim unto all the children of men those statutes by which man shall live and not die. Then didst Thou anoint Israel to be Thy servant, and in words of fire didst Thou engrave Thy truth upon his heart, that he might preserve the knowledge of Thee unto all generations. And to this day, O our Father, the echo of that ever memorable event resounds in the hearts of the descendants of Israel. For we know that not only with our fathers of yore, but also with us, who stand before Thee this day, with all who are not here this day, aye, even with all the generations of the future has this covenant of righteousness been made. We know, Eternal, that we also live by the strength and power of that covenant of the centuries, an ever growing knowledge of which comes to us when from year to year the sounds of the Shofar recall to us the days when Thy name was inscribed on Israel's banner, when they learned to live for Thee, and when they glorified Thee before all the nations. Then were they consecrated to carry the revealed truth even unto the furthest parts of the earth, seeking to win all Thy children for Thy truth and to bring them under Thy dominion. For Thy word exceeds the strength of mighty armies, and encompasses the power of beleaguered walls.

O grant that this word may still be our guide in our struggles for truth, until the power of Thy name shall have conquered the earth and subdued all nations. Then shall the sound of the Shofar announce the good tidings: Peace, peace, be unto them who are near, and unto them who are afar off. Then shall all the peoples of the earth be righteous and inherit peace, even the branch of Thy planting, the work of Thy hand, and forever glorified shall be the Eternal, who revealed His word and the covenant of truth unto Israel. Amen.

The Shofar is sounded.

Choir:

All ye dwellers on earth, when the Shofar is sounded, hark ye, and when the great trumpet is blown, come ye and worship the Lord at the holy mountain; the Lord of hosts shall be a shield unto you.

76 MORNING SERVICE FOR THE NEW YEAR.

Returning of the Scroll.

Minister:

O magnify the Lord with me and let us exalt His name together.

יְהַלְלוּ אֶת־שֵׁם יְיָ כִּי נִשְׂגָּב שְׁמוֹ לְבַדּוֹ:

Choir:

His glory is in the earth and in the heavens. He is the strength of all His servants, the praise of them that truly love Him. The hope of Israel whom He brought nigh to himself, Hallelujah.

הוֹדוֹ עַל אֶרֶץ וְשָׁמָיִם: וַיָּרֶם קֶרֶן לְעַמּוֹ תְּהִלָּה לְכָל חֲסִידָיו לִבְנֵי יִשְׂרָאֵל עַם קְרֹבוֹ הַלְלוּיָהּ:

Minister:

The law of the Lord is perfect, restoring the soul; the testimonies of the Lord are faithful, making wise the simple. The precepts of the Lord are plain, rejoicing the heart; the fear of the Lord is pure, enduring forever. Behold, a good doctrine has been given to you: forsake it not.

תּוֹרַת יְיָ תְּמִימָה. מְשִׁיבַת נָפֶשׁ. עֵדוּת יְיָ נֶאֱמָנָה. מַחְכִּימַת פֶּתִי: פִּקּוּדֵי יְיָ יְשָׁרִים. מְשַׂמְּחֵי לֵב. יִרְאַת יְיָ טְהוֹרָה. עוֹמֶדֶת לָעַד: כִּי לֶקַח טוֹב נָתַתִּי לָכֶם תּוֹרָתִי אַל תַּעֲזֹבוּ:

Choir:

It is a tree of life to them that lay hold of it and the supporters thereof are happy. Its ways are ways of pleasantness and all its paths are peace.

עֵץ־חַיִּים הִיא לַמַּחֲזִיקִים בָּהּ וְתֹמְכֶיהָ מְאֻשָּׁר:
דְּרָכֶיהָ דַרְכֵי נֹעַם וְכָל־נְתִיבוֹתֶיהָ שָׁלוֹם:

HYMN.

LO, our Father's tender care
   Slumbers not, nor sleepeth,
Gracious gifts His lavish hand
Daily on us heapeth.
Though fierce storms, though perils **lower**—
Is not God our sheltering tower?
     Tremble not!
At His word the storm is still,
Perils vanish at His will—
And His love ordains our lot.
Lo, our Guardian slumbers not.

Lo, our Father's gracious love
Slumbers not, nor sleepeth.
Trust with all thy heart in **Him**,
Who thy portion keepeth;
Who till now protection granted
And thy fortune wisely planted.
     Fear thou not!
God, who life and being grants
Kindly, too, supplies our wants.
Let but duty guide our lot.
Lo, our Guardian slumbers **not.**

ADORATION.

(Congregation standing.)

Minister:

LET us adore the ever-living God, and render praise unto Him who spread out the heavens and established the earth, whose glory is revealed in the heavens above and whose greatness is manifest throughout the world: He is our God, and there is none else.

We bow our head and bend our knee and magnify the King of kings, the Holy One, the Ever-blest.

Choir and Congregation:

וַאֲנַחְנוּ כֹּרְעִים וּמִשְׁתַּחֲוִים וּמוֹדִים לִפְנֵי מֶלֶךְ מַלְכֵי הַמְּלָכִים הַקָּדוֹשׁ בָּרוּךְ הוּא:

(Congregation sitting.)

Minister:

May the time not be far, O God, when Thy name shall be worshiped over all the earth, when unbelief shall disappear and error be no more. We fervently pray that the day may come upon which all men shall invoke Thy name, when corruption and evil shall give way to purity and goodness; when superstition shall no longer enslave the minds, nor idolatry blind their eyes, when all inhabitants of the earth shall perceive that to Thee alone every knee must bend and every tongue give homage. O may all, created in Thine image, recognize that they are brethren, so that they, one in spirit, and one in fellowship, may be forever united before Thee. Then shall Thy kingdom be established on earth, and the word of Thine ancient seer be fulfilled: The Eternal shall rule forever and aye.

Congregation:

On that day the Eternal shall be One, and His name shall be One.

Minister:

ALL you who mourn the loss of loved ones, and, at this hour, remember the goodness, the hope and the sweet companionship that have passed away with them, give ear to the word of comfort spoken to you in the name of your God. Only the body has died and has been laid in the dust. The spirit lives and will live on forever in the land of undisturbed peace and perfect happiness. But in this life, also, the loved ones continue in the remembrance of those to whom they were precious. Every act of goodness they performed, every true and beautiful word they spoke, is treasured up as an incentive to walk in the path of goodn ss.

And when you ask in your grief: Whence shall come my help and my comfort? then, in the strength of faith, answer with the Psalmist: "My help cometh from God," who will not forsake me, nor leave me in my grief. Upon Him I cast my burden, and He will grant me strength according to the days He has apportioned to me. All souls are His, and no power can take them out of His hands. Come, then, and in the midst of sympathizing fellow-worshipers, rise, and hallow with me the name of God.

(The mourners standing and speaking with the Minister.)

EXTOLLED and hallowed be the name of God throughout the world which He has created, and which He governs according to His righteous will. Just is He in all His ways, and wise are all His decrees. May His Kingdom come, and His will be done in all the earth.

Congregation:

Blessed be the Lord of life and righteous Judge forever more.

Minister:

To the departed whom we now remember, may peace and bliss be granted in the world of eternal life. There may they find grace and mercy before the Lord of heaven and earth. May their souls rejoice in that ineffable good which God has laid up for those that fear Him, and may their memory be a blessing unto those that cherish it.

Congregation:

Amen.

Minister:

May the Father of peace send peace to all troubled souls, and comfort all the bereaved among us.

Congregation:

Amen.

MORNING SERVICE FOR THE NEW YEAR.

(The mourners standing and speaking with the Minister.)

יִתְגַּדַּל וְיִתְקַדַּשׁ שְׁמֵהּ רַבָּא. בְּעָלְמָא דִי־בְרָא כִרְעוּתֵהּ. וְיַמְלִיךְ מַלְכוּתֵהּ. בְּחַיֵּיכוֹן וּבְיוֹמֵיכוֹן וּבְחַיֵּי דְכָל בֵּית יִשְׂרָאֵל. בַּעֲגָלָא וּבִזְמַן קָרִיב. וְאִמְרוּ אָמֵן:

Congregation:

יְהֵא שְׁמֵהּ רַבָּא מְבָרַךְ. לְעָלַם וּלְעָלְמֵי עָלְמַיָּא.

Minister:

יִתְבָּרַךְ וְיִשְׁתַּבַּח וְיִתְפָּאַר וְיִתְרוֹמַם וְיִתְנַשֵּׂא וְיִתְהַדָּר וְיִתְעַלֶּה וְיִתְהַלָּל שְׁמֵהּ דְּקוּדְשָׁא. בְּרִיךְ הוּא. לְעֵלָּא מִן כָּל בִּרְכָתָא וְשִׁירָתָא. תֻּשְׁבְּחָתָא וְנֶחֱמָתָא. דַּאֲמִירָן בְּעָלְמָא. וְאִמְרוּ אָמֵן:

עַל יִשְׂרָאֵל וְעַל צַדִּיקַיָּא. וְעַל־כָּל־מַן דְּאִתְפְּטַר מִן עָלְמָא הָדֵין כִּרְעוּתֵהּ דֶּאֱלָהָא. יְהֵא לְהוֹן שְׁלָמָא רַבָּא וְחוּלָקָא־טָבָא לְחַיֵּי עָלְמָא דְּאָתֵי. וְחִסְדָּא וְרַחֲמֵי מִן־קֳדָם מָרֵא שְׁמַיָּא וְאַרְעָא. וְאִמְרוּ אָמֵן:

יְהֵא שְׁלָמָא רַבָּא מִן־שְׁמַיָּא. וְחַיִּים. עָלֵינוּ וְעַל־כָּל־יִשְׂרָאֵל. וְאִמְרוּ אָמֵן:

עֹשֶׂה שָׁלוֹם בִּמְרוֹמָיו. הוּא יַעֲשֶׂה שָׁלוֹם עָלֵינוּ וְעַל כָּל יִשְׂרָאֵל. וְאִמְרוּ אָמֵן:

CLOSING HYMN.

WHO is like Thee, O universal Lord!
Who dare Thy praise and glory share?
Who is in heaven, Most High, like Thee adored?
Who can on earth with Thee compare?
Thou art the One true God alone,
And firmly founded is Thy throne.

Thy tender love embraces all mankind,
As children all by Thee are blest;
Repentant sinners with Thee mercy find,
Thy hand upholdeth the opprest;
All worlds attest Thy power sublime,
Thy glory shines in every clime.

And to Thy might and love is joined in Thee
The highest wisdom's living spring;
Whate'er to us is deepest mystery,
Is clear to Thee, our Lord and King.
O God of wisdom, love and might,
We worship Thee, Eternal Light.

BENEDICTION.

CLOSING HYMN.

אֵין כֵּאלֹהֵינוּ . אֵין כַּאדוֹנֵינוּ .
אֵין כְּמַלְכֵּנוּ . אֵין כְּמוֹשִׁיעֵנוּ:

מִי כֵאלֹהֵינוּ . מִי כַאדוֹנֵינוּ .
מִי כְמַלְכֵּנוּ . מִי כְמוֹשִׁיעֵנוּ:

נוֹדֶה לֵאלֹהֵינוּ . נוֹדֶה לַאדוֹנֵינוּ .
נוֹדֶה לְמַלְכֵּנוּ . נוֹדֶה לְמוֹשִׁיעֵנוּ:

בָּרוּךְ אֱלֹהֵינוּ . בָּרוּךְ אֲדוֹנֵינוּ .
בָּרוּךְ מַלְכֵּנוּ . בָּרוּךְ מוֹשִׁיעֵנוּ:

אַתָּה הוּא אֱלֹהֵינוּ . אַתָּה הוּא אֲדוֹנֵינוּ .
אַתָּה הוּא מַלְכֵּנוּ . אַתָּה הוּא מוֹשִׁיעֵנוּ:

BENEDICTION.

PARTING BENEDICTIONS.

O GOD, be merciful to us and bless us, and cause Thy face to shine upon us: that Thy doings may be known on the earth, and Thy saving power unto all nations. May God continue to be with us, and may all the ends of earth worship before Him.

The Lord is my shepherd: I shall not want. He reviveth my soul; He leadeth me in paths of safety, for His name's sake. Surely, goodness and mercy shall follow me all the days of my life, and I shall dwell in the house of God for ever.

Lord, Thy peace be with us, the peace that spreadeth out like the heavens, like a tent to dwell in. May there be peace within us; peace in our houses, that works and words of love be in them. Let us hear what God will speak; for Thou wilt speak peace unto Thy people.

Eternal One, Thou hast shown us what is good, and what Thou dost require of us, to do justly, to love mercy, and to walk humbly with Thee. Great peace have they who love Thy law, and nothing can offend them. Lord, give strength unto Thy people, O God, bless Thy people with peace. Amen.

Day of Atonement.

Evening Service for the Day of Atonement.

For Silent Devotion.

O LORD our God, who art merciful and gracious, long-suffering and abundant in kindness, look down upon us in this hour when we enter upon Thy worship, on the day set apart for the purification of our hearts and the renewal of our spiritual life.

We feel, O God, that our sins and transgressions are many and that we need Thy pardoning grace. For shouldst Thou strictly mark all our failings, O Lord, who would be able to stand before Thee? O help us to employ this holy time in accordance with its sacred purpose, that we may gather spiritual blessings which will make our future lives more abundant in goodness more free from sin, and more perfect in righteousness and in love. When we are oppressed with a sense of our unworthiness, we are comforted by the assurances given unto us in Thy word, that the sacrifice Thou desirest is a meek and contrite spirit, and that they who confess their sins and forsake them shall find mercy and pardon, and be again accepted by Thee. Even thus we desire to prepare ourselves to meet Thee, O God. Here, in

Thy sanctuary, we come to pour out our hearts with all the burdens that press them down, with all the cares that disquiet us, with all the anxieties that often consume our strength. O Father, to whom our innermost life is revealed, Thou, who art acquainted with all our thoughts, even with those which remain buried in our bosom, deal kindly with us, as we humble ourselves before Thee; and as we confess our transgressions and shortcomings before Thee, O pardon us, and give us peace!

And as we seek to be at peace with Thee, so may we strive to be at peace with all our fellow-men. If our conscience smites us because of any wrong or injustice done to them, may this day admonish us, that we dare not ask Thy pardon before we have done our utmost to pacify those against whom we have offended, until we have undone the evil we have caused. O give us the high courage to acknowledge our sins to our fellow-men also, and thus to restore the bonds of friendship and heal the wounds we have inflicted. Thus, reconciled to one another, may we appear before Thee, O Father, on this Day of Atonement as with one heart and one soul, and thus make our supplications acceptable to Thee. Be Thou, we beseech Thee, with the spirits of all who are assembled here, and send unto them that light and comfort for which they crave according to their trials and necessities. And may this day come as a messenger of peace and grace to all our brethren of the house of Israel throughout their habitations. Hear us, O God, answer us according to the fulness of Thy mercy. Amen.

DAY OF ATONEMENT.

HYMN.

Day of God
  O, come!
And fill all our spirits
With peace and with gladness from Heaven.
From the eventide to eventide
Let all earthly thoughts be sanctified
In prayer!
Upward to God, upward to God,
Sons of earth, together!

  Lift the voice of prayer and song,
  Heavenward borne on the current strong,
  Upward all aspire!
  In the angel choir
  Blend our prayers and praises.

Lord! God! See,—
See Thou our heart's contrition,
And bow Thine ear!
Hear, O hear the voice of my petition,
Banish our fear!
Blot out our evil ways,
Open the door of grace,
Bid us enter there!

Minister:

OUT of the depths I cry unto Thee, O Lord, listen to my voice, let Thine ear be attentive to my supplication. If Thou shouldst mark transgressions, O Lord, who shall stand before Thy judgment? But with Thee is forgiveness, that Thou mayest be feared. I wait for the Lord; my soul doth wait, and in His word do I hope. My soul waiteth for the Lord more than they who watch for the morning—I say more than they who watch for the morning. Let Israel hope in the Lord; for with the Lord there is mercy, and with Him is plenteous redemption. He shall redeem Israel from all his iniquities. [Psalm cxxx.]

Choir:

May forgiveness be granted unto all the congregation of Israel and unto the stranger that sojourneth among them, for all the people have sinned in ignorance.

Minister:

Forgive, I beseech Thee, the iniquity of this people according to the greatness of Thy love, even as Thou hast borne with this people from Egypt until now.

Choir:

And the Lord said, I have pardoned according to Thy word.

Minister:

Praise be to Thee, O God, Ruler of the world, who hast granted us life, hast preserved and sustained us and brought us unto this day.

Choir:—Amen

DAY OF ATONEMENT.

Minister:

מִמַּעֲמַקִּים קְרָאתִיךָ יְיָ: אֲדֹנָי שִׁמְעָה בְקוֹלִי.
תִּהְיֶינָה אָזְנֶיךָ קַשֻּׁבוֹת לְקוֹל תַּחֲנוּנָי: אִס־עֲוֹנוֹת
תִּשְׁמָר־יָהּ. אֲדֹנָי מִי יַעֲמֹד: כִּי־עִמְּךָ הַסְּלִיחָה.
לְמַעַן תִּוָּרֵא: קִוִּיתִי יְיָ קִוְּתָה נַפְשִׁי וְלִדְבָרוֹ
הוֹחָלְתִּי: נַפְשִׁי לַאדֹנָי מִשֹּׁמְרִים לַבֹּקֶר. שֹׁמְרִים
לַבֹּקֶר: יַחֵל יִשְׂרָאֵל אֶל־יְיָ. כִּי־עִם־אֲדֹנָי הַחֶסֶד.
וְהַרְבֵּה עִמּוֹ פְדוּת: וְהוּא יִפְדֶּה אֶת־יִשְׂרָאֵל מִכֹּל
עֲוֹנוֹתָיו:

Choir:

וְנִסְלַח לְכָל־עֲדַת בְּנֵי יִשְׂרָאֵל. וְלַגֵּר הַגָּר בְּתוֹכָם.
כִּי לְכָל־הָעָם בִּשְׁגָגָה:

Minister:

סְלַח־נָא לַעֲוֹן הָעָם הַזֶּה כְּגֹדֶל חַסְדֶּךָ: וְכַאֲשֶׁר
נָשָׂאתָה לָעָם הַזֶּה מִמִּצְרַיִם וְעַד־הֵנָּה:

Choir:

וַיֹּאמֶר יְהֹוָה סָלַחְתִּי כִּדְבָרֶךָ:

Minister:

בָּרוּךְ אַתָּה יְיָ אֱלֹהֵינוּ מֶלֶךְ הָעוֹלָם. שֶׁהֶחֱיָנוּ
וְקִיְּמָנוּ וְהִגִּיעָנוּ לַזְּמַן הַזֶּה:

Choir:—Amen.

(Congregation standing.)

Minister:

Praise ye the Lord, to whom all praise is due

Choir and Congregation:

Praised be the Lord from this time forth and forever

(Congregation sitting.)

Minister:

PRAISE be unto Thee, O Eternal, Ruler of the world, at whose words the shades of evening fall, and by whose will the gates of morn are opened. Thy wisdom established the changes of times and seasons, and ordered the ways of the stars in their heavenly courses. Creator of day and night, Lord of hosts is Thy name. Thou, ever-living God, wilt rule over us forever. Praise be unto Thee, O God, for the day and its work and for the night and its rest.

Infinite as is Thy power, even so is Thy Love. Thou didst manifest it unto Israel, Thy servant. By laws and commandments, by statutes and ordinances hast Thou led us into the way of righteousness and brought us to the light of truth. Therefore, at our lying down and our rising up we meditate on Thy teachings and, at all times, rejoice in Thy laws. In them is true life and length of days. O, that Thy love may never depart from our hearts. Praise be to Thee, O God, who hast revealed Thy love unto Israel.

DAY OF ATONEMENT.

(Congregation standing.)

Minister:

בָּרְכוּ אֶת יְיָ הַמְבֹרָךְ:

Choir and Congregation:

בָּרוּךְ יְיָ הַמְבֹרָךְ לְעוֹלָם וָעֶד:

(Congregation sitting.)

Minister:

בָּרוּךְ אַתָּה יְיָ אֱלֹהֵינוּ מֶלֶךְ הָעוֹלָם. אֲשֶׁר בִּדְבָרוֹ מַעֲרִיב עֲרָבִים. בְּחָכְמָה פּוֹתֵחַ שְׁעָרִים. וּבִתְבוּנָה מְשַׁנֶּה עִתִּים וּמַחֲלִיף אֶת הַזְּמַנִּים. וּמְסַדֵּר אֶת הַכּוֹכָבִים בְּמִשְׁמְרוֹתֵיהֶם בָּרָקִיעַ כִּרְצוֹנוֹ. בּוֹרֵא יוֹם וָלָיְלָה. יְיָ צְבָאוֹת שְׁמוֹ. אֵל חַי וְקַיָּם תָּמִיד יִמְלֹךְ עָלֵינוּ לְעוֹלָם וָעֶד. בָּרוּךְ אַתָּה יְיָ הַמַּעֲרִיב עֲרָבִים:

אַהֲבַת עוֹלָם בֵּית יִשְׂרָאֵל עַמְּךָ אָהָבְתָּ. תּוֹרָה וּמִצְוֹת חֻקִּים וּמִשְׁפָּטִים אוֹתָנוּ לִמַּדְתָּ. עַל כֵּן יְיָ אֱלֹהֵינוּ בְּשָׁכְבֵּנוּ וּבְקוּמֵנוּ נָשִׂיחַ בְּחֻקֶּיךָ. וְנִשְׂמַח בְּדִבְרֵי תוֹרָתֶךָ וּבְמִצְוֹתֶיךָ לְעוֹלָם וָעֶד. כִּי הֵם חַיֵּינוּ וְאֹרֶךְ יָמֵינוּ. וּבָהֶם נֶהְגֶּה יוֹמָם וָלָיְלָה. וְאַהֲבָתְךָ אַל תָּסִיר מִמֶּנּוּ לְעוֹלָמִים. בָּרוּךְ אַתָּה יְיָ אוֹהֵב עַמּוֹ יִשְׂרָאֵל:

(Congregation standing.)

Minister, then Choir and Congregation:

Hear, O Israel, the Lord our God, the Lord is One.
Praised be His glorious name forever and ever.

(Congregation sitting.)

Minister:

THOU shalt love the Lord, thy God, with all thy heart, with all thy soul, and with all thy might. And these words, which I command thee this day, shall be in thy heart. Thou shalt teach them diligently unto thy children, and shalt speak of them when thou sittest in thy house, when thou walkest by the way, when thou liest down, and when thou risest up. Bind them as a sign upon thy hand, and let them be as frontlets between thine eyes. Write them upon the doorposts of thy house and upon thy gates.

To the end that ye may remember to do according to all my commandments and your life shall be hallowed unto the Lord. I am the Lord your God.

For Alternate Reading or Chanting:

ETERNAL truth it is that Thou alone art God, and there is none besides;

And through Thy power alone has Israel been redeemed from the hands of oppressors.

Wonders without number hast Thou wrought for us, and hast protected us to this day.

Thou hast preserved our soul for life, and hast not suffered our foot to stumble.

DAY OF ATONEMENT.

(Congregation standing.)

Minister, then Choir and Congregation:

שְׁמַע יִשְׂרָאֵל יְהֹוָה אֱלֹהֵינוּ יְהֹוָה אֶחָד:

בָּרוּךְ שֵׁם כְּבוֹד מַלְכוּתוֹ לְעוֹלָם וָעֶד:

(Congregation sitting.)

Minister:

וְאָהַבְתָּ אֵת יְיָ אֱלֹהֶיךָ בְּכָל־לְבָבְךָ וּבְכָל־נַפְשְׁךָ וּבְכָל־מְאֹדֶךָ: וְהָיוּ הַדְּבָרִים הָאֵלֶּה אֲשֶׁר אָנֹכִי מְצַוְּךָ הַיּוֹם עַל־לְבָבֶךָ: וְשִׁנַּנְתָּם לְבָנֶיךָ וְדִבַּרְתָּ בָּם. בְּשִׁבְתְּךָ בְּבֵיתֶךָ וּבְלֶכְתְּךָ בַדֶּרֶךְ וּבְשָׁכְבְּךָ וּבְקוּמֶךָ: וּקְשַׁרְתָּם לְאוֹת עַל־יָדֶךָ. וְהָיוּ לְטֹטָפֹת בֵּין עֵינֶיךָ: וּכְתַבְתָּם עַל־מְזֻזוֹת בֵּיתֶךָ וּבִשְׁעָרֶיךָ:

לְמַעַן תִּזְכְּרוּ וַעֲשִׂיתֶם אֶת כָּל מִצְוֹתָי וִהְיִיתֶם קְדֹשִׁים לֵאלֹהֵיכֶם: אֲנִי יְיָ אֱלֹהֵיכֶם:

For Alternate Reading or Chanting:

אֱמֶת וֶאֱמוּנָה כָּל זֹאת וְקַיָּם עָלֵינוּ. כִּי הוּא יְיָ אֱלֹהֵינוּ וְאֵין זוּלָתוֹ. וַאֲנַחְנוּ יִשְׂרָאֵל עַמּוֹ.

הַפּוֹדֵנוּ מִיַּד מְלָכִים. מַלְכֵּנוּ הַגּוֹאֲלֵנוּ מִכַּף כָּל־הֶעָרִיצִים.

Thy love has watched over us in the night of oppression; and Thy mercy has sustained us in the hour of trial.

And now that we live in a land of freedom, may we continue to be faithful to Thee and Thy word.

May Thy love rule in the hearts of all Thy children, and Thy truth unite them in the bonds of fellowship.

Let the righteous of all nations rejoice in Thy grace, and exult in Thy justice.

O God, Thou art our refuge and our hope; we glorify Thy name now, as did our fathers in the ancient days:

Choir and Congregation:

Who is like unto Thee, O God, among the mighty? Who is like unto Thee, glorious in holiness, extolled in praises, working wonders?

God reigneth forever and ever.

Minister:

As Thou hast redeemed Israel and saved him from arms stronger than his, so mayest Thou redeem all who are oppressed and persecuted. Blessed art Thou, O God, Redeemer of Israel.

Choir:

On this day ye shall be forgiven and cleansed from all your sins; before God shall ye be pure.

DAY OF ATONEMENT.

הָעוֹשֶׂה גְדֹלוֹת עַד אֵין חֵקֶר. וְנִפְלָאוֹת עַד אֵין מִסְפָּר.

הַשָּׂם נַפְשֵׁנוּ בַּחַיִּים. וְלֹא נָתַן לַמּוֹט רַגְלֵנוּ.

הָעוֹשֶׂה לָנוּ נִסִּים בְּמִצְרָיִם. אוֹתוֹת וּמוֹפְתִים בְּאַדְמַת בְּנֵי חָם.

וַיִּרְאוּ בָנָיו גְּבוּרָתוֹ. שִׁבְּחוּ וְהוֹדוּ לִשְׁמוֹ.

Choir and Congregation:

מִי־כָמֹכָה בָּאֵלִים יְיָ. מִי כָּמֹכָה נֶאְדָּר בַּקֹּדֶשׁ. נוֹרָא תְהִלֹּת עֹשֵׂה־פֶלֶא:

Minister:

מַלְכוּתְךָ רָאוּ בָנֶיךָ. זֶה אֵלִי עָנוּ וְאָמְרוּ:

Choir and Congregation:

יְיָ יִמְלֹךְ לְעֹלָם וָעֶד:

Minister:

וְנֶאֱמַר כִּי פָדָה יְהוָֹה אֶת יַעֲקֹב וּגְאָלוֹ מִיַּד חָזָק מִמֶּנּוּ בָּרוּךְ אַתָּה יְיָ גָּאַל יִשְׂרָאֵל:

Choir:

כִּי בַיּוֹם הַזֶּה יְכַפֵּר עֲלֵיכֶם לְטַהֵר אֶתְכֶם מִכֹּל חַטֹּאתֵיכֶם לִפְנֵי יְיָ תִּטְהָרוּ:

Minister:

PRAISE be unto Thee, O Eternal, our God, God of our fathers, Abraham, Isaac and Jacob; the great, mighty, and most high God. Thou bestowest loving-kindness upon all Thy creatures; Thou rememberest the goodness of the fathers, and Thou sendest redemption to their descendants for the sake of Thy name.

Remember us unto life, O Sovereign who ordainest life, and inscribe us in the book of life, for Thy sake, O God of life. Thou art our helper, our redeemer and protector. Praise be to Thee, O God, shield of Abraham.

Thou art omnipotent, O Lord, and mighty to save. In Thy kindness Thou sustainest the living, upholdest the falling, healest the sick, and settest the captives free. Thou wilt of a surety fulfil Thy promise of immortal life unto those who sleep in the dust. Who is like unto Thee, Almighty, Author of life and death, Thou who sendest salvation.

Who is like unto Thee, Father of mercies, who rememberest Thy children unto life eternal. Praise be to Thee, O God, who hast implanted within us immortal life.

Holy art Thou and awe-inspiring is Thy name. There is no God beside Thee. The Lord of hosts is exalted in judgment and the Holy One is sanctified through righteousness. Praise be to Thee, O God, who rulest in holiness.

Choir:—Amen.

DAY OF ATONEMENT.

בָּרוּךְ אַתָּה יְיָ אֱלֹהֵינוּ וֵאלֹהֵי אֲבוֹתֵינוּ. אֱלֹהֵי אַבְרָהָם אֱלֹהֵי יִצְחָק וֵאלֹהֵי יַעֲקֹב. הָאֵל הַגָּדוֹל הַגִּבּוֹר וְהַנּוֹרָא. אֵל עֶלְיוֹן. גּוֹמֵל חֲסָדִים טוֹבִים. וְקֹנֵה הַכֹּל וְזוֹכֵר חַסְדֵי אָבוֹת. וּמֵבִיא גְאֻלָּה לִבְנֵי בְנֵיהֶם. לְמַעַן שְׁמוֹ בְּאַהֲבָה:

זָכְרֵנוּ לַחַיִּים. מֶלֶךְ חָפֵץ בַּחַיִּים. וְכָתְבֵנוּ בְּסֵפֶר הַחַיִּים. לְמַעַנְךָ אֱלֹהִים חַיִּים:

מֶלֶךְ עוֹזֵר וּמוֹשִׁיעַ וּמָגֵן. בָּרוּךְ אַתָּה יְיָ מָגֵן אַבְרָהָם:

אַתָּה גִבּוֹר לְעוֹלָם אֲדֹנָי. רַב לְהוֹשִׁיעַ. מְכַלְכֵּל חַיִּים בְּחֶסֶד. מְחַיֶּה הַכֹּל בְּרַחֲמִים רַבִּים. סוֹמֵךְ נוֹפְלִים וְרוֹפֵא חוֹלִים וּמַתִּיר אֲסוּרִים. וּמְקַיֵּם אֱמוּנָתוֹ לִישֵׁנֵי עָפָר. מִי כָמוֹךָ בַּעַל גְּבוּרוֹת. וּמִי דּוֹמֶה לָּךְ. מֶלֶךְ מֵמִית וּמְחַיֶּה. וּמַצְמִיחַ יְשׁוּעָה:

מִי כָמוֹךָ אַב הָרַחֲמִים. זוֹכֵר יְצוּרָיו לַחַיִּים בְּרַחֲמִים: בָּרוּךְ אַתָּה יְיָ נֹטֵעַ בְּתוֹכֵנוּ חַיֵּי עוֹלָם:

קָדוֹשׁ אַתָּה וְנוֹרָא שְׁמֶךָ. וְאֵין אֱלוֹהַּ מִבַּלְעָדֶיךָ. כַּכָּתוּב. וַיִּגְבַּה יְיָ צְבָאוֹת בַּמִּשְׁפָּט. וְהָאֵל הַקָּדוֹשׁ נִקְדָּשׁ בִּצְדָקָה. בָּרוּךְ אַתָּה יְיָ הַמֶּלֶךְ הַקָּדוֹשׁ:

Choir:—Amen.

HYMN.

UNTO Thee our prayers arise,
    When to darkness turns the light;
Give us peace, then, in the morning,
To allay the fears of night,
So that joy and comfort cheer us
When another day takes flight.

Let our voices praise Thy goodness
In the waning hours of day;
And Thy mercy come to meet us
At the early dawn's first ray;
That our lives show Thy salvation
When we close another day.

Over all our sins and failings
Our repenting spirits rise;
Then let Thy forgiveness follow
With the morning's sacrifice:
That our soul's desire be granted
When again the daylight flies.

May our supplications find Thee
In the quiet of the eve;
And Thy hand with each new morning
Send us succor and reprieve:
That Thy love and mercy guide us
When our earthly home we leave.

DAY OF ATONEMENT.

HYMN.

יַעֲלֶה תַחֲנוּנֵנוּ מֵעֶרֶב. וְיָבֹא שַׁוְעָתֵנוּ מִבֹּקֶר.
וְיֵרָאֶה רִנּוּנֵנוּ עַד עָרֶב:

יַעֲלֶה קוֹלֵנוּ מֵעֶרֶב. וְיָבֹא צִדְקָתֵנוּ מִבֹּקֶר.
וְיֵרָאֶה פִדְיוֹנֵנוּ עַד עָרֶב:

יַעֲלֶה עֲתִירָתֵנוּ מֵעֶרֶב. וְיָבֹא סְלִיחָתֵנוּ מִבֹּקֶר.
וְיֵרָאֶה בַקָּשָׁתֵנוּ עַד עָרֶב:

יַעֲלֶה יִשְׁעֵנוּ מֵעֶרֶב. וְיָבֹא טָהֳרֵנוּ מִבֹּקֶר.
וְיֵרָאֶה חִנּוּנֵנוּ עַד עָרֶב:

יַעֲלֶה דָפְקֵנוּ מֵעֶרֶב. וְיָבֹא גִילֵנוּ מִבֹּקֶר.
וְיֵרָאֶה הַדְרָתֵנוּ עַד עָרֶב:

יַעֲלֶה אֶנְקָתֵנוּ מֵעֶרֶב. וְיָבֹא אֵלֶיךָ מִבֹּקֶר:
וְיֵרָאֶה אֵלֵינוּ עַד עָרֶב:

Alternate Reading:

GIVE ear to my words, O Lord, have regard to my prayer.

Listen to the voice of my supplication, my King and my God, for to Thee do I pray.

Thou desirest mercy more than sacrifice and the knowledge of God rather than burnt-offering.

Who is like unto Thee, O God, gracious and plenteous of mercy, long-suffering and forgiving transgressions.

Thy mercy is above the heavens, and Thy truth extendeth unto the skies.

Who shall not stand in awe of Thee, O King of nations?

Among all the wise and the mighty there is none like unto Thee.

Justice and judgment are the pillars of Thy throne, love and truth are ever before Thee.

How precious is Thy loving kindness, O God. Therefore do the children of man seek shelter under the shadow of Thy wing.

Lead me, O Lord, in Thy righteousness, make Thy path straight before my face.

For with Thee is the fountain of life. In Thy light we behold light.

Choir:

Prepare to meet thy God, O Israel! Seek ye the Lord and ye shall live. Let justice flow forth as water, and righteousness as a mighty stream.

DAY OF ATONEMENT.

Minister and Congregation:

BE gracious unto me, O God, according to Thy loving kindness.

In Thine endless mercy blot out my transgressions.

Cleanse me, O Lord, and I shall be clean; purify me and I shall be whiter than snow.

Behold Thou desirest truth in our innermost heart —so teach me wisdom and right understanding.

I acknowledge my transgressions and my sin is ever before me.

Create in me a pure heart, O God, renew within me a steadfast spirit.

Cast me not away from Thy presence and take not Thy holy spirit from me.

The soul is Thine and the body is Thine; O, have compassion on Thy handiwork.

For Thy name's sake, O merciful God, pardon our iniquities, though they be many.

Let us search and try our ways and return again unto the Lord.

For Thee, O Lord, do we wait; in Thee, O Lord, do we hope, for with the Lord there is mercy and with Him is plenteous redemption.

Choir:

Like as a father pitieth his children so the Lord pitieth them that fear Him. High as the heaven is above the earth, so great is His mercy toward them that revere Him.

Minister:

וּבְכֵן תֵּן פַּחְדְּךָ

OUR God, and God of our fathers! May Thy presence be manifest to us in all Thy works, and may reverence for Thee fill the hearts of all Thy creatures; may all the children of men bow before Thee in humility and unite to do Thy will with perfect hearts, and all acknowledge that Thine is the kingdom, the power and the majesty, and that Thy name is exalted above all.

Grant hope, O Lord, to them that seek Thee; inspire with courage all who wait for Thee, and be nigh unto all who trust in Thy name; that all men may walk in the light of Thy truth, and recognize that they are children of One Father, that One God has created them all. Then shall the just rejoice and the righteous be glad; then shall iniquity be no more and all men will render homage to Thee alone as their God and King.

Eternal, our God, may Thy kingdom come speedily, and the worship of Thy name and obedience to Thy law unite all men in the bonds of brotherhood and peace, that every creature may know that Thou hast created it, and every living being exclaim: The Eternal, the God of Israel, ruleth and His dominion endureth forever.

Choir:—Amen.

אתה בחרתנו

We render thanksgiving unto Thee that Thou hast chosen our fathers from amongst all nations. Thou hast called us to Thy service, that through Israel, Thy holy name may be known over all the earth. In Thy love hast Thou given us this Day of Atonement, that we may obtain forgiveness of our sins and be reconciled to Thee and our fellow-men. For Thou desirest not the death of the sinner, but that he shall return to Thee and live.

O, that this pleading call may not be in vain, but move us rather to look earnestly within, to search through the hidden recesses of our hearts, that we may know ourselves as we are. May it arouse us to examine all our aims and purposes in the light of Thy truth, in the light of our conscience, that we may know wherein we have strayed from Thy way.

Dispel, we pray Thee, every cloud that veils our vision, that all our most secret sins may stand revealed before us. And when we have learned wherein we have fallen short, and are overcome with the misery of sin, grant us the strength and courage to turn from the evil of our ways and to seek the shelter of Thy paternal love. O Lord, enter not into judgment with us, for in Thy sight can no living man be justified. O let Thy mercy prevail with us. May Thine assistance come to us as we seek to purify our spirits; and may Thy loving-kindness protect and shield us even as we put our trust in Thee.

Choir:—Amen.

Minister:

OUR God and God of our fathers, on this Day of Atonement pardon our transgressions, remove our guilt and blot out our iniquities, as Thou hast promised: I, even I, blot out thine iniquities for mine own sake, and thy sins will I remember no more. I have made thy sins to vanish like a cloud and thy transgressions like a mist; return to me for I have redeemed thee. For on this day shall ye be forgiven and cleansed from all your sins ; before God shall ye be pure.

Minister and Choir:

Our God and God of our fathers, may our prayers come before Thee and turn not away from our supplications, for we are not so arrogant and stiff-necked as to say before Thee that we have not sinned, but aye, we have sinned.

Yea, we have sinned; yea we have transgressed; yea, we have done perversely.

Minister:

We have departed from Thy commandments and from Thy good ordinances, and it hath not profited us, but Thou art justified in all that has come upon us, for Thou doest justly; but we have done evil. What shall we say before Thee, O Most High, and what shall we plead before Thee, O Thou who dwellest in the heavens ? Behold all things secret and revealed

DAY OF ATONEMENT. 107

Minister:

אֱלֹהֵינוּ וֵאלֹהֵי אֲבוֹתֵינוּ. מְחַל לַעֲוֹנוֹתֵינוּ בְּיוֹם הַכִּפֻּרִים הַזֶּה. מְחֵה וְהַעֲבֵר פְּשָׁעֵינוּ וְחַטֹּאתֵינוּ מִנֶּגֶד עֵינֶיךָ. כָּאָמוּר. אָנֹכִי אָנֹכִי הוּא מֹחֶה פְשָׁעֶיךָ לְמַעֲנִי וְחַטֹּאתֶיךָ לֹא אֶזְכֹּר: וְנֶאֱמַר. מָחִיתִי כָעָב פְּשָׁעֶיךָ. וְכֶעָנָן חַטֹּאתֶיךָ. שׁוּבָה אֵלַי כִּי גְאַלְתִּיךָ: וְנֶאֱמַר. כִּי בַיּוֹם הַזֶּה יְכַפֵּר עֲלֵיכֶם. לְטַהֵר אֶתְכֶם מִכֹּל חַטֹּאתֵיכֶם. לִפְנֵי יְיָ תִּטְהָרוּ:

Minister and Choir:

אֱלֹהֵינוּ וֵאלֹהֵי אֲבוֹתֵינוּ.

תָּבֹא לְפָנֶיךָ תְּפִלָּתֵנוּ. וְאַל תִּתְעַלַּם מִתְּחִנָּתֵנוּ. שֶׁאֵין אֲנַחְנוּ עַזֵּי פָנִים וּקְשֵׁי עוֹרֶף. לוֹמַר לְפָנֶיךָ יְיָ אֱלֹהֵינוּ וֵאלֹהֵי אֲבוֹתֵינוּ. צַדִּיקִים אֲנַחְנוּ וְלֹא חָטָאנוּ. אֲבָל אֲנַחְנוּ חָטָאנוּ:

חָטָאנוּ עָוִינוּ. פָּשַׁעְנוּ:

Minister:

סַרְנוּ מִמִּצְוֹתֶיךָ וּמִמִּשְׁפָּטֶיךָ הַטּוֹבִים וְלֹא שָׁוָה לָנוּ. וְאַתָּה צַדִּיק עַל כָּל הַבָּא עָלֵינוּ. כִּי אֱמֶת עָשִׂיתָ וַאֲנַחְנוּ הִרְשָׁעְנוּ:

מַה־נֹּאמַר לְפָנֶיךָ יוֹשֵׁב מָרוֹם. וּמַה נְּסַפֵּר לְפָנֶיךָ שׁוֹכֵן שְׁחָקִים. הֲלֹא כָּל הַנִּסְתָּרוֹת וְהַנִּגְלוֹת אַתָּה יוֹדֵעַ:

Thou knowest. Thou knowest the secret things of the world and what is hidden in the minds of all the living.

Thou searchest the depths of the mind and triest all the intents of the heart. Nothing is concealed from Thine eyes.

Now may it be Thy will, O Lord our God, to forgive our transgressions and pardon our sins and blot out our trespasses:

Minister and Congregation:

The sin which we have sinned against Thee,
> willingly or unwittingly;
> publicly or secretly;
> presumptuously or ignorantly;

The sin which we have sinned against Thee,
> by the evil resolves of the heart;
> by the speech of the mouth;
> by a violent hand;

The sin which we have sinned against Thee.
> by the profanation of Thy name;
> by disregard for our parents and teachers;
> by deceit and treachery to our neighbor;

Minister and Congregation, then Choir:

For all of them, O God of forgiveness, grant us remission! Forgive us! Pardon us!

DAY OF ATONEMENT.

אַתָּה יוֹדֵעַ רָזֵי עוֹלָם. וְתַעֲלוּמוֹת סִתְרֵי כָל חָי.
אַתָּה חוֹפֵשׂ כָּל חַדְרֵי בָטֶן. וּבוֹחֵן כְּלָיוֹת וָלֵב. אֵין
דָּבָר נֶעְלָם מִמֶּךָּ. וְאֵין נִסְתָּר מִנֶּגֶד עֵינֶיךָ:

וּבְכֵן יְהִי רָצוֹן מִלְּפָנֶיךָ. יְיָ אֱלֹהֵינוּ וֵאלֹהֵי אֲבוֹתֵינוּ.
שֶׁתִּסְלַח לָנוּ עַל כָּל חַטֹּאתֵינוּ. וְתִמְחָל לָנוּ עַל
כָּל עֲוֹנוֹתֵינוּ. וּתְכַפֶּר לָנוּ עַל כָּל פְּשָׁעֵינוּ:

Minister and Congregation:

עַל חֵטְא שֶׁחָטָאנוּ לְפָנֶיךָ בְּאֹנֶס וּבְרָצוֹן:
עַל חֵטְא שֶׁחָטָאנוּ לְפָנֶיךָ בְּגָלוּי וּבַסֵּתֶר:
עַל חֵטְא שֶׁחָטָאנוּ לְפָנֶיךָ בְּזָדוֹן וּבִשְׁגָגָה:
עַל חֵטְא שֶׁחָטָאנוּ לְפָנֶיךָ בְּהִרְהוּר הַלֵּב:
עַל חֵטְא שֶׁחָטָאנוּ לְפָנֶיךָ בְּדִבּוּר פֶּה:
עַל חֵטְא שֶׁחָטָאנוּ לְפָנֶיךָ בְּחֹזֶק יָד:
עַל חֵטְא שֶׁחָטָאנוּ לְפָנֶיךָ בְּחִלּוּל הַשֵּׁם:
עַל חֵטְא שֶׁחָטָאנוּ לְפָנֶיךָ בְּזִלְזוּל הוֹרִים וּמוֹרִים:
עַל חֵטְא שֶׁחָטָאנוּ לְפָנֶיךָ בְּהוֹנָאַת וּצְדִיַּת רֵעַ:

וְעַל כֻּלָּם אֱלוֹהַּ סְלִיחוֹת.

Minister and Congregation, then Choir:

סְלַח לָנוּ. מְחַל לָנוּ. כַּפֵּר לָנוּ:

Minister:

O GOD, God of our fathers, forsake us not; may we not be put to shame. Lead us to the knowledge of Thy law, that we may understand and follow Thy ways. Incline our hearts to revere Thy name, and purify our soul by Thy love, that we may return to Thee in truth. Forgive our sins for the sake of Thy great name.

HEAR our voice, Lord our God, be gracious unto us, and in Thy mercy favorably accept our prayers.

CANTICLE.

We are Thy people, Thou art our King.

We are Thy children, Thou art our Father.

We are Thy possession, Thou art our Portion.

We are Thy flock, Thou art our Shepherd.

We are Thy vineyard, Thou art our Keeper.

We are Thy beloved, Thou art our Friend.

Minister:

Praised be Thou, O God, who forgivest transgressions; King of the world, who sanctifiest Israel and the Day of Atonement.

Choir:—Amen.

DAY OF ATONEMENT.

Minister:

אֱלֹהֵינוּ וֵאלֹהֵי אֲבוֹתֵינוּ . אַל תַּעַזְבֵנוּ . וְאַל תִּטְּשֵׁנוּ . וְאַל תַּכְלִימֵנוּ . וְאַל תָּפֵר בְּרִיתְךָ אִתָּנוּ . קָרְבֵנוּ לְתוֹרָתֶךָ . לַמְּדֵנוּ מִצְוֹתֶיךָ . הוֹרֵנוּ דְרָכֶיךָ . הַט לִבֵּנוּ לְיִרְאָה אֶת שְׁמֶךָ . וּמוֹל אֶת לְבָבֵנוּ לְאַהֲבָתֶךָ . וְנָשׁוּב אֵלֶיךָ בֶּאֱמֶת וּבְלֵב שָׁלֵם . וּלְמַעַן שִׁמְךָ הַגָּדוֹל תִּמְחוֹל וְתִסְלַח לַעֲוֹנֵינוּ:
שְׁמַע קוֹלֵנוּ יְיָ אֱלֹהֵינוּ . חוּס וְרַחֵם עָלֵינוּ . וְקַבֵּל בְּרַחֲמִים וּבְרָצוֹן אֶת תְּפִלָּתֵנוּ .

CANTICLE.

כִּי אָנוּ עַמֶּךָ	וְאַתָּה מַלְכֵּנוּ:
אָנוּ בָנֶיךָ	וְאַתָּה אָבִינוּ:
אָנוּ נַחֲלָתֶךָ	וְאַתָּה גוֹרָלֵנוּ:
אָנוּ צֹאנֶךָ	וְאַתָּה רוֹעֵנוּ:
אָנוּ כַרְמֶךָ	וְאַתָּה נוֹטְרֵנוּ:
אָנוּ רַעְיָתֶךָ	וְאַתָּה דוֹדֵנוּ:

Minister:

בָּרוּךְ אַתָּה יְיָ מֶלֶךְ מוֹחֵל וְסוֹלֵחַ לַעֲוֹנוֹתֵינוּ מֶלֶךְ עַל כָּל־הָאָרֶץ מְקַדֵּשׁ יִשְׂרָאֵל וְיוֹם הַכִּפּוּרִים:

Choir:—Amen.

Alternate Reading:

(Psalm cxxxix.)

O LORD! Thou hast searched me and known me; Thou knowest my sitting down and my rising-up; Thou understandest my thoughts from afar.

Thou seest my path and my lying down, and art acquainted with all my ways.

Whither shall I go from Thy spirit, and whither shall I flee from Thy presence?

If I ascend into heaven, Thou art there! If I make my bed in the underworld, behold, Thou art there!

If I take the wings of the morning, and dwell in the remotest part of the sea, even there shall Thy hand lead me, and Thy right hand shall hold me.

If I say, Surely the darkness shall cover me, even the night shall be light about me.

Yea, the darkness hideth not from Thee, but the night shineth as the day;

The darkness and the light are both alike to Thee.

How precious to me are Thy thoughts, O God! how great is the sum of them!

Search me, O God! and know my heart; try me and know my thoughts.

And see if the evil way be within me, and lead me in the way everlasting.

DAY OF ATONEMENT. 113

Minister:

שים שלום

GRANT us peace, Thy most precious gift, O Thou eternal source of peace, and enable Israel to be a messenger of peace unto the peoples of the earth. Bless our country that it may ever be a stronghold of peace, and be its advocate in the councils of nations. May contentment reign within its borders, health and happiness within its homes. Strengthen the nds of friendship and fellowship between all the inhabitants of our land. Plant virtue in every soul and may love of Thy name hallow every home and every heart.

Inscribe us in the book of life, and grant unto us a year of prosperity and joy. Blessed be Thou, O Lord, Giver of peace. Amen.

Silent Devotion:

אלהי נצור

O GOD, guard my tongue from evil and my lips from uttering deceit. Be my support when grief silences my voice, and my comfort when woe bends my spirit. Plant humility in my soul, and strengthen my heart with perfect faith in Thee. Help me to be strong when temptations and trials come, and to be meek when others wrong me, that I may readily forgive them. Guide me by the light of Thy counsel, and let me ever find rest in Thee, who art my Refuge and my Redeemer. Amen.

HYMN.

THY faithful servant, Lord, doth yearn
    For Thy consoling grace;
Spread over him its healing wing,
    His guilt do Thou efface.

Were not Thy word: Turn back from sin
    And I will turn to Thee,
I, like a helmsman in the storm,
    Would, helpless, face the sea.

To Thy despondent·servant show
    The path of penitents:
He striveth painfully for words
    To tell how he repents.

O God! I tremble when I mark
    How day on day is lost,
And yet my heart, by passions ruled,
    Still to and fro is tossed.

O let my penitence to-day
    Be my soul's surety;
Contrite I vow to serve Thee well;
    Be merciful to me!

DAY OF ATONEMENT.

Minister, then Congregation:

OUR Father, our King, grant us a year of happiness.

Choir:—Amen.

Our Father, our King, have mercy upon us and upon our children.

Choir:—Amen.

Our Father, our King, keep far from our country, sickness, war, and famine.

Choir:—Amen.

Our Father, our King, help us to lead a life of purity and goodness.

Choir:—Amen.

Our Father, our King, accept with mercy and with favor our supplication.

Choir:—Amen.

EVENING SERVICE FOR THE

ADORATION.

(Congregation standing.)

Minister:

LET us adore the ever-living God, and render praise unto Him who spread out the heavens and established the earth, whose glory is revealed in the heavens above and whose greatness is manifest throughout the world: He is our God, and there is none else.

We bow our head and bend our knee and magnify the King of kings, the Holy One, the Ever-blest.

Choir and Congregation:

וַאֲנַחְנוּ כֹּרְעִים וּמִשְׁתַּחֲוִים וּמוֹדִים לִפְנֵי מֶלֶךְ מַלְכֵי הַמְּלָכִים הַקָּדוֹשׁ בָּרוּךְ הוּא:

(Congregation sitting.)

Minister:

May the time not be far, O God, when Thy name shall be worshiped over all the earth, when unbelief shall disappear and error be no more. We fervently pray that the day may come upon which all men shall invoke Thy name, when corruption and evil shall give way to purity and goodness; when superstition shall no longer enslave the minds, nor idolatry blind the eyes, when all inhabitants of the earth shall perceive that to Thee alone every knee must bend and every tongue give homage. O may all, created in Thine image, recognize that they are brethren, so that they, one in spirit, and one in fellowship, may be forever united before Thee. Then shall Thy kingdom be established on earth, and the word of Thine ancient seer be fulfilled: The Eternal shall rule forever and aye.

Congregation:

On that day the Eternal shall **be One, and** His name shall be One.

Minister:

ALL you who mourn the loss of loved ones, and, at this hour, remember the goodness, the hope and the sweet companionship that have passed away with them, give ear to the word of comfort spoken to you in the name of your God. Only the body has died and has been laid in the dust. The spirit lives and will live on forever in the land of undisturbed peace and perfect happiness. But in this life, also, the loved ones continue in the remembrance of those to whom they were precious. Every act of goodness they performed, every true and beautiful word they spoke, is treasured up as an incentive to walk in the path of goodness.

And when you ask in your grief: "Whence shall come my help and my comfort?" then, in the strength of faith, answer with the Psalmist: "My help cometh from God," who will not forsake me, nor leave me in my grief. Upon Him I cast my burden, and He will grant me strength according to the days He has apportioned to me. All souls are His, and no power can take them out of His hands. Come, then, and in the midst of sympathizing fellow-worshipers, rise, and hallow with me the name of God.

(The mourners standing and speaking with the Minister.)

EXTOLLED and hallowed be the name of God throughout the world which He has created, and which He governs according to His righteous will. Just is He in all His ways, and wise are all His decrees. May His Kingdom come, and His will be done in all the earth.

Congregation:

Blessed be the Lord of life and righteous Judge forever more.

Minister:

To the departed whom we now remember, may peace and bliss be granted in the world of eternal life. There may they find grace and mercy before the Lord of heaven and earth. May their souls rejoice in that ineffable good which God has laid up for those that fear Him, and may their memory be a blessing unto those that cherish it.

Congregation:

Amen.

Minister:

May the Father of peace send peace to all troubled souls, and comfort all the bereaved among us.

Congregation:

Amen.

DAY OF ATONEMENT. 119

(The mourners standing and speaking with the Minister.)

יִתְגַּדַּל וְיִתְקַדַּשׁ שְׁמֵהּ רַבָּא. בְּעָלְמָא דִי־בְרָא כִרְעוּתֵהּ. וְיַמְלִיךְ מַלְכוּתֵהּ. בְּחַיֵּיכוֹן וּבְיוֹמֵיכוֹן וּבְחַיֵּי דְכָל בֵּית יִשְׂרָאֵל. בַּעֲגָלָא וּבִזְמַן קָרִיב. וְאִמְרוּ אָמֵן:

Congregation:

יְהֵא שְׁמֵהּ רַבָּא מְבָרַךְ. לְעָלַם וּלְעָלְמֵי עָלְמַיָּא.

Minister:

יִתְבָּרַךְ וְיִשְׁתַּבַּח וְיִתְפָּאַר וְיִתְרוֹמַם וְיִתְנַשֵּׂא וְיִתְהַדָּר וְיִתְעַלֶּה וְיִתְהַלָּל שְׁמֵהּ דְּקוּדְשָׁא. בְּרִיךְ הוּא. לְעֵלָּא מִן כָּל בִּרְכָתָא וְשִׁירָתָא. תֻּשְׁבְּחָתָא וְנֶחָמָתָא. דַּאֲמִירָן בְּעָלְמָא. וְאִמְרוּ אָמֵן:

עַל יִשְׂרָאֵל וְעַל צַדִּיקַיָּא. וְעַל־כָּל־מַן דְּאִתְפְּטַר מִן עָלְמָא הָדֵין כִּרְעוּתֵהּ דֶּאֱלָהָא. יְהֵא לְהוֹן שְׁלָמָא רַבָּא וְחוּלָקָא־טָבָא לְחַיֵּי עָלְמָא דְּאָתֵי. וְחִסְדָּא וְרַחֲמֵי מִן־קֳדָם מָרֵא שְׁמַיָּא וְאַרְעָא. וְאִמְרוּ אָמֵן:

יְהֵא שְׁלָמָא רַבָּא מִן־שְׁמַיָּא וְחַיִּים. עָלֵינוּ וְעַל־כָּל־יִשְׂרָאֵל. וְאִמְרוּ אָמֵן:

עֹשֶׂה שָׁלוֹם בִּמְרוֹמָיו. הוּא יַעֲשֶׂה שָׁלוֹם עָלֵינוּ וְעַל כָּל יִשְׂרָאֵל. וְאִמְרוּ אָמֵן:

CLOSING HYMN.

EXTOLLED be the living God and praised! He existeth, but His existence is not bounded by time.

He is One, but there is no unity like unto His unity; He is incomprehensible, and His unity is unending.

He hath no material form; He is incorporeal; and naught that is can be compared to Him in holiness.

He existed before all things that are created; He is the first, but there is no beginning to His existence.

Behold! He is the Lord of the world; and all the creation revealeth His power and His dominion.

The inspiration of prophecy did He bestow on the men of His chosen people.

There never arose a prophet in Israel like unto Moses, who beheld God's similitude.

A true law hath God given to His people, by the hand of His prophet who was faithful in His house

God will never alter nor change His law for any other.

He beholdeth and knoweth all secret things; for He vieweth the end of a thing at its commencement.

He bestoweth kindness on man according to his deeds, and recompenses the wicked according to their wickedness.

Life eternal He hath planted within us. Blessed be the name of His glory for evermore.

DAY OF ATONEMENT.

CLOSING HYMN.

יִגְדַּל אֱלֹהִים חַי וְיִשְׁתַּבַּח נִמְצָא וְאֵין עֵת אֶל מְצִיאוּתוֹ:

אֶחָד וְאֵין יָחִיד כְּיִחוּדוֹ נֶעְלָם וְגַם אֵין סוֹף לְאַחְדּוּתוֹ:

אֵין לוֹ דְמוּת הַגּוּף וְאֵינוֹ גוּף לֹא נַעֲרוֹךְ אֵלָיו קְדֻשָּׁתוֹ:

קַדְמוֹן לְכָל דָּבָר אֲשֶׁר נִבְרָא רִאשׁוֹן וְאֵין רֵאשִׁית לְרֵאשִׁיתוֹ:

הִנּוֹ אֲדוֹן עוֹלָם לְכָל נוֹצָר יוֹרֶה גְדֻלָּתוֹ וּמַלְכוּתוֹ:

שֶׁפַע נְבוּאָתוֹ נְתָנוֹ אֶל אַנְשֵׁי סְגֻלָּתוֹ וְתִפְאַרְתּוֹ:

לֹא קָם בְּיִשְׂרָאֵל כְּמֹשֶׁה עוֹד נָבִיא וּמַבִּיט אֶת תְּמוּנָתוֹ:

תּוֹרַת אֱמֶת נָתַן לְעַמּוֹ אֵל עַל יַד נְבִיאוֹ נֶאֱמַן בֵּיתוֹ:

לֹא יַחֲלִיף הָאֵל וְלֹא יָמִיר דָּתוֹ לְעוֹלָמִים לְזוּלָתוֹ:

צוֹפֶה וְיוֹדֵעַ סְתָרֵינוּ מַבִּיט לְסוֹף דָּבָר בְּקַדְמָתוֹ:

גּוֹמֵל לְאִישׁ חֶסֶד כְּמִפְעָלוֹ נוֹתֵן לְרָשָׁע רָע כְּרִשְׁעָתוֹ:

יִשְׁלַח לְקֵץ יָמִין פְּדוּת עוֹלָם כָּל חַי וְיֵשׁ יַכִּיר יְשׁוּעָתוֹ:

חַיֵּי עוֹלָם נָטַע בְּתוֹכֵנוּ. בָּרוּךְ עֲדֵי עַד שֵׁם תְּהִלָּתוֹ:

PARTING BENEDICTIONS.

THEY who trust in the Lord shall be as Mount Zion, which cannot be moved, which standeth forever. As the mountains are round about Jerusalem, so the Lord is round about his people, henceforth even forever!

Behold, how good and pleasant it is for brethren to dwell together in unity! It is like precious perfume upon the head, like the dew which descendeth upon the mountains of Zion. For there the Lord commandeth a blessing, even life for evermore.

Lift up your eyes to the heavens and look upon the earth beneath; the heavens shall vanish away like smoke, and the earth shall wax old like a garment; and they that dwell therein shall die in like manner; but the salvation of the Lord shall be forever, and His righteousness shall not fail.

Eternal One, Thou hast shown us what is good and what Thou dost require of us, to do justly, to love mercy, and to walk humbly with Thee. Great peace have they who love Thy law, and nothing can offend them. Lord, give strength unto Thy people, O God, bless Thy people with peace.

Morning Service for the Day of Atonement.

For Silent Devotion:

TO Thee, my God and Father, do I lift up my soul in this hour of self-inquiry. Bowed down by the consciousness of my sins I come into Thy house and approach Thy throne of justice, O most righteous Judge! Thou hast given me understanding to distinguish good from evil and hast revealed Thy commandments to me that I may do Thy will. But often have I not hearkened to Thy word nor heeded Thy commandment. Thou hast illumined my soul with the light of understanding, and often I have closed my eyes so as not to see it. Where, O God, shall I hide myself that Thy judging eye may not see me? Whither shall I flee, that the voice of Thy displeasure may not reach me? No distance can separate me from Thine omnipresence, no darkness can hide me from Thine all-seeing eye. But there is still one refuge for me, one hope that sustains me. I shall hide myself in the shadow of Thy mercy; I shall look for shelter under the wings of Thy grace; for Thy forbearance is everlasting and the fountain of Thy love flows forever.

Thou dost not desire the death of the sinner, but Thou dost graciously accept him when he returns to Thee with a changed heart; and never wilt Thou banish the repenting child from Thy presence.

Forgive my sins, O merciful Father! May I find peace in my inmost soul. May no false pride blind me to the defects in my character. Let me not appear righteous in my own sight, but help me to search my heart and know myself. Let me seek and find reconciliation with those of my fellow-men whom I have grieved. May I be worthy of their love. Remove hatred from my heart against those that wish me ill; may Thy love inspire me to forgive willingly those who have wronged me.

May I be reconciled, Lord, to Thee, to myself, and to all my fellow-men. O Thou, who art the loving Father of all, hear my prayer, and in Thy mercy answer me. Amen.

ANTHEM:

THE Lord of all did reign supreme
    Ere yet this world was made and formed.
When all was finished by His will,
Then was His name as King proclaimed.

And should these forms no more exist,
He still will rule in majesty.
He was, He is, He shall remain;
His glory never shall decrease.

And one is He, and none there is
To be compared or joined to Him.
He ne'er began, and ne'er will end,
To Him belong dominion's power.

He is my God, my living God;
To Him I flee when tried in grief;
My banner high, my refuge strong,
Who hears and answers when I call.

My spirit I commit to Him,
My body, too, and all I prize,
Both, when I sleep and when I wake;
He is with me, I shall not fear.

Minister:

RECEIVE us graciously in Thy presence, our God and Father, as we gather on this holiest of days in the abode sanctified by Thy name. As members of one great family, we come to renew our faith in Thee, and to strengthen the bonds of love which may have been weakened amid the strife and turmoil of daily life. Help us to purify our hearts, to subdue our passions, and to remove evil from our thoughts. We long for Thy presence, O God, and wait for Thy mercy. Hear our supplications, and accept in love the prayers we offer here from morning until evening. In Thy grace and truth answer us, O God of our salvation.

Congregation:—Amen.

Minister:

אלהי נשמה

MY God, the soul which Thou hast given unto me came pure from Thy hands. Thou hast created it; Thou hast formed it; Thou hast breathed it into me; Thou hast preserved it in this body and, at the appointed time, Thou wilt take it from this earth that it may enter upon the life everlasting. While the soul animates my being I will worship Thee, Sovereign of the world and Lord of all souls. Blessed be Thou, O Lord, in whose hands are the souls of all the living and the spirits of all flesh.

Congregation:—Amen.

Minister:

רבון כל העולמים

LORD of all the worlds! Not in reliance upon righteousness or merit in ourselves do we make our supplications to Thee, but trusting in Thine infinite mercy alone. For what are we, what is our life, what our goodness, what our power? What can we say in Thy presence? Are not all the mighty men as naught before Thee, and those of great renown as though they had never been; the wisest, as if without knowledge, and the men of understanding as if without discernment? Behold, nations are but as a drop of water, and accounted as a grain of dust in the balance. Many of our actions are vain, and our days pass away like shadows. Our life would be altogether vanity, were it not for the soul which, fashioned in Thine own image, gives us assurance of our higher destiny, and imparts to our fleeting days an abiding value.

We, therefore, beseech Thee, O our God! to help us banish from our hearts all pride and vain-glory, all confidence in worldly possessions, all self-sufficient leaning on our own reason. O give us the spirit of meekness and the grace of modesty, that we may become wise in Thy fear. May we never forget that all we have and prize is but lent to us, that we may use worthily every gift that cometh from Thee, to Thy honor, and the good of our fellow-men.

Congregation:—Amen.

Alternate Reading for Minister and Congregation:

(I Chron. xvi.)

GIVE thanks unto the Lord, call upon His name; make known His deeds among the people.

Sing unto Him; sing psalms unto Him; talk ye of all His wondrous works.

Glory ye in His holy name; let the heart of them rejoice that seek the Lord.

Seek the Lord and His strength; seek His face continually.

Remember His marvellous works that He hath done, His wonders and the judgments of His mouth;

O ye offspring of Israel, His servant, ye children of Jacob, His chosen ones.

He is the Lord, our God; His judgments are in all the earth.

Be ye mindful always of His covenant; the word which he commanded to a thousand generations;

Even of the covenant which He made with Abraham, and of His oath unto Isaac;

And hath confirmed the same to Jacob for a law, and to Israel for an everlasting covenant.

He suffered no man to do them wrong; yea, he reproved kings for their sakes,

Saying, Touch not mine anointed, and do my prophets no harm.

DAY OF ATONEMENT.

Alternate Reading for Minister and Congregation:

(I Chron. xvi.)

הוֹדוּ לַיָּ קִרְאוּ בִשְׁמוֹ. הוֹדִיעוּ בָעַמִּים עֲלִילֹתָיו:

שִׁירוּ לוֹ זַמְּרוּ־לוֹ. שִׂיחוּ בְּכָל־נִפְלְאֹתָיו:

הִתְהַלְלוּ בְּשֵׁם קָדְשׁוֹ. יִשְׂמַח לֵב מְבַקְשֵׁי יְיָ.

דִּרְשׁוּ יְיָ וְעֻזּוֹ. בַּקְּשׁוּ פָנָיו תָּמִיד.

זִכְרוּ נִפְלְאֹתָיו אֲשֶׁר עָשָׂה. מֹפְתָיו וּמִשְׁפְּטֵי־פִיהוּ:

זֶרַע יִשְׂרָאֵל עַבְדוֹ. בְּנֵי יַעֲקֹב בְּחִירָיו:

הוּא יְיָ אֱלֹהֵינוּ. בְּכָל־הָאָרֶץ מִשְׁפָּטָיו:

זִכְרוּ לְעוֹלָם בְּרִיתוֹ. דָּבָר צִוָּה לְאֶלֶף דּוֹר:

אֲשֶׁר כָּרַת אֶת־אַבְרָהָם. וּשְׁבוּעָתוֹ לְיִצְחָק:

וַיַּעֲמִידֶהָ לְיַעֲקֹב לְחֹק. לְיִשְׂרָאֵל בְּרִית עוֹלָם:

לֹא־הִנִּיחַ לְאִישׁ לְעָשְׁקָם. וַיּוֹכַח עֲלֵיהֶם מְלָכִים:

אַל תִּגְּעוּ בִמְשִׁיחָי. וּבִנְבִיאַי אַל־תָּרֵעוּ:

שִׁירוּ לַיָּ כָּל־הָאָרֶץ. בַּשְּׂרוּ מִיּוֹם־אֶל־יוֹם יְשׁוּעָתוֹ:

סַפְּרוּ בַגּוֹיִם אֶת־כְּבוֹדוֹ. בְּכָל־הָעַמִּים נִפְלְאֹתָיו:

Sing unto the Lord, all the earth; show forth from day to day His salvation.

Declare His glory among the heathen; His marvellous works among all nations.

For great is the Lord and greatly to be praised; He also is to be feared above all gods.

For all the gods of the people are idols: but the Lord made the heavens.

Glory and honor are in His presence; strength and gladness are in His place.

Give unto the Lord, ye kindreds of the people, give unto the Lord glory and strength.

Give unto the Lord the glory due unto His name; bring an offering, and come before Him;

Worship the Lord in the beauty of holiness.

Fear before Him, all the earth; the world also shall be stable, that it be not moved.

Let the heavens be glad, and let the earth rejoice; and let men say among the nations, The Lord reigneth.

Let the sea roar, and the fulness thereof; let the fields rejoice, and all that is therein.

Then shall the trees of the wood sing at the presence of the Lord, because He cometh to judge the earth.

O give thanks unto the Lord, for He is good; for His mercy endureth forever.

DAY OF ATONEMENT.

כִּי גָדוֹל יְיָ וּמְהֻלָּל מְאֹד. וְנוֹרָא הוּא עַל־כָּל אֱלֹהִים:

כִּי כָּל־אֱלֹהֵי הָעַמִּים אֱלִילִים. וַיְיָ שָׁמַיִם עָשָׂה:

הוֹד וְהָדָר לְפָנָיו. עֹז וְחֶדְוָה בִּמְקוֹמוֹ:

הָבוּ לַיְיָ מִשְׁפְּחוֹת עַמִּים. הָבוּ לַיְיָ כָּבוֹד וָעֹז:

הָבוּ לַיְיָ כְּבוֹד שְׁמוֹ. שְׂאוּ מִנְחָה וּבֹאוּ לְפָנָיו. הִשְׁתַּחֲווּ לַיְיָ בְּהַדְרַת־קֹדֶשׁ:

חִילוּ מִלְּפָנָיו כָּל־הָאָרֶץ. אַף־תִּכּוֹן תֵּבֵל בַּל־תִּמּוֹט:

יִשְׂמְחוּ הַשָּׁמַיִם וְתָגֵל הָאָרֶץ. וְיֹאמְרוּ בַגּוֹיִם יְיָ מָלָךְ:

יִרְעַם הַיָּם וּמְלֹאוֹ. יַעֲלֹץ הַשָּׂדֶה וְכָל־אֲשֶׁר־בּוֹ:

אָז יְרַנְּנוּ עֲצֵי הַיָּעַר מִלִּפְנֵי יְיָ. כִּי־בָא לִשְׁפּוֹט אֶת־הָאָרֶץ:

הוֹדוּ לַיְיָ כִּי טוֹב. כִּי לְעוֹלָם חַסְדּוֹ:

Choir:

Praised be the Lord, the God of Israel, from eternity to eternity, and let all people worship the Lord. Amen.

Minister and Congregation:

HAPPY are they who dwell in Thy house, they shall continually praise Thee.

Happy are they who thus know Him; happy the people whose God is the Eternal.

(Psalm cxlv.)

I will extol Thee, my God, O King, and I will bless Thy name forever and ever.

Every day I will bless Thee, and I will praise Thy name forever and ever.

Great is the Lord and highly to be praised; His greatness is unsearchable.

One generation shall praise Thy works to another, and shall declare Thy mighty deeds.

I will speak of the glorious honor of Thy majesty, and of Thy wonderful works.

And men shall speak of the might of Thy deeds, and I will declare Thy greatness.

They shall remember Thy great goodness, and sing of Thy righteousness.

The Lord is gracious and full of compassion, slow to anger, and rich in mercy.

The Lord is good to all, and His tender mercies are over all His works.

DAY OF ATONEMENT.

Choir:

בָּרוּךְ יְיָ אֱלֹהֵי יִשְׂרָאֵל ‏. מִן־הָעוֹלָם וְעַד־הָעוֹלָם ‏. וְיֹאמְרוּ כָל־הָעָם ‏. אָמֵן וְהַלֵּל לַיְיָ:

Minister and Congregation:

אַשְׁרֵי יוֹשְׁבֵי בֵיתֶךָ ‏. עוֹד יְהַלְלוּךָ סֶּלָה:
אַשְׁרֵי הָעָם שֶׁכָּכָה לּוֹ ‏. אַשְׁרֵי הָעָם שֶׁיְיָ אֱלֹהָיו:

(Psalm cxlv.)

אֲרוֹמִמְךָ אֱלוֹהַי הַמֶּלֶךְ ‏. וַאֲבָרְכָה שִׁמְךָ לְעוֹלָם וָעֶד:
בְּכָל־יוֹם אֲבָרְכֶךָ ‏. וַאֲהַלְלָה שִׁמְךָ לְעוֹלָם וָעֶד:
גָּדוֹל יְיָ וּמְהֻלָּל מְאֹד ‏. וְלִגְדֻלָּתוֹ אֵין חֵקֶר:
דּוֹר לְדוֹר יְשַׁבַּח מַעֲשֶׂיךָ ‏. וּגְבוּרֹתֶיךָ יַגִּידוּ:
הֲדַר כְּבוֹד הוֹדֶךָ וְדִבְרֵי נִפְלְאֹתֶיךָ אָשִׂיחָה:
וֶעֱזוּז נוֹרְאוֹתֶיךָ יֹאמֵרוּ ‏. וּגְדֻלָּתְךָ אֲסַפְּרֶנָּה:
זֵכֶר רַב־טוּבְךָ יַבִּיעוּ ‏. וְצִדְקָתְךָ יְרַנֵּנוּ:
חַנּוּן וְרַחוּם יְיָ ‏. אֶרֶךְ אַפַּיִם וּגְדָל־חָסֶד:
טוֹב יְיָ לַכֹּל ‏. וְרַחֲמָיו עַל־כָּל־מַעֲשָׂיו:
יוֹדוּךָ יְיָ כָּל־מַעֲשֶׂיךָ ‏. וַחֲסִידֶיךָ יְבָרְכוּכָה:
כְּבוֹד מַלְכוּתְךָ יֹאמֵרוּ ‏. וּגְבוּרָתְךָ יְדַבֵּרוּ:

All Thy works praise Thee, O God, and **Thy holy** ones bless Thee.

They proclaim the glory of Thy kingdom, and speak of Thy power.

Thy kingdom is an everlasting kingdom, and Thy dominion endureth from generation to generation.

The Lord upholdeth the falling and uplifteth those who are bowed down.

The eyes of all wait upon Thee, and Thou givest them their food in due season.

Thou openest Thy hand and satisfiest the desire of every living being.

The Lord is righteous in all His ways, and merciful in all His works.

The Lord is nigh to all who call upon Him, unto all who call upon Him in truth.

He fulfilleth the desire of those that fear Him; He will also hear their cry and save them.

My mouth shall utter the praises of the Lord; and let all flesh bless His holy name forever and ever.

And we will praise the Lord from henceforth and forever. Hallelujah!

(Psalm cxlvi.)

Hallelujah, praise the Lord, O my soul.

I will praise the Lord as long as I live; I will sing praises to my God while I have my being.

DAY OF ATONEMENT. 135

לְהוֹדִיעַ לִבְנֵי הָאָדָם גְּבוּרֹתָיו. וּכְבוֹד הֲדַר מַלְכוּתוֹ:

מַלְכוּתְךָ מַלְכוּת כָּל־עֹלָמִים. וּמֶמְשַׁלְתְּךָ בְּכָל־דּוֹר וָדֹר.

סוֹמֵךְ יְיָ לְכָל־הַנֹּפְלִים. וְזוֹקֵף לְכָל־הַכְּפוּפִים:

עֵינֵי כֹל אֵלֶיךָ יְשַׂבֵּרוּ וְאַתָּה נוֹתֵן־לָהֶם אֶת־אָכְלָם בְּעִתּוֹ:

פּוֹתֵחַ אֶת־יָדֶךָ. וּמַשְׂבִּיעַ לְכָל־חַי רָצוֹן:

צַדִּיק יְיָ בְּכָל־דְּרָכָיו. וְחָסִיד בְּכָל־מַעֲשָׂיו:

קָרוֹב יְיָ לְכָל־קֹרְאָיו. לְכֹל אֲשֶׁר יִקְרָאֻהוּ בֶאֱמֶת:

רְצוֹן־יְרֵאָיו יַעֲשֶׂה. וְאֶת־שַׁוְעָתָם יִשְׁמַע וְיוֹשִׁיעֵם:

שׁוֹמֵר יְיָ אֶת־כָּל־אֹהֲבָיו. וְאֵת כָּל־הָרְשָׁעִים יַשְׁמִיד:

תְּהִלַּת יְיָ יְדַבֶּר־פִּי. וִיבָרֵךְ כָּל־בָּשָׂר שֵׁם קָדְשׁוֹ לְעוֹלָם וָעֶד:

וַאֲנַחְנוּ נְבָרֵךְ יָהּ מֵעַתָּה וְעַד־עוֹלָם הַלְלוּיָהּ:

(Psalm cxlvi.)

הַלְלוּיָהּ הַלְלִי נַפְשִׁי אֶת־יְהוָֹה:

אֲהַלְלָה יְהוָֹה בְּחַיָּי. אֲזַמְּרָה לֵאלֹהַי בְּעוֹדִי:

Put not your trust in princes, in the son of man, in whom there is no help!

His breath goeth forth; he returneth to the dust; in that very day his plans perish.

Happy is he that hath the God of Jacob for his help;

Whose hope is in the Lord his God;

Who made heaven and earth, the sea, and all that is therein; who keepeth truth forever;

Who executeth judgment for the oppressed; who giveth food to the hungry.

The Lord setteth free the prisoners; the Lord openeth the eyes of the blind.

The Lord raiseth up them that are bowed down; the Lord loveth the righteous.

The Lord preserveth the strangers; he relieveth the fatherless and the widow.

Choir:

The Lord shall reign forever; Thy God, O Zion! to all generations! praise ye the Lord!

Minister and Congregation:

(Psalm cxlvii.)

PRAISE ye the Lord! for it is good to sing praise to our God; for it is pleasant, and praise is becoming.

He healeth the broken in heart, and bindeth up their wounds.

DAY OF ATONEMENT. 137

אַל־תִּבְטְחוּ בִנְדִיבִים . בְּבֶן־אָדָם שֶׁאֵין־לוֹ תְשׁוּעָה:
תֵּצֵא רוּחוֹ יָשֻׁב לְאַדְמָתוֹ . בַּיּוֹם הַהוּא אָבְדוּ עֶשְׁתֹּנֹתָיו:
אַשְׁרֵי שֶׁאֵל יַעֲקֹב בְּעֶזְרוֹ . שִׂבְרוֹ עַל־יְיָ אֱלֹהָיו:
עֹשֶׂה שָׁמַיִם וָאָרֶץ . אֶת־הַיָּם וְאֶת־כָּל־אֲשֶׁר בָּם . הַשֹּׁמֵר אֱמֶת לְעוֹלָם:
עֹשֶׂה מִשְׁפָּט לָעֲשׁוּקִים . נֹתֵן לֶחֶם לָרְעֵבִים . יְיָ מַתִּיר אֲסוּרִים:
יְיָ פֹּקֵחַ עִוְרִים . יְיָ זֹקֵף כְּפוּפִים . יְיָ אֹהֵב צַדִּיקִים:
יְהוָֹה שֹׁמֵר אֶת־גֵּרִים . יָתוֹם וְאַלְמָנָה יְעוֹדֵד . וְדֶרֶךְ רְשָׁעִים יְעַוֵּת:

Choir:

יִמְלֹךְ יְיָ לְעוֹלָם אֱלֹהַיִךְ צִיּוֹן לְדֹר וָדֹר הַלְלוּיָהּ:

Minister and Congregation:

(Psalm cxlvii.)

הַלְלוּיָהּ . כִּי־טוֹב זַמְּרָה אֱלֹהֵינוּ . כִּי־נָעִים נָאוָה תְהִלָּה:
הָרוֹפֵא לִשְׁבוּרֵי לֵב . וּמְחַבֵּשׁ לְעַצְּבוֹתָם:
מוֹנֶה מִסְפָּר לַכּוֹכָבִים . לְכֻלָּם שֵׁמוֹת יִקְרָא:

He counteth the number of the stars; He calleth them all by their names.

Great is our Lord, and mighty in power; His wisdom is infinite.

The Lord lifteth up the lowly; He casteth the wicked down to the ground.

Sing to the Lord with thanksgiving; sing praises upon the harp to our God!

Who covereth the heavens with clouds, who prepareth rain for the earth, who causeth grass to grow upon the mountains.

He giveth to the cattle their food, and to the young ravens, when they cry.

He delighteth not in the strength of the horse. He taketh not pleasure in the force of a man.

The Lord taketh pleasure in those who fear Him, in those who trust in His mercy:

Praise the Lord, O Jerusalem! Praise thy God, O Zion!

For He hath strengthened the bars of thy gates; He hath blessed thy children within thee.

He maketh peace in thy borders, and satisfieth thee with the finest of the wheat.

He sendeth forth His command to the earth; His word runneth swiftly.

He giveth snow like wool, and scattereth the hoarfrost like ashes.

He casteth forth His ice like morsels; who can stand before His cold?

גָּדוֹל אֲדוֹנֵינוּ וְרַב־כֹּחַ. לִתְבוּנָתוֹ אֵין מִסְפָּר:

מְעוֹדֵד עֲנָוִים יְהֹוָה. מַשְׁפִּיל רְשָׁעִים עֲדֵי אָרֶץ:

עֱנוּ לַיהוָה בְּתוֹדָה. זַמְּרוּ לֵאלֹהֵינוּ בְכִנּוֹר:

הַמְכַסֶּה שָׁמַיִם בְּעָבִים. הַמֵּכִין לָאָרֶץ מָטָר. הַמַּצְמִיחַ הָרִים חָצִיר:

נוֹתֵן לִבְהֵמָה לַחְמָהּ. לִבְנֵי עֹרֵב אֲשֶׁר יִקְרָאוּ:

לֹא בִגְבוּרַת הַסּוּס יֶחְפָּץ. לֹא־בְשׁוֹקֵי הָאִישׁ יִרְצֶה:

רוֹצֶה יְהֹוָה אֶת יְרֵאָיו. אֶת הַמְיַחֲלִים לְחַסְדּוֹ:

שַׁבְּחִי יְרוּשָׁלַיִם אֶת יְהֹוָה. הַלְלִי אֱלֹהַיִךְ צִיּוֹן:

כִּי חִזַּק בְּרִיחֵי שְׁעָרָיִךְ: בֵּרַךְ בָּנַיִךְ בְּקִרְבֵּךְ:

הַשָּׂם גְּבוּלֵךְ שָׁלוֹם. חֵלֶב חִטִּים יַשְׂבִּיעֵךְ:

הַשֹּׁלֵחַ אִמְרָתוֹ אָרֶץ. עַד מְהֵרָה יָרוּץ דְּבָרוֹ:

הַנֹּתֵן שֶׁלֶג כַּצָּמֶר. כְּפוֹר כָּאֵפֶר יְפַזֵּר:

מַשְׁלִיךְ קַרְחוֹ כְפִתִּים. לִפְנֵי קָרָתוֹ מִי יַעֲמֹד:

יִשְׁלַח דְּבָרוֹ וְיַמְסֵם. יַשֵּׁב רוּחוֹ יִזְּלוּ מָיִם:

מַגִּיד דְּבָרָיו לְיַעֲקֹב. חֻקָּיו וּמִשְׁפָּטָיו לְיִשְׂרָאֵל:

He sendeth forth His word, and melteth them; He causeth His wind to blow, and the waters flow.

He published His word to Jacob, His statutes and laws to Israel.

He hath dealt in this manner with no other nation; and, as for His ordinances, they have not known them. Hallelujah!

Choir:

Amen. Hallelujah!

Minister and Congregation:

(Psalm cxlviii.)

PRAISE ye the Lord! praise the Lord from the heavens! praise Him in the heights.

Praise Him, all ye His angels! praise Him, all ye His hosts!

Praise ye Him, sun and moon! praise Him, all ye stars of light!

Praise Him, ye heavens of heavens! ye waters, that are above the heavens!

Let them praise the name of the Lord; for He commanded, and they were created.

He hath also established them forever; He hath given them a law and they transgress it not.

Praise the Lord from the earth, ye sea-monsters, and all deeps!

DAY OF ATONEMENT.

לֹא עָשָׂה כֵן לְכָל־גּוֹי. וּמִשְׁפָּטִים בַּל יְדָעוּם. הַלְלוּיָהּ:

Choir:

Amen. Hallelujah.

Minister and Congregation:

(Psalm cxlviii.)

הַלְלוּיָהּ . הַלְלוּ אֶת יְיָ מִן הַשָּׁמַיִם . הַלְלוּהוּ בַּמְּרוֹמִים:

הַלְלוּהוּ כָל־מַלְאָכָיו. הַלְלוּהוּ כָּל־צְבָאָיו:

הַלְלוּהוּ שֶׁמֶשׁ וְיָרֵחַ . הַלְלוּהוּ כָּל־כּוֹכְבֵי אוֹר:

הַלְלוּהוּ שְׁמֵי הַשָּׁמָיִם . וְהַמַּיִם אֲשֶׁר מֵעַל הַשָּׁמָיִם:

יְהַלְלוּ אֶת שֵׁם יְהוָֹה . כִּי הוּא צִוָּה וְנִבְרָאוּ:

וַיַּעֲמִידֵם לָעַד לְעוֹלָם . חָק־נָתַן וְלֹא יַעֲבוֹר:

הַלְלוּ אֶת יְהוָֹה מִן־הָאָרֶץ . תַּנִּינִים וְכָל־תְּהֹמוֹת:

אֵשׁ וּבָרָד שֶׁלֶג וְקִיטוֹר . רוּחַ סְעָרָה עֹשָׂה דְבָרוֹ:

הֶהָרִים וְכָל גְּבָעוֹת . עֵץ פְּרִי וְכָל אֲרָזִים:

הַחַיָּה וְכָל בְּהֵמָה . רֶמֶשׂ וְצִפּוֹר כָּנָף:

Fire and hail, snow and vapor; thou tempest, that fulfillest His word!

Ye mountains, and all hills! fruit-trees, and all cedars!

Ye wild beasts, and all cattle! ye creeping things, and winged birds!

Ye kings, and all peoples, princes, and all judges of the earth!

Young men and maidens, old men and children!

Let them praise the name of the Lord! for His name alone is exalted;

His glory is above the earth and the heavens.

He exalteth the honor of his people, the glory of the children of Israel, a people near unto Him. Praise ye the Lord!

Choir:

Amen. Hallelujah!

Minister and Congregation:

(Psalm xxxiv.)

I WILL bless the Lord at all times; His praise shall be continually in my mouth.

In the Lord doth my soul boast; let the afflicted hear, and rejoice!

O magnify the Lord with me, and let us exalt His name together!

I sought the Lord, and He heard me and delivered me from my fears.

מַלְכֵי־אֶרֶץ וְכָל לְאֻמִּים. שָׂרִים וְכָל־שֹׁפְטֵי אָרֶץ:
בַּחוּרִים וְגַם־בְּתוּלוֹת. זְקֵנִים עִם־נְעָרִים:
יְהַלְלוּ אֶת־שֵׁם יְיָ. כִּי־נִשְׂגָּב שְׁמוֹ לְבַדּוֹ. הוֹדוֹ עַל־אֶרֶץ וְשָׁמָיִם:
וַיָּרֶם קֶרֶן לְעַמּוֹ. תְּהִלָּה לְכָל־חֲסִידָיו. לִבְנֵי יִשְׂרָאֵל עַם קְרֹבוֹ. הַלְלוּיָהּ:

Choir:

Amen. Hallelujah.

Minister and Congregation:

(Psalm xxxiv.)

אֲבָרְכָה אֶת־יְהֹוָה בְּכָל־עֵת. תָּמִיד תְּהִלָּתוֹ בְּפִי:
בַּיהֹוָה תִּתְהַלֵּל נַפְשִׁי. יִשְׁמְעוּ עֲנָוִים וְיִשְׂמָחוּ:
גַּדְּלוּ לַיהֹוָה אִתִּי. וּנְרוֹמְמָה שְׁמוֹ יַחְדָּו:
דָּרַשְׁתִּי אֶת־יְהֹוָה וְעָנָנִי. וּמִכָּל־מְגוּרוֹתַי הִצִּילָנִי:
הִבִּיטוּ אֵלָיו וְנָהָרוּ. וּפְנֵיהֶם אַל־יֶחְפָּרוּ:
זֶה עָנִי קָרָא וַיהֹוָה שָׁמֵעַ. וּמִכָּל־צָרוֹתָיו הוֹשִׁיעוֹ:
חֹנֶה מַלְאַךְ־יְהֹוָה סָבִיב לִירֵאָיו וַיְחַלְּצֵם:
טַעֲמוּ וּרְאוּ כִּי טוֹב יְהֹוָה. אַשְׁרֵי הַגֶּבֶר יֶחֱסֶה־בּוֹ:

Look up to Him, and ye shall have light; your faces shall never be ashamed.

The afflicted man cried, and the Lord heard, and saved him from all his troubles.

The angels of the Lord encamp around those who fear Him, and deliver them.

O taste, and see how good is the Lord! happy the man who trusteth in Him!

O fear the Lord, ye His servants! for to those who fear Him there shall be no want.

Come, ye children, hearken to me! I will teach you the fear of the Lord.

Who is he that loveth life, and desireth many days, in which he may see good?

Guard well thy tongue from evil, and thy lips from speaking guile!

Depart from evil, and do good; seek peace, and pursue it!

The eyes of the Lord are upon the righteous, and His ears are open to their cry.

The Lord is near to them that are of a broken heart; And saveth such as are of a contrite spirit.

Many are the afflictions of the righteous: but the Lord delivereth him from them all.

Choir:

The Lord redeemeth the soul of His servants, and none that put their trust in Him will He abandon.

DAY OF ATONEMENT.

יְראוּ אֶת־יְהֹוָה קְדֹשָׁיו ۰ כִּי אֵין מַחְסוֹר לִירֵאָיו:

כְּפִירִים רָשׁוּ וְרָעֵבוּ ۰ וְדֹרְשֵׁי יְהֹוָה לֹא־יַחְסְרוּ כָל־טוֹב:

לְכוּ־בָנִים שִׁמְעוּ־לִי ۰ יִרְאַת יְהֹוָה אֲלַמֶּדְכֶם:

מִי־הָאִישׁ הֶחָפֵץ חַיִּים ۰ אֹהֵב יָמִים לִרְאוֹת טוֹב:

נְצֹר לְשׁוֹנְךָ מֵרָע ۰ וּשְׂפָתֶיךָ מִדַּבֵּר מִרְמָה:

סוּר מֵרָע וַעֲשֵׂה־טוֹב ۰ בַּקֵּשׁ שָׁלוֹם וְרָדְפֵהוּ:

עֵינֵי יְהֹוָה אֶל־צַדִּיקִים ۰ וְאָזְנָיו אֶל־שַׁוְעָתָם:

פְּנֵי יְהֹוָה בְּעֹשֵׂי רָע ۰ לְהַכְרִית מֵאֶרֶץ זִכְרָם:

צָעֲקוּ וַיהֹוָה שָׁמֵעַ ۰ וּמִכָּל־צָרוֹתָם הִצִּילָם:

קָרוֹב יְהֹוָה לְנִשְׁבְּרֵי־לֵב ۰ וְאֶת־דַּכְּאֵי־רוּחַ יוֹשִׁיעַ:

רַבּוֹת רָעוֹת צַדִּיק ۰ וּמִכֻּלָּם יַצִּילֶנּוּ יְהֹוָה:

שֹׁמֵר כָּל־עַצְמוֹתָיו ۰ אַחַת מֵהֵנָּה לֹא נִשְׁבָּרָה:

תְּמוֹתֵת רָשָׁע רָעָה ۰ וְשֹׂנְאֵי צַדִּיק יֶאְשָׁמוּ:

Choir:

פּוֹדֶה יְהֹוָה נֶפֶשׁ עֲבָדָיו ۰ וְלֹא יֶאְשְׁמוּ כָּל הַחוֹסִים

Minister and Congregation:

(Psalm xxxiii.)

REJOICE, O ye righteous, in the Lord! for praise becometh the upright.

Thank the Lord with psaltery and harp; sing a new song unto Him.

For the word of the Lord is right, and all His acts are faithful.

He loveth justice and equity; the earth is full of the goodness of the Lord.

By the word of the Lord were the heavens made, and all the hosts of them by the breath of His mouth.

He gathereth the waters of the sea as a heap; He layeth up the deep in storehouses.

Let all the earth fear the Lord; let all the inhabitants of the world stand in awe of Him!

For He spake, and it was done; He commanded, and it stood fast.

The purposes of the Lord stand forever; the designs of His heart to all generations.

Happy is the nation whose God is the Lord; the people whom He hath chosen for His inheritance.

The Lord looketh down from heaven; He beholdeth all the children of man;

He that formed the hearts of all, and observeth all their works.

DAY OF ATONEMENT.

Minister and Congregation:

(Psalm xxxiii.)

רַנְּנוּ צַדִּיקִים בַּיְיָ. לַיְשָׁרִים נָאוָה תְהִלָּה:

הוֹדוּ לַיְיָ בְּכִנּוֹר. בְּנֵבֶל עָשׂוֹר זַמְּרוּ לוֹ:

שִׁירוּ לוֹ שִׁיר חָדָשׁ. הֵיטִיבוּ נַגֵּן בִּתְרוּעָה:

כִּי יָשָׁר דְּבַר יְיָ. וְכָל מַעֲשֵׂהוּ בֶּאֱמוּנָה:

אֹהֵב צְדָקָה וּמִשְׁפָּט. חֶסֶד יְיָ מָלְאָה הָאָרֶץ:

בִּדְבַר יְיָ שָׁמַיִם נַעֲשׂוּ. וּבְרוּחַ פִּיו כָּל צְבָאָם:

כֹּנֵס כַּנֵּד מֵי הַיָּם. נֹתֵן בְּאוֹצָרוֹת תְּהוֹמוֹת:

יִירְאוּ מֵיְיָ כָּל־הָאָרֶץ. מִמֶּנּוּ יָגוּרוּ כָּל יֹשְׁבֵי תֵבֵל:

כִּי הוּא אָמַר וַיֶּהִי. הוּא צִוָּה וַיַּעֲמֹד:

יְיָ הֵפִיר עֲצַת גּוֹיִם. הֵנִיא מַחְשְׁבוֹת עַמִּים:

עֲצַת יְיָ לְעוֹלָם תַּעֲמֹד. מַחְשְׁבוֹת לִבּוֹ לְדֹר וָדֹר:

אַשְׁרֵי הַגּוֹי אֲשֶׁר יְיָ אֱלֹהָיו. הָעָם בָּחַר לְנַחֲלָה לוֹ:

מִשָּׁמַיִם הִבִּיט יְיָ. רָאָה אֶת־כָּל־בְּנֵי הָאָדָם:

מִמְּכוֹן שִׁבְתּוֹ הִשְׁגִּיחַ. אֶל כָּל יֹשְׁבֵי הָאָרֶץ:

הַיֹּצֵר יַחַד לִבָּם. הַמֵּבִין אֶל־כָּל־מַעֲשֵׂיהֶם:

אֵין הַמֶּלֶךְ נוֹשָׁע בְּרָב־חָיִל. גִּבּוֹר לֹא יִנָּצֵל בְּרָב־כֹּחַ:

A king is not saved by the number of his hosts, nor a hero by the greatness of his strength.

Behold the eye of the Lord is upon them that fear Him, upon them that trust in His goodness;

To save them from the power of death, and keep them alive in famine.

The hope of our souls is in the Lord; He is our help and our shield.

Yea, in Him doth our heart rejoice; in His holy name we put our trust.

Choir:

May Thy goodness be upon us, O Lord! according as we hope in Thee!

Minister and Congregation:

(Psalm xix.)

THE heavens declare the glory of God; the firmament showeth forth the work of His hands.

Day uttereth instruction unto day,

And night showeth knowledge unto night.

There is no speech nor language where their voice is not heard.

Their sound goeth forth to all the earth, and their words to the ends of the world.

In them hath He set a tabernacle for the sun,

Who like a bridegroom cometh forth from his chamber, and rejoiceth, like a hero, to run his course.

DAY OF ATONEMENT. 149

שֶׁקֶר הַסּוּס לִתְשׁוּעָה. וּבְרֹב חֵילוֹ לֹא יְמַלֵּט:

הִנֵּה עֵין יְיָ אֶל־יְרֵאָיו. לַמְיַחֲלִים לְחַסְדּוֹ:

לְהַצִּיל מִמָּוֶת נַפְשָׁם. וּלְחַיּוֹתָם בָּרָעָב:

נַפְשֵׁנוּ חִכְּתָה לַיְיָ. עֶזְרֵנוּ וּמָגִנֵּנוּ הוּא:

כִּי־בוֹ יִשְׂמַח לִבֵּנוּ. כִּי בְשֵׁם קָדְשׁוֹ בָטָחְנוּ:

Choir:

יְהִי חַסְדְּךָ יְיָ עָלֵינוּ. כַּאֲשֶׁר יִחַלְנוּ לָךְ:

Minister and Congregation:

(Psalm xix.)

הַשָּׁמַיִם מְסַפְּרִים כְּבוֹד אֵל. וּמַעֲשֵׂה יָדָיו מַגִּיד הָרָקִיעַ:

יוֹם לְיוֹם יַבִּיעַ אֹמֶר. וְלַיְלָה לְּלַיְלָה יְחַוֶּה דָּעַת:

אֵין אֹמֶר וְאֵין דְּבָרִים. בְּלִי נִשְׁמָע קוֹלָם:

בְּכָל הָאָרֶץ יָצָא קַוָּם. וּבִקְצֵה תֵבֵל מִלֵּיהֶם. לַשֶּׁמֶשׁ שָׂם אֹהֶל בָּהֶם:

וְהוּא כְּחָתָן יֹצֵא מֵחֻפָּתוֹ. יָשִׂישׂ כְּגִבּוֹר לָרוּץ אֹרַח:

He goeth forth from the extremity of heaven, and maketh his circuit to the end of it; and nothing is hid from his heat.

The law of the Lord is perfect, reviving the soul;

The precepts of the Lord are sure, making wise the simple.

The statutes of the Lord are right, rejoicing the heart;

The commandments of the Lord are pure, enlightening the eyes.

The fear of the Lord is pure, enduring forever;

The judgments of the Lord are true and righteous altogether.

More precious are they than gold; yea, than much fine gold; sweeter than honey and the honeycomb.

By them also is Thy servant warned, and in the keeping of them, there is great reward.

Who knoweth His own offences? O, cleanse Thou me from secret faults!

Keep back also Thy servant from presumptuous sins; let them not have dominion over me!

Then shall I be perfect, and free from great transgression.

Choir.

May the words of my mouth and the meditation of my heart be acceptable before Thee, O Lord, my strength and my redeemer.

מִקְצֵה הַשָּׁמַיִם מוֹצָאוֹ. וּתְקוּפָתוֹ עַל־קְצוֹתָם. וְאֵין נִסְתָּר מֵחַמָּתוֹ:

תּוֹרַת יְיָ תְּמִימָה. מְשִׁיבַת נָפֶשׁ. עֵדוּת יְיָ נֶאֱמָנָה' מַחְכִּימַת פֶּתִי:

פִּקּוּדֵי יְיָ יְשָׁרִים. מְשַׂמְּחֵי־לֵב. מִצְוַת יְיָ בָּרָה. מְאִירַת עֵינָיִם:

יִרְאַת יְיָ טְהוֹרָה. עוֹמֶדֶת לָעַד. מִשְׁפְּטֵי־יְיָ אֱמֶת. צָדְקוּ יַחְדָּו:

הַנֶּחֱמָדִים מִזָּהָב וּמִפַּז רָב. וּמְתוּקִים מִדְּבַשׁ וְנֹפֶת צוּפִים:

גַּם־עַבְדְּךָ נִזְהָר בָּהֶם. בְּשָׁמְרָם עֵקֶב רָב:

שְׁגִיאוֹת מִי־יָבִין. מִנִּסְתָּרוֹת נַקֵּנִי:

גַּם מִזֵּדִים חֲשֹׂךְ עַבְדֶּךָ. אַל־יִמְשְׁלוּ־בִי. אָז אֵיתָם. וְנִקֵּיתִי מִפֶּשַׁע רָב:

Choir:

יִהְיוּ לְרָצוֹן אִמְרֵי־פִי. וְהֶגְיוֹן לִבִּי לְפָנֶיךָ. יְיָ צוּרִי וְגוֹאֲלִי:

Minister:

THINE alone, O Lord, is the greatness and the glory. Riches and honor come from Thee; in Thy hand are strength and power. Every living soul shall praise Thee; the spirit of all flesh shall glorify Thy name. Thou art God from everlasting to everlasting and besides Thee there is no redeemer nor savior. Thou art the first and the last, the Lord of all generations. Thou rulest the world in kindness and all Thy creatures in mercy. Thou art our guardian who sleepeth not and slumbereth not. To Thee alone we give thanks. Yet, though our lips would overflow with song, and our tongues with joyous praise, we would still be unable to thank Thee even for a thousandth part of the bounties which Thou hast bestowed upon us and our fathers. Thou hast been our protector and our savior in every trial and peril. Thy mercy has watched over us and Thy loving-kindness has never failed us.

Praised be Thy holy name. Thou hast made Thine eternal law our portion, and hast given us a goodly heritage. Thou didst appoint us to proclaim Thy truth unto the nations and win them for Thy law of righteousness. Sanctify us for the service to which Thou hast called us, O Heavenly Father, that Thy name may be hallowed through us in all the world. Gather all Thy children around Thy banner of truth that Thy praise may resound from one end of the earth to the other, and that through Israel the entire human family may be blessed with truth and peace.

Choir:—Amen.

DAY OF ATONEMENT.

Minister:

נִשְׁמַת כָּל־חַי תְּבָרֵךְ אֶת־שִׁמְךָ יְיָ אֱלֹהֵינוּ. וְרוּחַ כָּל־בָּשָׂר תְּפָאֵר וּתְרוֹמֵם זִכְרְךָ מַלְכֵּנוּ תָּמִיד: מִן־הָעוֹלָם וְעַד־הָעוֹלָם אַתָּה אֵל. וּמִבַּלְעָדֶיךָ אֵין לָנוּ מֶלֶךְ גּוֹאֵל וּמוֹשִׁיעַ פּוֹדֶה וּמַצִּיל. וּמְפַרְנֵס וּמְרַחֵם. בְּכָל־עֵת צָרָה וְצוּקָה. אֵין לָנוּ מֶלֶךְ אֶלָּא אָתָּה: אֱלֹהֵי הָרִאשׁוֹנִים וְהָאַחֲרוֹנִים. הַמְּנַהֵג עוֹלָמוֹ בְּחֶסֶד וּבְרִיּוֹתָיו בְּרַחֲמִים. לְךָ לְבַדְּךָ אֲנַחְנוּ מוֹדִים: אִלּוּ פִינוּ מָלֵא שִׁירָה כַּיָּם. וּלְשׁוֹנֵנוּ רִנָּה כַּהֲמוֹן גַּלָּיו. וְשִׂפְתוֹתֵינוּ שֶׁבַח כְּמֶרְחֲבֵי רָקִיעַ אֵין אֲנַחְנוּ מַסְפִּיקִים לְהוֹדוֹת לְךָ יְיָ אֱלֹהֵינוּ וֵאלֹהֵי אֲבוֹתֵינוּ. עַל־כָּל הַטּוֹבוֹת שֶׁעָשִׂיתָ עִם־אֲבוֹתֵינוּ וְעִמָּנוּ: מִמִּצְרַיִם גְּאַלְתָּנוּ יְיָ אֱלֹהֵינוּ וּמִבֵּית עֲבָדִים פְּדִיתָנוּ. בְּרָעָב זַנְתָּנוּ. וּבְשָׂבָע כִּלְכַּלְתָּנוּ: מֵחֶרֶב הִצַּלְתָּנוּ וּמִדֶּבֶר מִלַּטְתָּנוּ. וּמֵחֳלָיִם רָעִים וְנֶאֱמָנִים דִּלִּיתָנוּ: עַד־הֵנָּה עֲזָרוּנוּ רַחֲמֶיךָ. וְלֹא־עֲזָבוּנוּ חֲסָדֶיךָ. וְאַל־תִּטְּשֵׁנוּ יְיָ אֱלֹהֵינוּ לָנֶצַח: עַל־כֵּן נְהַלֶּלְךָ וּנְשַׁבֵּחֲךָ וּנְפָאֶרְךָ וּנְבָרֵךְ אֶת־שֵׁם קָדְשֶׁךָ. בָּרוּךְ אַתָּה יְיָ. אֵל מֶלֶךְ גָּדוֹל בַּתִּשְׁבָּחוֹת. אֵל הַהוֹדָאוֹת. אֲדוֹן הַנִּפְלָאוֹת. הַבּוֹחֵר בְּשִׁירֵי זִמְרָה. מֶלֶךְ אֵל חֵי הָעוֹלָמִים:

Choir:—Amen.

(Congregation standing.)

Minister:

Praise ye the Lord, to whom all praise is due!

Choir and Congregation:

Praised be the Lord from this time forth and forever.

(Congregation sitting.)

Minister:

PRAISE be to Thee, O Lord, our God, Ruler of the world, who in Thy mercy causest light to shine over the earth and all its inhabitants, and renewest daily in kindness the works of creation. How manifold are Thy works, O Eternal; in wisdom hast Thou made them all, the earth is full of Thy possessions. The heavens declare Thy glory and the firmament showeth Thy handiwork. Thou formest light and darkness, ordainest good and evil, bringest harmony into nature, and peace to the heart of man.

With love abounding hast Thou guided us, O our God, and with great compassion hast Thou borne with us. Because our fathers believed and trusted in Thee, therefore hast Thou taught them the laws of life, and shown them the way of wisdom. We beseech Thee, O merciful Father, to grant us discernment, that we may understand and fulfill all the teachings of Thy word. Make us gladly obedient to Thy commandments and fill our hearts with love and reverence for Thee. In Thee we put our trust; we rejoice and delight in Thy help; for with Thee alone is salvation. Thou hast appointed us as the teachers of

DAY OF ATONEMENT. 155

(Congregation standing.)
Minister:

בָּרְכוּ אֶת יְיָ הַמְבֹרָךְ:

Choir and Congregation:

בָּרוּךְ יְיָ הַמְבֹרָךְ לְעוֹלָם וָעֶד:

(Congregation sitting.)
Minister:

בָּרוּךְ אַתָּה יְיָ אֱלֹהֵינוּ מֶלֶךְ הָעוֹלָם. יוֹצֵר אוֹר וּבוֹרֵא חֹשֶׁךְ. עֹשֶׂה שָׁלוֹם וּבוֹרֵא אֶת הַכֹּל:

הַמֵּאִיר לָאָרֶץ וְלַדָּרִים עָלֶיהָ בְּרַחֲמִים. וּבְטוּבוֹ מְחַדֵּשׁ בְּכָל־יוֹם תָּמִיד מַעֲשֵׂה־בְרֵאשִׁית. מָה רַבּוּ מַעֲשֶׂיךָ יְיָ. כֻּלָּם בְּחָכְמָה עָשִׂיתָ. מָלְאָה הָאָרֶץ קִנְיָנֶךָ: תִּתְבָּרַךְ יְיָ אֱלֹהֵינוּ עַל־שֶׁבַח מַעֲשֵׂה יָדֶיךָ: וְעַל־מְאוֹרֵי־אוֹר שֶׁעָשִׂיתָ יְפָאֲרוּךָ סֶּלָה: בָּרוּךְ אַתָּה יְיָ יוֹצֵר הַמְּאוֹרוֹת:

אַהֲבָה רַבָּה אֲהַבְתָּנוּ יְיָ אֱלֹהֵינוּ. חֶמְלָה גְדוֹלָה וִיתֵרָה חָמַלְתָּ עָלֵינוּ. אָבִינוּ מַלְכֵּנוּ. בַּעֲבוּר אֲבוֹתֵינוּ שֶׁבָּטְחוּ בָךְ. וַתְּלַמְּדֵם חֻקֵּי חַיִּים. כֵּן תְּחָנֵּנוּ וּתְלַמְּדֵנוּ: הָאֵר עֵינֵינוּ בְּתוֹרָתֶךָ. וְדַבֵּק לִבֵּנוּ בְּמִצְוֹתֶיךָ. וְיַחֵד לְבָבֵנוּ לְאַהֲבָה וּלְיִרְאָה שְׁמֶךָ. וְלֹא נֵבוֹשׁ לְעוֹלָם וָעֶד: כִּי בְשֵׁם קָדְשְׁךָ בָּטָחְנוּ. נָגִילָה

Thy law; Thou hast chosen us for a holy mission unto mankind; therefore do we joyfully lift up our voices and proclaim Thy unity. Blessed be Thou, O God, who hast revealed Thy truth through Israel.

(Congregation standing.)

Minister, then Choir and Congregation:

Hear, O Israel, the Lord our God, the Lord is One. Praised be His glorious name forever and ever.

(Congregation sitting.)

Minister:

THOU shalt love the Lord, thy God, with all thy heart, with all thy soul, and with all thy might. And these words, which I command thee this day, shall be in thy heart. Thou shalt teach them diligently unto thy children, and shalt speak of them when thou sittest in thy house, when thou walkest by the way, when thou liest down, and when thou risest up. Bind them as a sign upon thy hand, and let them be as frontlets between thine eyes. Write them upon the doorposts of thy house and upon thy gates.

To the end that ye may remember to do according to all my commandments and your life shall be hallowed unto the Lord. I am the Lord your God.

TRUE it is that the God of all the world is our Ruler; He is the rock of Israel, the shield of our salvation. Unto all generations shall He alone endure, and His kingdom shall abide forever. His words are words of life and are established for all time. They are faithful and precious unto all generations.

DAY OF ATONEMENT. 157

וְנִשְׂמְחָה בִּישׁוּעָתֶךָ . כִּי אֵל פּוֹעֵל יְשׁוּעוֹת אָתָּה ,
וּבָנוּ בָחַרְתָּ וְקֵרַבְתָּנוּ לְשִׁמְךָ הַגָּדוֹל סֶלָה בֶּאֱמֶת
לְהוֹדוֹת לְךָ וּלְיַחֶדְךָ בְּאַהֲבָה . בָּרוּךְ אַתָּה יְיָ
הַבּוֹחֵר בְּעַמּוֹ יִשְׂרָאֵל בְּאַהֲבָה:

(Congregation standing.)

Minister, then Choir and Congregation:

שְׁמַע יִשְׂרָאֵל יְהוָֹה אֱלֹהֵינוּ יְהוָֹה אֶחָד:

בָּרוּךְ שֵׁם כְּבוֹד מַלְכוּתוֹ לְעוֹלָם וָעֶד:

(Congregation sitting.)

Minister:

וְאָהַבְתָּ אֵת יְיָ אֱלֹהֶיךָ בְּכָל־לְבָבְךָ וּבְכָל־נַפְשְׁךָ
וּבְכָל־מְאֹדֶךָ: וְהָיוּ הַדְּבָרִים הָאֵלֶּה אֲשֶׁר אָנֹכִי
מְצַוְּךָ הַיּוֹם עַל־לְבָבֶךָ: וְשִׁנַּנְתָּם לְבָנֶיךָ וְדִבַּרְתָּ
בָּם . בְּשִׁבְתְּךָ בְּבֵיתֶךָ וּבְלֶכְתְּךָ בַדֶּרֶךְ וּבְשָׁכְבְּךָ
וּבְקוּמֶךָ: וּקְשַׁרְתָּם לְאוֹת עַל־יָדֶךָ . וְהָיוּ לְטֹטָפֹת
בֵּין עֵינֶיךָ: וּכְתַבְתָּם עַל־מְזוּזוֹת בֵּיתֶךָ וּבִשְׁעָרֶיךָ:

לְמַעַן תִּזְכְּרוּ וַעֲשִׂיתֶם אֶת כָּל מִצְוֹתָי וִהְיִיתֶם
קְדוֹשִׁים לֵאלֹהֵיכֶם:

אֱמֶת . אֱלֹהֵי עוֹלָם מַלְכֵּנוּ . צוּר יַעֲקֹב מָגֵן יִשְׁעֵנוּ .
לְדוֹר וָדוֹר הוּא קַיָּם וּשְׁמוֹ קַיָּם . וְכִסְאוֹ נָכוֹן
וּמַלְכוּתוֹ וֶאֱמוּנָתוֹ לָעַד קַיָּמֶת . וּדְבָרָיו חָיִים

True it is that He is our God, our Creator, and the rock of our salvation. Our redeemer and our savior is He forever, and there is no one besides, in whom we can put our trust. He is the first and the last. He has redeemed our fathers from the bondage of Egypt, and rescued them from the hand of their oppressor. Therefore did they praise and extol the Lord.

Choir and Congregation:

Who is like unto Thee, O God, among the mighty?
   Who is like unto Thee glorious in holiness, extolled in praises, working wonders?
God reigneth forever and ever.

Minister:

O Rock of Israel, be pleased to redeem them that are oppressed, and deliver them that are persecuted.

Praise be unto Thee, our redeemer, the Holy One of Israel.

Choir:—Amen.

Minister:

PRAISE be unto Thee, O Eternal, our God, God of our fathers Abraham, Isaac and Jacob, the great, mighty, and most high God. Thou bestowest lovingkindness upon all Thy creatures; Thou rememberest the goodness of the fathers, and Thou sendest redemption to their descendants for the sake of Thy name.

Remember us unto life, O Sovereign, who ordainest life, and inscribe us in the book of life, for Thy sake,

וְקַיָּמִים. נֶאֱמָנִים וְנֶחֱמָדִים לָעַד וּלְעוֹלְמֵי עוֹלָמִים:
אֱמֶת אַתָּה הוּא רִאשׁוֹן וְאַתָּה הוּא אַחֲרוֹן. וּמִבַּלְעָדֶיךָ אֵין לָנוּ מֶלֶךְ גּוֹאֵל וּמוֹשִׁיעַ. מִמִּצְרַיִם גְּאַלְתָּנוּ יְיָ אֱלֹהֵינוּ. וּמִבֵּית עֲבָדִים פְּדִיתָנוּ. עַל־זֹאת שִׁבְּחוּ אֲהוּבִים וְרוֹמְמוּ אֵל:

Choir and Congregation:

מִי־כָמֹכָה בָּאֵלִים יְיָ. מִי כָּמֹכָה נֶאְדָּר בַּקֹּדֶשׁ. נוֹרָא תְהִלֹּת עֹשֵׂה־פֶלֶא:

Minister:

מַלְכוּתְךָ רָאוּ בָנֶיךָ. זֶה אֵלִי עָנוּ וְאָמְרוּ:

Choir and Congregation:

יְיָ יִמְלֹךְ לְעֹלָם וָעֶד:

Minister:

צוּר יִשְׂרָאֵל. קוּמָה בְּעֶזְרַת יִשְׂרָאֵל. גְּאָלֵנוּ יְיָ צְבָאוֹת. שְׁמוֹ קְדוֹשׁ יִשְׂרָאֵל. בָּרוּךְ אַתָּה יְיָ גָּאַל יִשְׂרָאֵל:

בָּרוּךְ אַתָּה יְיָ אֱלֹהֵינוּ וֵאלֹהֵי אֲבוֹתֵינוּ. אֱלֹהֵי אַבְרָהָם אֱלֹהֵי יִצְחָק וֵאלֹהֵי יַעֲקֹב. הָאֵל הַגָּדוֹל הַגִּבּוֹר וְהַנּוֹרָא. אֵל עֶלְיוֹן. גּוֹמֵל חֲסָדִים טוֹבִים. וְקֹנֵה הַכֹּל וְזוֹכֵר חַסְדֵי אָבוֹת. וּמֵבִיא גְאֻלָּה לִבְנֵי בְנֵיהֶם. לְמַעַן שְׁמוֹ בְּאַהֲבָה:

O God of life. Thou art our helper, our redeemer and protector. Praise be to Thee, O God, shield of Abraham.

Thou art omnipotent, O Lord, and mighty to save. In Thy kindness Thou sustainest the living, upholdest the falling, healest the sick, and settest the captive free. Thou wilt, of a surety, fulfil Thy promise of immortal life unto those who sleep in the dust. Who is like unto Thee, Almighty, Author of life and death, Thou who sendest salvation.

Who is like unto Thee, Father of mercies, who rememberest Thy children unto life eternal. Praise be to Thee, O God, who hast implanted within us immortal life.

SANCTIFICATION.

(Congregation standing.)

We hallow Thy name on earth, even as it is hallowed in heaven; and with the prophet say in humble adoration:

Choir and Congregation:

Holy, holy, holy is the Lord of Hosts, the whole earth is full of His glory.

Minister:

God our strength, God our Lord, how excellent is Thy name in all the earth.

DAY OF ATONEMENT.

זָכְרֵנוּ לַחַיִּים. מֶלֶךְ חָפֵץ בַּחַיִּים. וְכָתְבֵנוּ בְּסֵפֶר הַחַיִּים. לְמַעַנְךָ אֱלֹהִים חַיִּים:

מֶלֶךְ עוֹזֵר וּמוֹשִׁיעַ וּמָגֵן. בָּרוּךְ אַתָּה יְיָ מָגֵן אַבְרָהָם:

אַתָּה גִבּוֹר לְעוֹלָם אֲדֹנָי. רַב לְהוֹשִׁיעַ. מְכַלְכֵּל חַיִּים בְּחֶסֶד. מְחַיֵּה הַכֹּל בְּרַחֲמִים רַבִּים. סוֹמֵךְ נוֹפְלִים וְרוֹפֵא חוֹלִים וּמַתִּיר אֲסוּרִים. וּמְקַיֵּם אֱמוּנָתוֹ לִישֵׁנֵי עָפָר. מִי כָמוֹךָ בַּעַל גְּבוּרוֹת. וּמִי דוֹמֶה-לָּךְ. מֶלֶךְ מֵמִית וּמְחַיֶּה וּמַצְמִיחַ יְשׁוּעָה:

מִי כָמוֹךָ אַב הָרַחֲמִים. זוֹכֵר יְצוּרָיו לְחַיִּים בְּרַחֲמִים: בָּרוּךְ אַתָּה יְיָ נָטַע בְּתוֹכֵנוּ חַיֵּי עוֹלָם:

(Congregation standing.)

נְקַדֵּשׁ אֶת שִׁמְךָ בָּעוֹלָם. כְּשֵׁם שֶׁמַּקְדִּישִׁים אוֹתוֹ בִּשְׁמֵי מָרוֹם. כַּכָּתוּב עַל-יַד נְבִיאֶךָ. וְקָרָא זֶה אֶל-זֶה וְאָמַר:

Choir and Congregation:

קָדוֹשׁ קָדוֹשׁ קָדוֹשׁ יְיָ צְבָאוֹת. מְלֹא כָל-הָאָרֶץ כְּבוֹדוֹ:

Minister:

אַדִּיר אַדִּירֵנוּ יְיָ אֲדוֹנֵנוּ מָה-אַדִּיר שִׁמְךָ בְּכָל הָאָרֶץ:

Choir and Congregation:

In all places of Thy dominion Thy name is praised and glorified.

Minister:

Our God is One; He is our Father; He is our King; He is our Helper; and in His mercy He will answer our petition in the sight of all the living.

Choir and Congregation:

God will reign forever, thy God, O Zion, from generation to generation.—Hallelujah!

(Congregation sitting.)

Minister:

Holy art Thou and awe-inspiring is Thy name. There is no God beside Thee. The Lord of hosts is exalted in judgment and the Holy One is sanctified through righteousness. Praise be to Thee, O God, who rulest in holiness.

Choir:—Amen.

Minister:

SANCTIFY us through Thy commandments, and enlighten us by Thy law. Satisfy us with Thy goodness, and gladden us with Thy help. May we serve Thee in purity of heart and in truth. Praised be Thou, O God, who forgivest our transgressions, King of the world, who sanctifiest Israel, and the Day of Atonement.

Choir:—Amen.

DAY OF ATONEMENT.

Choir and Congregation:

בָּרוּךְ כְּבוֹד יְיָ מִמְּקוֹמוֹ:

Minister:

אֶחָד הוּא אֱלֹהֵינוּ. הוּא אָבִינוּ. הוּא מַלְכֵּנוּ. וְהוּא מוֹשִׁיעֵנוּ: וְהוּא יַשְׁמִיעֵנוּ בְּרַחֲמָיו לְעֵינֵי כָּל־חָי:

Choir and Congregation:

יִמְלֹךְ יְיָ לְעוֹלָם אֱלֹהַיִךְ צִיּוֹן לְדֹר וָדֹר הַלְלוּיָהּ:

(Congregation sitting.)

Minister:

קָדוֹשׁ אַתָּה וְנוֹרָא שְׁמֶךָ. וְאֵין אֱלוֹהַּ מִבַּלְעָדֶיךָ. כַּכָּתוּב. וַיִּגְבַּהּ יְיָ צְבָאוֹת בַּמִּשְׁפָּט. וְהָאֵל הַקָּדוֹשׁ נִקְדַּשׁ בִּצְדָקָה. בָּרוּךְ אַתָּה יְיָ הַמֶּלֶךְ הַקָּדוֹשׁ:

Choir:—Amen.

Minister:

אֱלֹהֵינוּ וֵאלֹהֵי אֲבוֹתֵינוּ. קַדְּשֵׁנוּ בְּמִצְוֹתֶיךָ· וְתֵן חֶלְקֵנוּ בְּתוֹרָתֶךָ. שַׂבְּעֵנוּ מִטּוּבֶךָ. וְשַׂמְּחֵנוּ בִּישׁוּעָתֶךָ. וְטַהֵר לִבֵּנוּ לְעָבְדְּךָ בֶּאֱמֶת. כִּי אַתָּה סָלְחָן לְיִשְׂרָאֵל וּמִבַּלְעָדֶיךָ אֵין לָנוּ מֶלֶךְ מוֹחֵל וְסוֹלֵחַ:

בָּרוּךְ אַתָּה יְיָ מֶלֶךְ מוֹחֵל וְסוֹלֵחַ לַעֲוֹנוֹתֵינוּ. מֶלֶךְ עַל־כָּל־הָאָרֶץ מְקַדֵּשׁ יִשְׂרָאֵל וְיוֹם הַכִּפֻּרִים:

Minister:

OUR God, and God of our fathers! May Thy presence be manifest to us in all Thy works, and may reverence for Thee fill the hearts of all Thy creatures; may all the children of men bow before Thee in humility and unite to do Thy will with perfect hearts, and all acknowledge that Thine is the kingdom, the power and the majesty, and that Thy name is exalted above all.

Grant hope, O Lord, to them that seek Thee; inspire with courage all who wait for Thee, and be nigh unto all who trust in Thy name; that all men may walk in the light of Thy truth, and recognize that they are children of One Father, that One God has created them all. Then shall the just rejoice and the righteous be glad; then shall iniquity be no more and all men will render homage to Thee alone as their God and King.

Eternal, our God, may Thy kingdom come speedily, and the worship of Thy name and obedience to Thy law unite all men in the bonds of brotherhood and peace, that every creature may know that Thou hast created it, and every living being exclaim: The Eternal, the God of Israel, ruleth and His dominion endureth forever.

Choir:—Amen.

DAY OF ATONEMENT.

Minister:

וּבְכֵן תֵּן פַּחְדְּךָ יְיָ אֱלֹהֵינוּ עַל כָּל־מַעֲשֶׂיךָ וְאֵימָתְךָ עַל כָּל־מַה־שֶּׁבָּרָאתָ וְיִירָאוּךָ כָּל־הַמַּעֲשִׂים וְיִשְׁתַּחֲווּ לְפָנֶיךָ כָּל־הַבְּרוּאִים וְיֵעָשׂוּ כֻלָּם אֲגֻדָּה אֶחָת לַעֲשׂוֹת רְצוֹנְךָ בְּלֵבָב שָׁלֵם כְּמוֹ שֶׁיָּדַעְנוּ יְיָ אֱלֹהֵינוּ שֶׁהַשָּׁלְטוֹן לְפָנֶיךָ עֹז בְּיָדְךָ וּגְבוּרָה בִּימִינֶךָ וְשִׁמְךָ נוֹרָא עַל כָּל־מַה־שֶּׁבָּרָאתָ:

וּבְכֵן תֵּן כָּבוֹד יְיָ לְעַמֶּךָ תְּהִלָּה לִירֵאֶיךָ וְתִקְוָה לְדוֹרְשֶׁיךָ וּפִתְחוֹן פֶּה לַמְיַחֲלִים לָךְ. שִׂמְחָה לְכָל יֹשְׁבֵי תֵבֵל אַרְצֶךָ וּצְמִיחַת קֶרֶן לִמְיַחֲדֵי שְׁמֶךָ. בִּמְהֵרָה בְיָמֵינוּ:

וּבְכֵן צַדִּיקִים יִרְאוּ וְיִשְׂמָחוּ וִישָׁרִים יַעֲלוֹזוּ וַחֲסִידִים בְּרִנָּה יָגִילוּ וְעוֹלָתָה תִּקְפָּץ־פִּיהָ. וְכָל־הָרִשְׁעָה כֻּלָּהּ כְּעָשָׁן תִּכְלֶה. כִּי תַעֲבִיר מֶמְשֶׁלֶת זָדוֹן מִן־הָאָרֶץ:

וְתִמְלוֹךְ אַתָּה יְיָ לְבַדֶּךָ עַל כָּל־מַעֲשֶׂיךָ. כַּכָּתוּב בְּדִבְרֵי קָדְשֶׁךָ יִמְלֹךְ יְיָ לְעוֹלָם אֱלֹהַיִךְ צִיּוֹן לְדֹר וָדֹר הַלְלוּיָהּ:

Chour:—Amen.

LOOK down with compassion, O Lord, upon Israel, Thy servant, and in Thy love accept his worship offered Thee at all times. Praise be to Thee, O Lord, whom alone we will serve in reverence.

We gratefully acknowledge, O Lord, our God, that Thou art our creator and preserver, the rock of our life and the shield of our help. We render thanks unto Thee for our lives which are in Thy hands, for our souls which are ever in Thy keeping, for Thy wondrous providence and for Thy continuous goodness, which Thou bestowest upon us day by day. Truly, Thy mercies never fail and Thy loving-kindness never ceases. Therefore in Thee do we forever put our trust.

OUR God, and God of our fathers, may Thy blessing rest upon us, according to the gracious promise of Thy word, spoken by the priests, ministering at Thy holy altar, saying:

May the Lord bless thee and keep thee!

Choir:—Amen.

May the Lord let his countenance shine upon thee and be gracious unto thee!

Choir:—Amen.

May the Lord lift up His countenance upon thee and give thee peace!

Choir:—Amen.

DAY OF ATONEMENT.

רְצֵה יְיָ אֱלֹהֵינוּ בְּעַמְּךָ יִשְׂרָאֵל. וּתְפִלָּתָם בְּאַהֲבָה תְקַבֵּל. וּתְהִי לְרָצוֹן תָּמִיד עֲבוֹדַת יִשְׂרָאֵל עַמֶּךָ. בָּרוּךְ אַתָּה יְיָ שֶׁאוֹתְךָ לְבַדְּךָ בְּיִרְאָה נַעֲבוֹד:

מוֹדִים אֲנַחְנוּ לָךְ. שָׁאַתָּה הוּא יְיָ אֱלֹהֵינוּ וֵאלֹהֵי אֲבוֹתֵינוּ לְעוֹלָם וָעֶד. צוּר חַיֵּינוּ מָגֵן יִשְׁעֵנוּ. אַתָּה הוּא לְדוֹר וָדוֹר. נוֹדֶה לְךָ וּנְסַפֵּר תְּהִלָּתֶךָ. עַל חַיֵּינוּ הַמְּסוּרִים בְּיָדֶךָ. וְעַל נִשְׁמוֹתֵינוּ הַפְּקוּדוֹת לָךְ. וְעַל נִסֶּיךָ שֶׁבְּכָל־יוֹם עִמָּנוּ. וְעַל נִפְלְאוֹתֶיךָ שֶׁבְּכָל־עֵת. עֶרֶב וָבֹקֶר וְצָהֳרָיִם. הַטּוֹב כִּי לֹא־כָלוּ רַחֲמֶיךָ. וְהַמְרַחֵם כִּי לֹא־תַמּוּ חֲסָדֶיךָ. מֵעוֹלָם קִוִּינוּ לָךְ:

אֱלֹהֵינוּ וֵאלֹהֵי אֲבוֹתֵינוּ. בָּרְכֵנוּ בַּבְּרָכָה הַמְשֻׁלֶּשֶׁת הַכְּתוּבָה בַּתּוֹרָה:

יְבָרֶכְךָ יְיָ וְיִשְׁמְרֶךָ:

Choir:—Amen.

יָאֵר יְיָ פָּנָיו אֵלֶיךָ וִיחֻנֶּךָּ:

Choir:—Amen.

יִשָּׂא יְיָ פָּנָיו אֵלֶיךָ וְיָשֵׂם לְךָ שָׁלוֹם:

Choir:—Amen.

Alternate Reading for Minister and Congregation:

O COME, let us return unto the Lord; for He hath wounded and He will heal us; He hath smitten and He will restore us.

He will revive us, and will raise us up, and we shall live in His presence.

Let us therefore know Him; let us strive to know the Lord;

His coming forth is sure as the morning.

Return, O Israel, to the Lord, thy God, for Thou hast stumbled by thine iniquity.

Let us return to the Lord, saying: "Forgive all our iniquities and receive us graciously."

We will render to Thee the sacrifices of our lips, and no more will we say to the works of our hands, "Ye are our gods."

I will not execute the fierceness of my anger, saith the Lord; I will not abandon thee, O Israel.

I will ransom thee from the power of the grave; I will redeem thee from death.

I will heal their rebellion and love them truly; for mine anger is turned away from them.

I, the Lord, will be like the dew to Israel; that they shall blossom as the lily, and strike root like Lebanon.

Who is wise and will understand these things; prudent, that he may know them?

The ways of the Lord are right; the righteous walk in them; but in them transgressors stumble.

Wherewith shall I come before the Lord, and bow myself before God, the Most High?

He hath told thee, O man, what is good; what the Lord doth require of thee, but to do justly, to love mercy and to walk humbly with thy God!

Who is like Thee, O God, that pardoneth iniquity and forgiveth transgressions?

He retaineth not His anger for ever, for He delighteth in mercy.

He will again have compassion on us; He will pardon our sins and blot our iniquities.

Thou wilt show faithfulness to Jacob, and mercy to the house of Israel, as Thou hast promised to our fathers in the days of old.

Choir:

Turn us again to Thee, O Lord, that we may be restored; renew our life as in the days of our innocence.

Minister and Congregation:

I KNOW, O Lord, that the way of man is not within his power, that it is not within him to establish his steps.

Chasten me, O Lord, but in measure; not in Thine anger, lest Thou bring me to naught.

O **Lord,** Thou knowest me; Thou hast seen me and tried my heart, whether it cleaves unto Thee.

Thou, O Lord, knowest all my doings; O remember me, and have regard for me.

Heal me, O Lord, and I shall be healed; save me, and I shall be saved; for Thou art my praise.

The Lord is my portion, saith my soul; therefore do I hope in Him.

The Lord is good to them that trust in Him; to the soul that seeketh Him.

It is good that a man hope, and quietly wait for the salvation of the Lord.

It is good for a man that he bear the yoke in his youth, that he sit alone and keep silence, since God layeth it upon him.

For the Lord will not cast off forever; for though He causeth grief, yet doth He have compassion.

For He doth not willingly afflict the children of men, for He is a merciful God.

Yea, His compassion faileth not; it is new every morning; great is His faithfulness.

Cometh not evil as well as good from the hand of the Most High?

Wherefore then murmureth the living man? Let him murmur at his own sin.

Let us search and try our ways and turn again to the Lord.

Let us lift up our hearts unto God and say: We have sinned, we have transgressed; we have rebelled against Thy word.

We acknowledge our iniquity; we have rebelled against the Lord, our God.

Let us seek good and not evil, that we may live; then shall the Lord, the God of hosts be with us.

If thou wilt return unto me, O Israel, saith the Lord, thou shalt stand before me.

If thou wilt separate the precious from the vile, thou shalt be my priest.

I will forgive their iniquity, saith the Lord; I will remember their sin no more.

Choir:

I, the Lord, search the heart and try the thoughts, to give to every man according to his ways, and according to the fruit of his doings.

Minister:

אנוש מה יזכה

WHAT is man, Almighty, that Thou art mindful of him, and the son of man that Thou rememberest him? Yet, till the day of his death Thou desirest that he should repent and return to Thee. How can mortal man appear pure and blameless bef re Thee? Even the hosts of heaven are not perfect in Thy sight. And shall man, born of the dust, whose days are as a passing shadow, count himself pure in Thy presence? If the mighty cedars are consumed in flames, how shall the dry grass withstand the fire?

Though we have virtue before men who judge after the appearance, yet who shall boast himself before Thee who searchest the heart, to whom the darkness is as the light, and from whose eye nothing is hid? Thou art veiled from the eyes of all creatures; but their inmost ways lie open to Thee. Even that which shall be is known unto Thee, and Thou readest the future as Thou dost the past. As Thou seest and knowest all, so art Thou the judge of all. Who shall question Thy judgments, or who shall say to Thee, What doest Thou? Over all nations and over men Thou stretchest the line, and who shall stay Thy measurements? O, that man would think of this, and that he would seek that which is good, and turn from that which is evil! O, that he would consider whither he goeth, and to whom he must give account at last! His days are as vanity, and his nights bring him no peace. His plans run to naught; he walketh as in a dream, and findeth no rest until the grave closeth over him. But why should man murmur at his life? Though he be called to toil and to trouble, yet his faithfulness shall not fail of reward, and the goal shall crown his course. Happy, therefore, the man who maketh Divine wisdom his guide, and whose reverence of God is from the heart.

For all things stand revealed at last, and each shall witness to his doings. Then the truth is made manifest, and all deception is ended forever. He who doeth the works of justice and benevolence will be led by Thee to the abode of everlasting peace. His gains surpass all earthly treasures and dignities. A good name is his here below, and the crown of life eternal beyond. For him the day of death is better than the day of birth.

CONFESSION.

For Silent Devotion.

O God and Father, Maker of heaven and earth, I bow myself before Thee in lowly adoration and prayer, and in the presence of Thy perfect holiness I would penitently acknowledge my sins, seeking help and deliverance, desiring to learn what is Thy will concerning me, and resolving to devote myself more faithfully to Thy holy service.

O God of ceaseless goodness and mercy, on this sacred spot, on the holiest of days, invited by Thy fatherly love to come to Thee, I cover my face in shame that I have been so ungrateful, and so slow to hearken to Thy call which goeth forth on every day and at every hour. I have sinned against my better knowledge and my resolves, against Thy promises and Thy warnings. Thine infinite grace has given me life and endowed me with power over all living things. Yet have I been led away by desires and purposes which I could not ask Thee to bless. Nor did I strive to know Thy word and Thy truth, and to manifest such knowledge in all my words and deeds;

the aim of my life has been to satisfy earthly desires and to gather the goods of this world, which I have worshiped as my idol. For pleasure and for gain, I have toiled with all the strength of my soul. To them, I have given my thoughts and my labor year after year, by day and by night, at my lying down and at my rising up. How few were the hours devoted to Thee and Thy work, how scarce the moments used for ennobling my spiritual self! And what is man, what is his strength, what are his hopes without Thine assistance? Is not everything I am and have, Thine? Thou hast watched over me and cared for me from the beginning of my life. Thou providest for my daily needs the food that nourishes me, the repose that restores my strength, the raiment that clothes me and the house that shelters me and mine. From Thee, all my joys and comforts come; and Thou crownest my days with loving-kindnesses and tender mercies. And when my pathway is darkened, and Thou triest me with affliction, still I am sure that it has been in mercy that Thou hast so dealt with me; and if Thou sendest me forth to sow in tears, bearing precious seed, I shall come back rejoicing, bringing my sheaves with me. But how little, O Father, did I esteem Thy boundless love and mercy. In the abundance of earthly goods and when my most ardent wishes were fulfilled, I praised not Thee, but myself, boasted of my wisdom, my strength and my industry, and forgot to show my gratitude and to repay part of my indebtedness by assisting those of Thy children who were less favored than I. And in the midst of trials and sorrows, I murmured against Thy wise rule, looked with envy at the success of evil-doers and complained that Thou hadst forsaken me, while it was my own folly and the evil inclination of my heart that had plunged me in misery. For I walked after the desires of mine eyes and was guided by the blind impulses of my passions, despising those enjoyments which spring from the consciousness of duty well fulfilled, and from the sweet approbation of conscience. How shamefully did I neglect these real enjoyments which make man truly happy, for the wild excitement of an hour, for the hasty draught from the cup of such pleasures which end in gall and wormwood. And thus indulging in impure thoughts and guilty desires, I wasted the splendid opportunities placed within my reach, to become a useful member of the family, of the community.

With deep humiliation do I remember how often in unbridled frivolity I violated the reverence due to Thee and Thy holy name. That holy name whose honor and glory fills the whole world and which no creature should dare to pronounce without a thrill of devotion, without awe and adoration—that holy name I bore thoughtlessly, many times, on my lips, as a hollow utterance; I used it as a sanction for vows which had no echo in my heart, and which often remained unfulfilled; I profaned it by using it as a seal to resolutions of anger and passion and revenge.

I have also forgotten my duty to those to whom I

am connected by the most sacred ties, and my conscience bears witness against me. I remember with shame my shortcomings in my relations with some who are still among the living, and with others who now rest in the grave. Instead of treating my father and mother with profound reverence and tender consideration, how often did I requite their sweet, self-sacrificing love with ingratitude. My disobedience, my cold indifference caused those eyes to shed tears of grief and agony which through so many nights had watched at the side of my bed; my conduct wounded, and perhaps broke, the heart which never grew weary in its love, and which had set its dearest and brightest hopes in its beloved child.

And the dear companion placed at my side by Thee in inseparable union, to share my joys and sorrows, and to support and comfort me in all the storms and vicissitudes of life—even that dear companion have I not rewarded with a due measure of fidelity, love and care. Often did I not shrink from grieving, by word or deed, the heart so closely linked to mine, nor refrain from violating the most sacred duties of matrimonial life by indifference or carelessness. And not seldom was I selfish enough to accept the offerings of tender love and touching devotion with a callous heart, a gloomy look and sullen coldness.

Nor have I been more mindful of my sacred duties towards my children, the most precious gifts Thy love has entrusted to me. I neglected to devote the right care to their education and their training. I failed to set them an example worthy of imitation, and to impart to them teachings apt to smooth for them the rocky path of life. I even omitted to do what was in my power to secure their worldly welfare, and have been still more negligent of their spiritual needs. I laid more stress upon their external beauty than upon their inner worth; more upon their outward success than upon the nobility of their heart, the firmness of their character, their spiritual and lasting welfare. I was more anxious to bring them up for the vanity of the world, than for God, for virtue and truth. Thus, I had not set my household in order, nor arranged my affairs so as to be fully prepared to depart hence without anxiety even in regard to those nearest and dearest to me.

And when I examine my conduct to my fellow-men, to the members of the whole human family, to all my brothers and sisters on earth, to all the children of my heavenly Father, with each of whom I am connected by sacred ties; when I reflect how often harsh words fell from my lips like barbed arrows into timid and trembling hearts; how often my tongue darted the deadly poison of calumny against the innocent; how often I treated the poor heartlessly, and instead of lifting them up with kindness, bent them still lower to the ground by my haughtiness and overbearing; how often I did thoughtlessly, or from envy and vindictiveness, throw the firebrand of discord between brother and brother, between friend and friend; when I reflect how little I cared to promote the welfare and honor of Israel, the prosperity and progress of my community, the usefulness and glory of this house of God; how, on the contrary, I reflected dishonor upon the name of Israel by my indifference to our religious interests, by my hypocritical observance, lip-service and mock-holiness—when I consider all this, then, O God, nothing remains to me but to cast down my eyes before Thy holy throne, and to hide my face in deep shame and repentance.

But no, I cannot hide myself; I will invoke Thee from the dust, O God, with whom is pity and forgiveness; for I desire to forsake the evil of my ways and to return to Thee from whom I have departed so often and so far. Let Thy care watch over me that I fall not again into any sin of which I have repented. Grant that I may never forget to be grateful and kind. Let not the allurements of the world, or any false counsel, or bad example so prevail with my weakness as to draw me to do anything which would dishonor Thee, or wrong my neighbor, or offend against my own manhood. Cause me to hate all fraud and deceit, all malice and envy, all slander and evil speaking, and every offense against Thy law of truth and love. Let me never deface Thine image in my soul by yielding myself as a slave to appetites and passions, but may I keep myself in purity and temperance, in simplicity and sincerity of heart. Give me grace, thus to seek Thee and righteousness. Hear me in mine anguish; draw nigh to my soul and relieve me in my distress. Amen.

Minister:

OUR God and Father, Thou hast summoned us to appear before Thy judgment-seat, to render an account of our doings before Thee, the All-just and All-holy. What shall we say in Thy presence? How can we attempt to justify ourselves? We blush with shame and are bowed down with humiliation, for we know our unworthiness. Thou, O Father, searchest and knowest us; Thou compassest our paths and art acquainted with all our ways; our most secret thoughts are not hidden before Thee. Therefore, Thou dost not call upon us to justify ourselves, but to examine our conduct, acknowledge our sins, and forsake the evil. Thou hast summoned us this day that we should judge ourselves in the light of truth. Not to punish, but to pardon is Thy holy will; not to destroy us in Thine anger, but to forgive us in Thy love hast Thou appointed this Day of Atonement. Lord, our God, though trembling before Thee, we hope in Thee; though stricken with awe at the call of Thy judgment, we look for the light of Thy compassion. We are bowed down with the burden of our sins. Judge us, O Father, in Thy mercy; let us not die in our guilt; let each day be to us a day of repentance, and every hour as the hour of death, which calls us to appear before Thy throne of judgment.

Before the hour has passed, let us hasten in deep humility and contrition of soul to make confession to God, and with sincere vows resolve so to mend our ways that we shall not be moved from his path Amen.

Minister:

OUR God and God of our fathers, on this Day of Atonement pardon our transgressions; remove our guilt and blot out our iniquities, as Thou hast promised: I, even I, blot out thine iniquities for mine own sake, and thy sins will I remember no more. I have made thy sins to vanish like a cloud and thy transgressions like a mist; return to me for I have redeemed thee. For on this day shall ye be forgiven and cleansed from all your sins; before God shall ye be pure.

Minister and Choir:

Our God and God of our fathers, may our prayers come before Thee and turn not away from our supplications, for we are not so arrogant and stiff-necked as to say before Thee that we have not sinned, but aye, we have sinned.

Yea, we have sinned; yea, we have transgressed; yea, we have done perversely.

Minister:

We have departed from Thy commandments and from Thy good ordinances, and it hath not profited us; but Thou art justified in all that has come upon us, for Thou doest justly, but we have done evil. What shall we say before Thee, O Most High, and what shall we plead before Thee, O Thou who dwellest in the heavens? Behold all things secret and revealed

DAY OF ATONEMENT. 181

Minister:

אֱלֹהֵינוּ וֵאלֹהֵי אֲבוֹתֵינוּ. מְחַל לַעֲוֹנוֹתֵינוּ בְּיוֹם הַכִּפֻּרִים הַזֶּה. מְחֵה וְהַעֲבֵר פְּשָׁעֵינוּ וְחַטֹּאתֵינוּ מִנֶּגֶד עֵינֶיךָ. כָּאָמוּר. אָנֹכִי אָנֹכִי הוּא מֹחֶה פְשָׁעֶיךָ לְמַעֲנִי וְחַטֹּאתֶיךָ לֹא אֶזְכֹּר: וְנֶאֱמַר. מָחִיתִי כָעָב פְּשָׁעֶיךָ. וְכֶעָנָן חַטֹּאתֶיךָ. שׁוּבָה אֵלַי כִּי גְאַלְתִּיךָ: וְנֶאֱמַר. כִּי בַיּוֹם הַזֶּה יְכַפֵּר עֲלֵיכֶם. לְטַהֵר אֶתְכֶם מִכֹּל חַטֹּאתֵיכֶם. לִפְנֵי יְיָ תִּטְהָרוּ:

Minister and Choir:

אֱלֹהֵינוּ וֵאלֹהֵי אֲבוֹתֵינוּ.

תָּבֹא לְפָנֶיךָ תְּפִלָּתֵנוּ. וְאַל תִּתְעַלַּם מִתְּחִנָּתֵנוּ. שֶׁאֵין אֲנַחְנוּ עַזֵּי פָנִים וּקְשֵׁי עוֹרֶף. לוֹמַר לְפָנֶיךָ יְיָ אֱלֹהֵינוּ וֵאלֹהֵי אֲבוֹתֵינוּ. צַדִּיקִים אֲנַחְנוּ וְלֹא חָטָאנוּ. אֲבָל אֲנַחְנוּ חָטָאנוּ:

חָטָאנוּ עָוִינוּ. פָּשַׁעְנוּ:

Minister:

סַרְנוּ מִמִּצְוֹתֶיךָ וּמִמִּשְׁפָּטֶיךָ הַטּוֹבִים וְלֹא שָׁוָה לָנוּ. וְאַתָּה צַדִּיק עַל כָּל הַבָּא עָלֵינוּ. כִּי אֱמֶת עָשִׂיתָ וַאֲנַחְנוּ הִרְשָׁעְנוּ:

מַה־נֹּאמַר לְפָנֶיךָ יוֹשֵׁב מָרוֹם. וּמַה נְּסַפֵּר לְפָנֶיךָ שׁוֹכֵן שְׁחָקִים. הֲלֹא כָּל הַנִּסְתָּרוֹת וְהַנִּגְלוֹת אַתָּה יוֹדֵעַ:

Thou knowest. Thou knowest the secret things of the world and what is hidden in the minds of all the living.

Thou searchest the depths of the mind and triest all the intents of the heart. Nothing is concealed from Thine eyes.

Now may it be Thy will, O Lord our God, to forgive our transgressions and pardon our sins and blot out our trespasses:

Minister and Congregation:

The sin which we have sinned against Thee,
  willingly or unwittingly;
  publicly or secretly;
  presumptuously or ignorantly;

The sin which we have sinned against Thee,
  by the evil resolves of the heart;
  by the speech of the mouth;
  by a violent hand;

The sin which we have sinned against Thee,
  by the profanation of Thy name;
  by disregard for our parents and teachers;
  by deceit and treachery to our neighbor;

Minister and Congregation, then Choir:

For all of them, O God of forgiveness, grant us remission! Forgive us! Pardon us!

DAY OF ATONEMENT.

אַתָּה יוֹדֵעַ רָזֵי עוֹלָם . וְתַעֲלוּמוֹת סִתְרֵי כָּל חָי.
אַתָּה חוֹפֵשׂ כָּל חַדְרֵי בָטֶן . וּבוֹחֵן כְּלָיוֹת וָלֵב. אֵין
דָּבָר נֶעְלָם מִמֶּךָ . וְאֵין נִסְתָּר מִנֶּגֶד עֵינֶיךָ:

וּבְכֵן יְהִי רָצוֹן מִלְּפָנֶיךָ . יְיָ אֱלֹהֵינוּ וֵאלֹהֵי אֲבוֹתֵינוּ.
שֶׁתִּסְלַח לָנוּ עַל כָּל חַטֹּאתֵינוּ . וְתִמְחָל לָנוּ עַל
כָּל עֲוֹנוֹתֵינוּ . וּתְכַפֶּר לָנוּ עַל כָּל פְּשָׁעֵינוּ:

Minister and Congregation:

עַל חֵטְא שֶׁחָטָאנוּ לְפָנֶיךָ בְּאֹנֶס וּבְרָצוֹן:
עַל חֵטְא שֶׁחָטָאנוּ לְפָנֶיךָ בְּגָלוּי וּבַסָּתֶר:
עַל חֵטְא שֶׁחָטָאנוּ לְפָנֶיךָ בְּזָדוֹן וּבִשְׁגָגָה:
עַל חֵטְא שֶׁחָטָאנוּ לְפָנֶיךָ בְּהַרְהוֹר הַלֵּב:
עַל חֵטְא שֶׁחָטָאנוּ לְפָנֶיךָ בְּדִבּוּר פֶּה:
עַל חֵטְא שֶׁחָטָאנוּ לְפָנֶיךָ בְּחֹזֶק יָד:
עַל חֵטְא שֶׁחָטָאנוּ לְפָנֶיךָ וּבְחִלּוּל הַשֵּׁם:
עַל חֵטְא שֶׁחָטָאנוּ לְפָנֶיךָ בְּזִלְזוּל הוֹרִים וּמוֹרִים:
עַל חֵטְא שֶׁחָטָאנוּ לְפָנֶיךָ בְּהוֹנָאַת וּצְדִיַּת רָע:

וְעַל כֻּלָּם אֱלוֹהַּ סְלִיחוֹת.

Minister and Congregation, then **Choir:**

סְלַח לָנוּ . מְחַל לָנוּ . כַּפֶּר לָנוּ:

CANTICLE.

We are Thy people, Thou art our King.

We are Thy children, Thou art our Father.

We are Thy possession, Thou art our Portion.

We are Thy flock, Thou art our Shepherd.

We are Thy vineyard, Thou art our Keeper.

We are Thy beloved, Thou art our Friend.

Minister:

The Lord is our Judge, the Lord is our Law-giver, the Lord is our King; He will save us.

Minister and Congregation:

O SUPREME Judge of the whole earth, which Thou wilt arraign in judgment, we beseech Thee that life and favor may be granted to us, and may this morning prayer be accepted as like the daily burnt-offering:

Congregation:

As the regular burnt-offering of the morning.

O Thou who art invested and surrounded with righteousness! to Thee alone appertaineth supremacy; though we are destitute of meritorious works, O! remember those who sleep in Hebron; and may

DAY OF ATONEMENT.
CANTICLE.

כִּי אָנוּ עַמֶּךָ   וְאַתָּה מַלְכֵּנוּ:

אָנוּ בָנֶיךָ   וְאַתָּה אָבִינוּ:

אָנוּ נַחֲלָתֶךָ   וְאַתָּה גוֹרָלֵנוּ:

אָנוּ צֹאנֶךָ   וְאַתָּה רוֹעֵנוּ:

אָנוּ כַרְמֶךָ   וְאַתָּה נוֹטְרֵנוּ:

אָנוּ רַעְיָתֶךָ   וְאַתָּה דוֹדֵנוּ:

Minister:

יְיָ שֹׁפְטֵנוּ. יְיָ מְחוֹקְקֵנוּ. יְיָ מַלְכֵּנוּ. הוּא יוֹשִׁיעֵנוּ:

Minister and Congregation:

שׁוֹפֵט כָּל הָאָרֶץ וְאוֹתָהּ בְּמִשְׁפָּט יַעֲמִיד. נָא־חַיִּים וָחֶסֶד. עַל עַם עָנִי תַּצְמִיד. וְאֶת תְּפִלַּת הַשַּׁחַר בִּמְקוֹם עוֹלָה תַעֲמִיד:

Congregation:

עוֹלַת הַבֹּקֶר אֲשֶׁר לְעוֹלַת הַתָּמִיד:

לוֹבֵשׁ צְדָקָה מַעֲטֶה. לְךָ לְבַד הַיִּתְרוֹן. אִם

their merits ascend as a grateful memorial before Thee, O Lord, continually:

Congregation:

As the regular burnt-offering of the morning.

O Thou who art ever inclined to mercy and disposed to lead man to life, incline towards Thy people with mercy: deal bountifully with them, and grant them life: inscribe a living token, which may be on their foreheads perpetually:

Congregation:

As the regular burnt-offering in the morning.

Deal kindly in Thy favor with Israel and Judah, and confer strength and glory on Thy law and its mission, and let gloom and darkness vanish before it, that light may increase continually:

Congregation:

As the regular burnt-offering in the morning.

Be ye of good courage, and fortify your hearts, O my people, in God and His strength: He will pardon your sins, and will remember mercy in His anger: Seek ye the Lord, and His protection: implore His presence continually:

Congregation:

As the regular burnt-offering of the morning.

DAY OF ATONEMENT. 187

אֵין בָּנוּ מַעֲשִׂים ׃ זָכְרָה יְשֵׁנֵי חֶבְרוֹן ׃ וְהֵם יַעֲלוּ לְזִכָּרוֹן ׃ לִפְנֵי יְיָ תָּמִיד׃

Congregation:

עוֹלַת הַבֹּקֶר אֲשֶׁר לְעוֹלַת הַתָּמִיד׃

מַטֵּה כְּלַפֵּי חֶסֶד ׃ לְהַטּוֹת אִישׁ לִתְחִיָּה ׃ עַמָּךְ לְחֶסֶד הַטֵּה ׃ גְּמוֹל נָא עָלָיו וְחָיָה ׃ כְּתוֹב עָלָיו תָּו חַיִּים ׃ וְהָיָה עַל מִצְחוֹ תָּמִיד׃

Congregation:

עוֹלַת הַבֹּקֶר אֲשֶׁר לְעוֹלַת הַתָּמִיד׃

הֵטִיבָה בִרְצוֹנְךָ ׃ יִשְׂרָאֵל וִיהוּדָה ׃ וְנָתַתָּ יָד וָשֵׁם ׃ לַתּוֹרָה וְלִתְעוּדָה ׃ וְסַר חֹשֶׁךְ וַעֲלָטָה ׃ לְהַעֲלוֹת נֵר תָּמִיד׃

Congregation:

עוֹלַת הַבֹּקֶר אֲשֶׁר לְעוֹלַת הַתָּמִיד׃

חִזְקוּ וְאִמְצוּ לְבַבְכֶם ׃ עַמִּי בְּאֵל מָעֻזּוֹ ׃ יְכַפֵּר בְּעַד חַטֹּאתֵיכֶם ׃ וְיִזְכֹּר רַחֵם בְּרָגְזוֹ ׃ דִּרְשׁוּ יְיָ וְעֻזּוֹ ׃ בַּקְּשׁוּ פָנָיו תָּמִיד׃

Congregation:

עוֹלַת הַבֹּקֶר אֲשֶׁר לְעוֹלַת הַתָּמִיד׃

Minister:

שים שלום

GRANT us peace, Thy most precious gift, O Thou eternal source of peace, and enable Israel to be a messenger of peace unto the peoples of the earth. Bless our country that it may ever be a stronghold of peace, and be its advocate in the councils of nations. May contentment reign within its borders, health and happiness within its homes. Strengthen the bonds of friendship and fellowship between all the inhabitants of our land. Plant virtue in every soul and may love of Thy name hallow every home and every heart.

Inscribe us in the book of life, and grant unto us a year of prosperity and joy. Blessed be Thou, O Lord, Giver of peace. Amen.

Silent Devotion:

אלהי נצור

O GOD, guard my tongue from evil and my lips from uttering deceit. Be my support when grief silences my voice, and my comfort when woe bends my spirit. Plant humility in my soul, and strengthen my heart with perfect faith in Thee. Help me to be strong when temptations and trials come, and to be meek when others wrong me, that I may readily forgive them. Guide me by the light of Thy counsel, and let me ever find rest in Thee, who art my refuge and my redeemer. Amen.

READING OF THE SCRIPTURE.

Minister:

WHO shall ascend the hill of the Lord? and who shall stand in His holy place? He that hath clean hands and a pure heart; who hath not inclined his soul to falsehood, nor sworn deceitfully. He shall receive a blessing from the Lord, and favor from the God of his salvation. This is the generation of those that seek Thee; those that seek Thy face, O God of Israel.

[Psalm xxiv.]

Choir:

| Lift up your heads, O ye gates, and be ye lifted up, ye everlasting doors, for the King of glory shall enter. Who is the King of glory? The Lord of hosts —He is the King of glory. | שְׂאוּ שְׁעָרִים רָאשֵׁיכֶם. וּשְׂאוּ פִּתְחֵי עוֹלָם. וְיָבֹא מֶלֶךְ הַכָּבוֹד: מִי הוּא זֶה מֶלֶךְ הַכָּבוֹד. יְיָ צְבָאוֹת. הוּא מֶלֶךְ הַכָּבוֹד סֶלָה: |

(Congregation standing.)

Minister, then Choir:

| The Lord, the Lord God, merciful and gracious, long-suffering and abundant in goodness and ever-true; keeping mercy for thousands, forgiving iniquity, transgression and sin. | יְהֹוָה יְהֹוָה אֵל רַחוּם וְחַנּוּן אֶרֶךְ אַפַּיִם וְרַב־חֶסֶד וֶאֱמֶת. נֹצֵר חֶסֶד לָאֲלָפִים נֹשֵׂא עָוֹן וָפֶשַׁע וְחַטָּאָה: |

Minister, then Congregation:

Our Father, our King, we have sinned before Thee.

Our Father, our King, none is our Lord but Thee.

Our Father, our King, renew the year unto us for good.

Our Father, our King, keep far from our country sickness, war and famine.

Our Father, our King, help us to lead a good and pure life.

Our Father, our King, O pardon and blot out our sins.

Our Father, our King, accept graciously our petitions.

Our Father, our King, O be merciful and answer us; and though we can plead no merit, deal with us according to Thy loving kindness and help us.

Choir:—Amen.

(Minister takes the Scroll from the Ark, and turning to the congregation says:)

The Torah which God gave through Moses is the heritage of the house of Israel. Come ye and let us walk in the light of the Lord, that we may receive the spirit of wisdom and understanding, the spirit of counsel and strength, the spirit of knowledge and the fear of God.

Minister and Congregation:

Hear, O Israel, the Lord, our God, the Lord **is One.**

(Congregation sitting.)

DAY OF ATONEMENT. 191

Minister, then Congregation:

אָבִינוּ מַלְכֵּנוּ חָטָאנוּ לְפָנֶיךָ׃

אָבִינוּ מַלְכֵּנוּ אֵין לָנוּ מֶלֶךְ אֶלָּא אָתָּה׃

אָבִינוּ מַלְכֵּנוּ חַדֵּשׁ עָלֵינוּ שָׁנָה טוֹבָה׃

אָבִינוּ מַלְכֵּנוּ כַּלֵּה דֶּבֶר וְחֶרֶב וְרָעָב וּמַשְׁחִית מֵעָלֵינוּ׃

אָבִינוּ מַלְכֵּנוּ כָּתְבֵנוּ בְּסֵפֶר חַיִּים טוֹבִים׃

אָבִינוּ מַלְכֵּנוּ זָכְרֵנוּ לִגְאֻלָּה וְלִישׁוּעָה׃

אָבִינוּ מַלְכֵּנוּ סְלַח וּמְחַל לְכָל עֲוֹנוֹתֵינוּ׃

אָבִינוּ מַלְכֵּנוּ קַבֵּל בְּרַחֲמִים וּבְרָצוֹן אֶת תְּפִלָּתֵנוּ׃

אָבִינוּ מַלְכֵּנוּ חָנֵּנוּ וַעֲנֵנוּ כִּי אֵין בָּנוּ מַעֲשִׂים עֲשֵׂה עִמָּנוּ צְדָקָה וָחֶסֶד וְהוֹשִׁיעֵנוּ׃

Choir:—Amen.

(Minister takes the Scroll from the Ark, and turning to the congregation says:)

תּוֹרָה צִוָּה לָנוּ מֹשֶׁה ׃ מוֹרָשָׁה קְהִלַּת יַעֲקֹב׃

בֵּית יַעֲקֹב לְכוּ וְנֵלְכָה בְּאוֹר יְהֹוָה׃

Minister and Congregation:

שְׁמַע יִשְׂרָאֵל יְהֹוָה אֱלֹהֵינוּ יְהֹוָה אֶחָד׃

(Congregation sitting.)

Choir:

Thine, O Lord, is the greatness and the power, the glory, and the victory, and the majesty; for all that is in the heavens and in the earth is Thine, Thine is dominion, and Thou art exalted above all.

(Before reading from the Torah.)

Minister:

Blessed be Thou, O Lord, our God, Ruler of the world, who hast called Israel from amongst the nations and given him Thy Law. Praise be to Thee, O God, Giver of the Law.

(Deuteronomy xxix, 10 to xxx, 6.)

YE stand this day, all of you, before the Lord your God; your heads, your tribes, your elders, and your officers, even all the men of Israel, your little ones, your wives, and thy stranger that is in the midst of thy camps, from the hewer of thy wood unto the drawer of thy water: that thou shouldst enter into the covenant of the Lord thy God, and into his oath, which the Lord thy God maketh with thee this day: that He may establish thee this day unto Himself for a people, and that He may be unto thee a God, as He spake unto thee, and as he sware unto thy fathers, to Abraham, to Isaac, and to Jacob.

Neither with you only do I make this covenant and this oath; but with him that standeth here with us this day before the Lord our God, and also with him that is not here with us this day: (for ye know how we dwelt in the land of Egypt; and how we

DAY OF ATONEMENT.

Choir:

לְךָ יְיָ הַגְּדֻלָּה וְהַגְּבוּרָה . וְהַתִּפְאֶרֶת וְהַנֵּצַח וְהַהוֹד כִּי כֹל בַּשָּׁמַיִם וּבָאָרֶץ . לְךָ יְיָ הַמַּמְלָכָה . וְהַמִּתְנַשֵּׂא לְכֹל לְרֹאשׁ:

(Before reading from the Torah.)

Minister:

בָּרוּךְ אַתָּה יְיָ אֱלֹהֵינוּ מֶלֶךְ הָעוֹלָם . אֲשֶׁר בָּחַר בָּנוּ מִכָּל־הָעַמִּים וְנָתַן לָנוּ אֶת־תּוֹרָתוֹ . בָּרוּךְ אַתָּה יְיָ נוֹתֵן הַתּוֹרָה:

דברים כט׳

אַתֶּם נִצָּבִים הַיּוֹם כֻּלְּכֶם לִפְנֵי יְהֹוָה אֱלֹהֵיכֶם רָאשֵׁיכֶם שִׁבְטֵיכֶם זִקְנֵיכֶם וְשֹׁטְרֵיכֶם כֹּל אִישׁ יִשְׂרָאֵל: טַפְּכֶם נְשֵׁיכֶם וְגֵרְךָ אֲשֶׁר בְּקֶרֶב מַחֲנֶיךָ מֵחֹטֵב עֵצֶיךָ עַד שֹׁאֵב מֵימֶיךָ: לְעָבְרְךָ בִּבְרִית יְהֹוָה אֱלֹהֶיךָ וּבְאָלָתוֹ אֲשֶׁר יְהֹוָה אֱלֹהֶיךָ כֹּרֵת עִמְּךָ הַיּוֹם: לְמַעַן הָקִים־אֹתְךָ הַיּוֹם לוֹ לְעָם וְהוּא יִהְיֶה־לְּךָ לֵאלֹהִים כַּאֲשֶׁר דִּבֶּר־לָךְ וְכַאֲשֶׁר נִשְׁבַּע לַאֲבֹתֶיךָ לְאַבְרָהָם לְיִצְחָק וּלְיַעֲקֹב: וְלֹא אִתְּכֶם לְבַדְּכֶם אָנֹכִי כֹּרֵת אֶת־הַבְּרִית הַזֹּאת וְאֶת־הָאָלָה

came through the midst of the nations through which ye passed; and ye have seen their abominations, and their idols, wood and stone, silver and gold, which were among them;) lest there should be among you man, or woman, or family, or tribe, whose heart turneth away this day from the Lord our God, to go to serve the gods of those nations; lest there should be among you a root that beareth gall and wormwood; and it come to pass, when he heareth the words of this oath, that he bless himself in his heart, saying, I shall have peace, though I walk in the stubbornness of mine heart, to add drunkenness to thirst: the Lord will not pardon him; but then the anger of the Lord and His jealousy shall awake against that man, and all the curse that is written in this book shall lie upon him, and the Lord shall blot out his name from under heaven. And the Lord shall separate him unto evil out of all the tribes of Israel, according to all the curses of the covenant that is written in this book of the law. And the generation to come, your children that shall rise up after you, and the foreigner that shall come from a far land, shall say, when they see the plagues of that land, and the sicknesses wherewith the Lord hath made it sick; and that the whole land thereof is brimstone, and salt, and a burning, that it is not sown, nor beareth, nor any grass groweth therein, like the overthrow of Sodom and Gomorrah, Admah and Zeboiim, which the Lord overthrew in His anger, and in His wrath: even all the nations shall say, Wherefore hath the Lord done this unto this

DAY OF ATONEMENT. 195

הַזֹּאת: כִּי אֶת־אֲשֶׁר יֶשְׁנוֹ פֹּה עִמָּנוּ עֹמֵד הַיּוֹם
לִפְנֵי יְהֹוָה אֱלֹהֵינוּ וְאֵת אֲשֶׁר אֵינֶנּוּ פֹּה עִמָּנוּ
הַיּוֹם: כִּי־אַתֶּם יְדַעְתֶּם אֵת אֲשֶׁר־יָשַׁבְנוּ בְּאֶרֶץ
מִצְרָיִם וְאֵת אֲשֶׁר־עָבַרְנוּ בְּקֶרֶב הַגּוֹיִם אֲשֶׁר
עֲבַרְתֶּם: וַתִּרְאוּ אֶת־שִׁקּוּצֵיהֶם וְאֵת גִּלֻּלֵיהֶם עֵץ
וָאֶבֶן כֶּסֶף וְזָהָב אֲשֶׁר עִמָּהֶם: פֶּן־יֵשׁ בָּכֶם אִישׁ
אוֹ־אִשָּׁה אוֹ מִשְׁפָּחָה אוֹ־שֵׁבֶט אֲשֶׁר לְבָבוֹ פֹנֶה
הַיּוֹם מֵעִם יְהֹוָה אֱלֹהֵינוּ לָלֶכֶת לַעֲבֹד אֶת־אֱלֹהֵי
הַגּוֹיִם הָהֵם פֶּן־יֵשׁ בָּכֶם שֹׁרֶשׁ פֹּרֶה רֹאשׁ וְלַעֲנָה:
וְהָיָה בְּשָׁמְעוֹ אֶת־דִּבְרֵי הָאָלָה הַזֹּאת וְהִתְבָּרֵךְ
בִּלְבָבוֹ לֵאמֹר שָׁלוֹם יִהְיֶה־לִּי כִּי בִּשְׁרִרוּת לִבִּי
אֵלֵךְ לְמַעַן סְפוֹת הָרָוָה אֶת־הַצְּמֵאָה: לֹא־יֹאבֶה
יְהֹוָה סְלֹחַ לוֹ כִּי אָז יֶעְשַׁן אַף־יְהֹוָה וְקִנְאָתוֹ
בָּאִישׁ הַהוּא וְרָבְצָה בּוֹ כָּל־הָאָלָה הַכְּתוּבָה בַּסֵּפֶר
הַזֶּה וּמָחָה יְהֹוָה אֶת־שְׁמוֹ מִתַּחַת הַשָּׁמָיִם:
וְהִבְדִּילוֹ יְהֹוָה לְרָעָה מִכֹּל שִׁבְטֵי יִשְׂרָאֵל כְּכֹל
אָלוֹת הַבְּרִית הַכְּתוּבָה בְּסֵפֶר הַתּוֹרָה הַזֶּה: וְאָמַר
הַדּוֹר הָאַחֲרוֹן בְּנֵיכֶם אֲשֶׁר יָקוּמוּ מֵאַחֲרֵיכֶם
וְהַנָּכְרִי אֲשֶׁר יָבֹא מֵאֶרֶץ רְחוֹקָה וְרָאוּ אֶת־מַכּוֹת
הָאָרֶץ הַהִוא וְאֶת־תַּחֲלֻאֶיהָ אֲשֶׁר־חִלָּה יְהֹוָה בָּהּ:

land? What meaneth the heat of this great anger? Then men shall say, Because they forsook the covenant of the Lord, the God of their fathers, which He made with them when He brought them forth out of the land of Egypt; and went and served other gods, and worshiped them, gods whom they knew not, and whom He had not given unto them: therefore the anger of the Lord was kindled against this land, to bring upon it all the oath that is written in this book: and the Lord rooted them out of their land in anger, and in wrath, and in great indignation, and cast them into another land, as at this day. The secret things belong unto the Lord our God; but the things that are revealed belong unto us and to our children forever, that we may do all the words of this law.

(After Reading from the Torah.)

Praise be to Thee, O Eternal, our God, Ruler of the universe, who hast given us a law of truth and implanted eternal life within us. Praise be to Thee, O God, Giver of the Law. Amen.

DAY OF ATONEMENT. 197

גָפְרִית וָמֶלַח שְׂרֵפָה כָל־אַרְצָהּ לֹא תִזָּרַע וְלֹא
תַצְמִחַ וְלֹא־יַעֲלֶה בָהּ כָּל־עֵשֶׂב כְּמַהְפֵּכַת סְדֹם
וַעֲמֹרָה אַדְמָה וּצְבוֹיִם אֲשֶׁר הָפַךְ יְהֹוָה בְּאַפּוֹ
וּבַחֲמָתוֹ: וְאָמְרוּ כָּל־הַגּוֹיִם עַל־מֶה עָשָׂה יְהֹוָה
כָּכָה לָאָרֶץ הַזֹּאת מֶה חֳרִי הָאַף הַגָּדוֹל הַזֶּה:
וְאָמְרוּ עַל אֲשֶׁר עָזְבוּ אֶת־בְּרִית יְהֹוָה אֱלֹהֵי אֲבֹתָם
אֲשֶׁר כָּרַת עִמָּם בְּהוֹצִיאוֹ אֹתָם מֵאֶרֶץ מִצְרָיִם:
וַיֵּלְכוּ וַיַּעַבְדוּ אֱלֹהִים אֲחֵרִים וַיִּשְׁתַּחֲווּ לָהֶם אֱלֹהִים
אֲשֶׁר לֹא־יְדָעוּם וְלֹא חָלַק לָהֶם: וַיִּחַר־אַף יְהֹוָה
בָּאָרֶץ הַהִוא לְהָבִיא עָלֶיהָ אֶת־כָּל־הַקְּלָלָה
הַכְּתוּבָה בַּסֵּפֶר הַזֶּה: וַיִּתְּשֵׁם יְהֹוָה מֵעַל אַדְמָתָם
בְּאַף וּבְחֵמָה וּבְקֶצֶף גָּדוֹל וַיַּשְׁלִכֵם אֶל־אֶרֶץ
אַחֶרֶת כַּיּוֹם הַזֶּה: הַנִּסְתָּרֹת לַיהֹוָה אֱלֹהֵינוּ
וְהַנִּגְלֹת לָנוּ וּלְבָנֵינוּ עַד־עוֹלָם לַעֲשׂוֹת אֶת־כָּל־
דִּבְרֵי הַתּוֹרָה הַזֹּאת:

(After reading from the Torah.)

בָּרוּךְ אַתָּה יְיָ אֱלֹהֵינוּ מֶלֶךְ הָעוֹלָם . אֲשֶׁר נָתַן
לָנוּ תּוֹרַת אֱמֶת וְחַיֵּי עוֹלָם נָטַע בְּתוֹכֵנוּ .
בָּרוּךְ אַתָּה יְיָ נוֹתֵן הַתּוֹרָה:

(Before reading the Haphtarah.)

Blessed be the Lord our God, for the law of truth revealed in Israel and for the words of the prophets filled with His spirit and for the teachings of the masters and the preachers of righteousness, whom He raised up aforetime and in these days. They made His word a light to our feet and a lamp on our paths. May we hear it reverently, read it understandingly, and follow it willingly to the nurture and refreshment of the spiritual life which God has planted within us.

Reading of Haphtarah:

(Isaiah lvii, 14,-lviii, 14.)

CAST up, cast up, and prepare the way, take up the stumbling-block out of the way of my people. For thus saith the high and lofty One that inhabiteth eternity, whose name is holy: I dwell in the high and holy place, with him also that is of a contrite and humble spirit, to revive the spirit of the humble, and to revive the heart of the contrite ones. For I will not contend forever, neither will I be always wroth, for the spirit should fail before me, and the souls which I have made. For the iniquity of his covetousness was I wroth, and smote him; I hid me, and was wroth, and he went on forwardly in the way of his heart. I have seen his ways and will heal him; I will lead him also, and restore comforts unto him and to his mourners. I create the fruit of the lips: Peace, peace to him that is far off, and to him that is near, saith the Lord; and I will heal him. But the wicked are like the troubled sea, when it cannot rest, whose waters cast up mire and mud. There is no peace, saith my God, to the wicked.

Cry aloud, spare not, lift up thy voice like a trumpet, and show my people their transgressions and the house of Jacob their sins. Yet they seek me daily, and delight to know my ways: as a nation that has done righteousness, and forsaken not the ordinances of their God, they ask of me the ordinances of justice, they take delight in approaching God. Wherefore have we fasted, say they, and Thou seest not? Wherefore have we afflicted ourselves, and Thou takest no knowledge? Behold, in the day of your fast ye seek pleasure, and exact all your labors. Behold, ye fast for strife and debate, and to smite with the fist of wickedness: ye do not fast on this day, so as to make your voice to be heard on high. Is it such a fast that I have chosen? A day for a man to afflict himself? Is it to bow down his head as a bulrush, and to clothe himself with sackcloth and ashes? Wilt thou call this a fast, and an acceptable day to the Lord? Is not this the fast that I have chosen? to loose the bands of wickedness, to undo the heavy burdens, and to let the oppressed go free, and that ye break every yoke? Is it not to deal thy bread to the hungry, and that thou bring the poor, that are cast out, to thy house? When thou seest the naked, that thou cover him; and that thou hide not thyself from thine own flesh? Then shall thy light break forth as the morning, and thy health shall spring forth speedily; and thy righteousness shall go before thee; the glory of the Lord shall be thy rear-ward. Then shalt thou call, and the Lord will answer; thou shalt cry, and He will say, Here I am. If thou take away from the midst of thee the yoke, the putting forth of the finger, and speaking vanity; and if thou draw out thy soul to the hungry, and satisfy the afflicted soul; then shall light rise on thy obscurity, and thy darkness be as the noonday. The Lord shall guide thee continually, and satisfy thy soul in drought, and strengthen thy bones; and thou shalt be like a watered garden, and like a spring whose waters fail not. And they that shall be of thee shall build up the old waste places; thou shalt raise up the foundations of many generations; and thou shalt be called the repairer of the breach, the restorer of paths to dwell by. If thou turn away thy foot on the Sabbath from doing thy pleasure on my holy day; and call the Sabbath a delight, the holy of the Lord, honorable; and shalt honor Him, not doing thine own ways, nor seeking thine own pleasure, nor speaking thine own words; then shalt thou delight thyself in the Lord; and I will cause thee to ride upon the high places of the earth, and feed thee with the heritage of Jacob, thy father: for the mouth of the Lord hath spoken it.

DAY OF ATONEMENT.

Returning of the Scroll.

Minister:

O magnify the Lord with me and let us exalt His name together.

יְהַלְלוּ אֶת־שֵׁם יְיָ כִּי נִשְׂגָּב שְׁמוֹ לְבַדּוֹ׃

Choir:

His glory is in the earth and in the heavens. He is the strength of all His servants, the praise of them that truly love Him. The hope of Israel whom He brought nigh to Himself, Hallelujah.

הוֹדוֹ עַל אֶרֶץ וְשָׁמָיִם׃ וַיָּרֶם קֶרֶן לְעַמּוֹ תְּהִלָּה לְכָל חֲסִידָיו לִבְנֵי יִשְׂרָאֵל עַם קְרֹבוֹ הַלְלוּיָהּ׃

Minister·

The law of the Lord is perfect, restoring the soul; the testimonies of the Lord are faithful, making wise the simple. The precepts of the Lord are plain, rejoicing the heart; the fear of the Lord is pure, enduring forever. Behold, a good doctrine has been given to you: forsake it not.

תּוֹרַת יְיָ תְּמִימָה. מְשִׁיבַת נָפֶשׁ. עֵדוּת יְיָ נֶאֱמָנָה. מַחְכִּימַת פֶּתִי׃ פִּקּוּדֵי יְיָ יְשָׁרִים. מְשַׂמְּחֵי לֵב. יִרְאַת יְיָ טְהוֹרָה. עוֹמֶדֶת לָעַד׃ כִּי לֶקַח טוֹב נָתַתִּי לָכֶם תּוֹרָתִי אַל תַּעֲזֹבוּ׃

Choir:

It is a tree of life to them that lay hold of it and the supporters thereof are happy. Its ways are ways of pleasantness and all its paths are peace.

עֵץ־חַיִּים הִיא לַמַּחֲזִיקִים בָּהּ וְתוֹמְכֶיהָ מְאֻשָּׁר: דְּרָכֶיהָ דַרְכֵי נֹעַם וְכָל־נְתִיבוֹתֶיהָ שָׁלוֹם:

HYMN.

GIVE forth thine earnest cry,
O conscience, voice of God!
To young and old, to low and high,
Proclaim His will abroad.

Within the human breast
Thy strong monitions plead,
Still thunder thy divine protest
Against th' unrighteous deed.

Show the true way of peace
O thou, our guiding light!
From bondage of the wrong release
To service of the right.

THE SINNER'S TEAR.

MY soul is faint with grief and pain,
   My sins depress this frame of dust;
I know I am a mortal vain,
   And Thou, O God, art great and just;
The suns to Thee impure appear.
   My God, behold the sinner's tear.

The sting of guilt, the sinner's rod,
   Dejects my heart to nameless woe;
I know Thou art my righteous God,
   And I—the passion's hunted roe.
Too great my guilt, too great to bear,
   My Lord, behold the sinner's tear.

Repentance fills the contrite heart,
   Consumes my bones, bedims my way:
Transgressions bid my joys depart,
   And darkness hides the light of day
Be gracious, Lord, my pleading hear,
   O Father, dry the sinner's tear.

CHARITY.

STERN winter comes with icy footsteps speedy,
And many hearts are filled with doubts and fear;
Our duty 'tis to aid the poor and needy,
Who have no home, or but a chamber drear.
Let us fulfil the sacred word once spoken:
That he who giveth, lendeth to the Lord.
O freely give! This word shall ne'er be broken,
The giver's heart shall feel divine reward.
Go! lovely charity with blessings 'bounding,
Go! lend thine aid unto all in distress;
And let thy voice repeat in tones resounding:
Give to the poor! yourself you'll bless!

Whene'er the cry of poverty resoundeth,
Sweet charity, O hasten thy relief!
Pursue thy noble task! for want aboundeth.
Thou driest tears and calmest bitter grief,
Let all the world thy fair example follow.
All things are proved by the still voice within;
And they who give to those oppressed with sorrow,
A higher prize than gold can buy shall win.
Go! lovely charity with blessings 'bounding;
Go! lend thine aid unto all in distress;
And let thy voice repeat in tones resounding:
Give to the poor! yourself you'll bless!

Afternoon Service for the Day of Atonement.

Meditation:

אליך תשוקתי

FOR Thee, O Lord, is my longing, towards Thee all my thoughts are turned. My mind and my heart cling to Thee, who alone givest them their being. The body with all its members, the spirit soaring on ethereal wings to the most sublime; the heart, with its manifold sensations which influence its deepest recesses, everything that moves and lives within me, are gifts of grace from Thee. Therefore, with trembling reverence I offer my bodily and spiritual life on the flaming altar of devotion, as a burnt-offering to Thee, only One, whom no eye can behold, whose supreme greatness no mind can conceive: to Thee, Sovereign of the world, to whom no one can be sufficiently grateful.

With Thee are might and power and glory. In Thy presence submission alone is becoming. I bow to Thy will, and supplicate Thee both aloud and in silence. O strengthen me; feeble that I am;

suffer me to awaken to wisdom. Give health to my weak heart and heal my wounds. As long as there is breath within me, until all that is mortal in me perishes, I will look up to Thy greatness and pray for Thine aid. I wait and cease not to hope, till Thy grace reaches me, O till Thou removest my bitterness, and enlightenest my darkness.

Behold! I bow and kneel in repentance. My soul weeps by reason of its faithlessness. Before Thy holiness no one is pure. God of grace, have mercy on me. Woe is me, if I should gather the fruits of the seed which I have sown, and if Thou shouldst judge me according to my deserts. My evil inclination stands up to accuse me. In the guise of the defrauder and the seducer it lures me to destruction, and boldly enslaves me in the bonds of wickedness. O, when in the silence of night I review the evil of my ways, and think in sadness of mine own perversity, trembling possesses me and agony seizes on my heart. How can I go into eternity, with the consciousness of unpardoned guilt upon me!

When, the path of my time closing behind me and the day of retribution approaching, I hear Thy voice, O Lord! how overwhelmed with shame, shall I lift up my face? how stand in Thy presence and render an account unto Thee? I, who have so greatly transgressed, acted with duplicity, sinned against God and man, and neglected mine own salvation: I, who have wasted my strength and mine intellect on vanity, and built me a frail habitation upon sand, and heaped up evil deeds which now stand between Thee and me as a wall of separation: I, who have omitted so many occasions to do good, and have wasted precious time in idleness; carelessly disposed of Thy great bounties and misapplied what Thou hast confided to my care. In my youth, I stumbled in a mist of sensuous deception, and in old age I bound myself in the fetters of apathy and ease. I have murmured against Thy teachings and preferred to walk after the dictates of mine own heart. Thy precepts seldom animated me, and I delighted to walk in the paths of pleasure. Only the fleeting moment and the appetite of my senses swayed me, and I forgot the approaching end.

Must not then the blush of shame suffuse my countenance? Would that I might flee from Thy presence. But there is no escape from before Thee. For a just God art Thou, but also a gracious God; strict in judgment, but abounding in mercy. And thus am I encouraged to hope, and with a contrite heart and deep devotion, with a broken spirit and with frame bowed down, to appear even as a penitent child in prayer before Thee. O lend Thine ear to this my supplication. Behold my tribulation, and leave me not to perish. Let Thy grace prevail, and make an end of mine agony. Let me see Thy help before I die; that I may do good and eschew evil. Should my foot stumble, O be Thou my support! Should my soul falter, O give what will sustain it! Be Thou my strength in my hour of temptation, and though I lose all earthly pleasure, let me find my joy in Thee. Be Thou my delight and my hope, my light and my life, my comfort and my consolation in all mine aspirations.

This is the purpose of my prayers; for this flow all my tears. O, that they may be accepted and may wash away my sins, that my strength might be renewed to strive against passion and to conquer it. O grant when the soul shall leave its earthly habitation, even though it deserve and dare claim no reward, it may trust that it has been cleansed of all guilt, and may hasten to Thee, free and glad and pure. Then let Thine angels of peace receive it, singing in joyful chorus, Peace be Thy coming. There may it find its habitation in the blissful light of the spiritual world and its portion in unmeasured eternity and unending happiness. Amen.

Alternate Reading for Minister and Congregation:

(Psalms cxliii and xxv.)

Hear my prayer, O Lord; give ear to my supplications.

> In Thy faithfulness, and in Thy righteousness, answer me.

Enter not into judgment with Thy servant; for in Thy sight shall no man living be justified.

> My spirit is overwhelmed within me; my heart is desolate.

I remember the days of old; I meditate on all Thy works; I muse on the work of Thy hands.

I stretch forth my hands unto Thee; my soul thirsteth for Thee, like a parched land for rain.

Cause me to see Thy loving-kindness speedily; for in Thee do I trust.

Make known to me the way which I should walk; for to Thee do I lift up my soul.

Deliver me, O Lord, from mine enemies; for in Thee do I seek refuge.

Teach me to do Thy will; for Thou art my God. Let Thy good spirit lead me in a plain path.

Quicken me, O Lord, for Thy name's sake; for Thy righteousness' sake bring me out of my distress.

To Thee, O Lord, do I lift up my soul.

O my God, I trust in Thee; let me not be put to shame.

Yea, let none that wait on Thee be put to shame.

Cause me to know Thy ways, O Lord; teach me Thy paths; lead me in Thy truth.

For Thou art the God from whom cometh my help; in Thee do I trust at all times.

Remember Thy loving-kindness, O Lord, and Thy tender mercy, which Thou hast exercised of old.

Remember not the faults and transgressions of my youth.

According to Thy mercy remember Thou me, for Thy goodness sake, O Lord!

Good and righteous is the Lord; therefore showeth He to sinners the way.

The humble He guideth in judgment, and the contrite He teacheth His way.

All the paths of the Lord are mercy and truth to those who keep His covenant and His testimonies.

For Thy name's sake, O Lord, pardon mine iniquity; for it is great.

Who is the man that feareth the Lord? Him doth He show the way which he should choose.

The secret of the Lord is with them that fear Him, and He will teach them His covenant.

Mine eyes are ever directed to the Lord, for He will pluck my feet out of the net.

Look upon me and have pity upon me; for I am desolate and afflicted.

Lighten the sorrows of my heart, and deliver me from my troubles.

Look upon mine affliction and distress, and forgive all my sins.

Guard Thou my life, and deliver me; let me not be put to shame, for I have trusted in Thee.

Let integrity and uprightness preserve me, for on Thee do I rest my hope.

Choir:

Redeem Israel, O God, from all his sorrows.

Minister and Congregation:

(Psalm ci.)

I will sing of mercy and judgment; to Thee, O Lord, will I sing.

I will behave myself wisely in a perfect way; O, when wilt Thou come unto me?

I will walk within my house with a perfect heart.

I will set no wicked thing before mine eyes.

I hate the work of evil doers, it shall not cleave to me.

The perverse in heart shall be far from me, I will not know a wicked person.

Whoso slandereth his neighbor in secret, him will I remove.

Him that hath a haughty look and a proud heart, I will not endure.

Mine eyes shall be upon the faithful that they may dwell with me.

He who practiceth deceit shall not tarry in my house;

He who speaketh falsehood shall not remain in my sight.

Choir:

And I, through righteousness, shall see Thy face, I shall be satisfied with the light of Thy countenance.

Minister:

(Job viii and xi.)

DOTH God pervert judgment or doth the Almighty pervert justice? If thou wouldst seek unto God betimes, and make thy supplication to the Almighty; if thou wert pure and upright; surely now He would strive for thee, and make the habitation of thy righteousness prosperous. Though thy beginning was small, yet thy latter end should greatly increase. For inquire, I pray thee, of former ages, and apply thyself to that which their fathers have searched out: for we are but of yesterday, and know nothing, because our days upon earth are a shadow: Shall not they teach thee, and tell thee, and utter words out of their heart? Can the rush grow up without the mire? can the flag grow without the water? Whilst it is yet in its greenness, and not cut down, it withereth before any other herb. So are the paths of all that forget God; and the hope of the godless man shall perish. His hope shall be cut off, and his trust shall be a spider's web. He shall lean upon his house, but it shall not stand; he shall hold it fast, but it shall not endure. If he be destroyed from his place, then it shall deny him, saying, I have not seen thee. Behold, this is the joy of his way, and out of the earth shall others grow.

God will not cast away a perfect man, neither will he help the evil-doers. He will yet fill thy mouth with laughing and thy lips with rejoicing. They that hate thee shall be clothed with shame; and the dwelling-place of the wicked shall come to naught. Would that God would show thee the secrets of wisdom, that it is manifold in effectual working! Know, therefore, that God exacteth of thee less than thine iniquity deserveth.

Canst thou, by searching, find out God? Canst thou find out the Almighty unto perfection? It is as high as heaven; what canst thou do? deeper than the nether-world; what canst thou know? The measure thereof is longer than the earth, and broader than the sea. If He pass by and arrest, or gather together, then who can hinder Him? For He knoweth vain men: He seeth the wicked and the foolish.

If thou set thy heart aright, and stretch thy hands toward Him; if iniquity be in thy hand, put it far away, and let not wickedness dwell in thy tents; surely then shalt thou lift up thy face without spot; yea, thou shalt be steadfast, and shalt not fear; because thou shalt forget thy misery, and remember it as waters that pass away. And thine age shall be clearer than the noonday; though there be darkness, it shall be as the morning. And thou shalt be secure, because there is hope; yea, thou shalt search about thee, and thou shalt take thy rest in safety. Also thou shalt lie down, and none shall make thee afraid.

Minister and Congregation:

אלהים אלי אתה

ALMIGHTY, Thou art my God! I will invoke Thee in the assembly of Thy chosen; I will proclaim Thy truth and Thy greatness. Hear me on this solemn day, when I call on Thee in the midst of Thy congregation.

Congregation:

Open my lips, that they may speak Thy praise.

Before Thee, O God, my deepest secrets are unveiled; my soul and my body tremble in Thy presence. Hear me on this solemn day, when the erring yearn for Thy love.

Congregation:

Thy children are longing for Thy mercy.

Mercy is Thy garment, O God; therefore, let me not incur shame while striving to fulfil my sacred mission. Hear me on this solemn day, on which Thou hast promised to deliver me from the hand of the oppressor, and to heal my wounds.

Congregation:

Guide my heart, that it may be perfect with Thee and Thy law.

Guard, O God, my thoughts, that they may not stray from the exalted mark; guard my lips, that they may not draw me into a snare. Hear me, O God, on this solemn day, when only Thy praise, the

DAY OF ATONEMENT.

joy inspired by Thy greatness and love, can make me forget my deep sorrow.

Congregation:

May Thy light and Thy truth lead me unto the end.

Thou art my hope, my immovable rock, Thou support of the powerless. Hear me, O God, on this solemn day, on which Thou hast promised to purify the sinner and efface his guilt.

Congregation:

Create unto me a pure heart, O God, and renew within me an upright spirit.

Out of the depths, O God, I cry to Thee, whose throne is on measureless heights. Hear me, O God, on this solemn day, when the needy take refuge in Thy sanctuary.

Congregation:

I seek shelter from evil under the wings of Thy mercy.

Thou hast prepared a healing balm for my wounds: the sacred hour of atonement, which crowns us with Thy mercy. Hear me, O God, on this solemn day, on which I strive to shake off the iron fetters of sin.

Congregation:

O purify me from guilt and cleanse my heart from wrong.

The deepest depth in my heart is moved with longing toward Thee, and my spirit, so proud in former days, is now deeply bent. Hear me, O God, on this solemn day, on which all delusions vanish.

Congregation:

I lift up my heart to Thee, my Heavenly Father.

Most gracious God, worshiped by the circling hosts of heaven; remember me when my thoughts soar aloft to Thy throne. Hear me, O God, on this solemn day, on which I offer my supplications in the midst of Thy faithful children.

Congregation:

Let all living creatures praise and glorify Thy name, O God.

Alternate Reading for Minister and Congregation:

(Isaiah.)

O LORD, Thou art my God; I will exalt Thee, I will praise Thy name;

For Thou hast done wonderful things; Thine ancient purposes are faithfulness and truth.

Thou hast been a defence to the poor, a defence to the needy in their distress, a refuge from the storm, a shadow from the heat;

When the rage of tyrants was like a storm against the wall.

He will destroy death forever; the Lord will wipe away the tears from all faces;

And the reproach of His people shall He take away from the whole earth.

Then shall we sing: Behold, this is our God, we waited for Him, and He hath saved us.

This is the Lord, for whom we waited, let us rejoice and exult in His salvation.

Open ye the gates, that the righteous nation may enter in, the nation that keepeth the truth.

We have a strong city; His aid doth God appoint for walls and bulwarks.

Trust ye in the Lord forever, for the Lord is an everlasting rock.

Him that is steadfast in mind wilt Thou keep in continual peace, because he trusteth in Thee.

The way of the upright is a smooth way; Thou, O most righteous, dost level the path of the upright.

In the way of Thy judgments, O Lord, we have waited for Thee.

The desire of our souls is to Thy name, and to the remembrance of Thee.

My soul longeth for Thee in the night, and my spirit within me seeketh Thee in the morning.

For when Thy judgments are in the earth, the inhabitants of the world learn righteousness.

Though favor be shown to the wicked, he will not **learn righteousness.**

In the land of uprightness will he deal unjustly, and have no regard to the majesty of the Lord.

Thou, O Lord, wilt give us peace; for all our work Thou doest for us.

The effect of righteousness shall be peace; and the fruit of righteousness quiet and security forever.

Then shall the people dwell in peaceful habitations, in secure dwellings, and in quiet places.

There shall be security in Thy times: wisdom and knowledge shall be the store of thy prosperity, and the fear of the Lord shall be thy treasure.

Choir:

They shall not hurt, nor destroy in all my holy mountain, for the earth shall be full of the knowledge of the Lord, as the waters cover the sea.

Minister and Congregation:

(Psalm lxxxvi.)

INCLINE Thine ear, O Lord, and hear me, for I am in distress.

Have pity upon me, O Lord; for to Thee do I cry all the day.

Revive the soul of Thy servant, for to Thee, O Lord, do I lift up my soul.

Thou art good, and ready to forgive; **yea, rich in** mercy to all that call upon Thee.

Give ear, O Lord, to my prayer, and attend to the voice of my supplication.

In the day of my trouble I call upon Thee, for Thou wilt answer me.

There is none like unto Thee among the mighty, O Lord, and there are no works like Thy works.

All the nations which Thou hast made shall come and worship before Thee, O Lord;

For great art Thou, and wondrous are Thy works; Thou alone art God.

Teach me, O Lord, Thy way, that I may walk in Thy truth; unite all my heart to fear Thy name.

I will praise Thee, O Lord, my God, with my whole heart; I will give glory to Thy name forever.

For Thy kindness to me hath been great; Thou hast delivered me from the lowest pit.

Thou, O Lord, art a God full of compassion and kindness;

Long-suffering and rich in mercy and truth.

Give Thy strength to Thy servant, and save the son of Thy handmaid.

Choir:

Show me a token for good; because Thou, O Lord, helpest and comfortest me!

Minister and Congregation:

(Psalm xviii.)

I LOVE Thee, O Lord, my strength, my shield, my strong defense, my high tower.

I will call upon the Lord, who is worthy to be praised; so shall I be saved from mine enemies.

The snares of death encompassed me; the floods of destruction filled me with dismay.

In my distress I called upon the Lord, and cried unto my God.

He heard my voice from His place, and my cry came before Him.

He stretched forth His hand from above; He took me and drew me out of deep waters.

He delivered me from my strong enemy; from my adversaries who were too powerful for me.

They fell upon me in the day of my calamity; but the Lord was my stay.

With the merciful Thou wilt show Thyself merciful; with the upright Thou wilt show Thyself upright.

With the pure Thou wilt show Thyself pure, and with the perverse Thou wilt contend.

For Thou savest the afflicted people, but the haughty countenance Thou bringest down.

Thou causest my lamp to shine; the Lord, my God, enlighteneth my darkness.

For through Thee I have broken through troops; through my God I conquered mine enemies.

The ways of God are just and true; His word is tried and pure.

He is a shield to all who put their trust in Him.

Who then is God save the Eternal, and who is a deliverer save our God?

It is God that girded me with strength and made my way plain.

Thou gavest me the shield of Thy protection.

Thy right hand held me up, and Thy goodness made me great.

Thou hast saved me from the assaults of nations, from the violence of men.

Thou hast delivered me from mine enemies, yea, Thou hast lifted me up above mine adversaries.

The Lord is the living God; blessed be my rock; exalted be the God of my salvation.

Therefore will I give thanks to Thee, O Lord, among the nations, and sing praises to Thy name.

Choir:

The Lord giveth strength to His people, and showeth mercy to His anointed, to Israel, His servant, forever, Hallelujah!

Minister and Congregation:

Psalms lxv and xxxvi. (Abridged.)

TO Thee belongeth trust, to Thee praise, O God in Zion, and to Thee shall the vow be performed.

O Thou that hearest prayer, to Thee shall all flesh come and worship.

Happy is he whom Thou choosest, and bringest near Thee to dwell in Thy courts.

May we be satisfied with the blessings of Thy house, Thy holy temple.

By wonderful deeds dost Thou answer us in Thy goodness, O God, our salvation.

Thy goodness, O Lord, reacheth to the heavens, and Thy faithfulness to the clouds.

Thy righteousness is like the high mountains; Thy judgments are like the great deep.

Thou, O Lord, preservest man and beast.

How precious is Thy loving-kindness, O God; yea, the sons of men seek refuge under the shadows of Thy wings.

Thou causest them to drink of the full stream of Thy pleasures.

For with Thee is the fountain of life; through Thy light we see light.

Choir:

O continue Thy loving-kindness to them that know Thee, and Thy favor to the upright in heart!

Minister and Congregation:

(Psalm xl.)

I TRUSTED steadfastly in the Lord, and he listened, and heard my cry.

He hath put into my mouth a new song, a song of praise to our God.

Many shall see, and fear, and put their trust in the Lord.

Happy the man who maketh the Lord his trust, and resorteth not to men of pride and falsehood.

Many, O Lord, my God, are the wonderful works which thou hast done;

Many have been Thy gracious purposes toward me; none can be compared to Thee.

Would I declare and rehearse them, they are more than can be numbered.

In sacrifice and oblation Thou hast no pleasure; my ears Thou hast opened;

Burnt-offering and sin-offering Thou requirest not.

O my God, to do Thy will is my delight, and Thy law dwelleth in my heart;

May Thy loving-kindness and Thy truth continually preserve me.

Choir:

Let all who seek Thee be glad and rejoice in Thee; let those who love Thy protection ever say, Great is the Lord!

Minister:

WE will declare the greatness and the holiness of this Day, for thereon Thy kingdom is exalted, Thy throne established in mercy, and Thou judgest in truth. It is true that Thou art the Judge; Thou reprovest; Thou knowest all; Thou bearest witness, recordest and sealest: Thou also rememberest all things that seem to be forgotten; and all that enter the world must pass before Thee, even as the shepherd causes his sheep to pass under his rod. Thou numberest and countest, and visitest every living soul, appointest the limitations of all Thy creatures, and recordest the sentence of their judgment:

Minister and Choir:

How many are to pass away, and how many are to come into existence; who are to live and who are to die; who are to accomplish the full number of their days, and who are not to accomplish them;

Who are to perish by water and who by fire; who by the sword and who by hunger; who by earthquake and who by plagues;

Who shall have repose and who shall be troubled; who shall be tranquil and who shall be disturbed; who shall be prosperous and who shall be afflicted;

Who shall become poor and who shall become rich; who shall be cast down and who shall be exalted.

But Repentance, Prayer and Charity avert the evil decree.

DAY OF ATONEMENT

Minister:

וּנְתַנֶּה תֹּקֶף קְדֻשַּׁת הַיּוֹם. כִּי הוּא נוֹרָא וְאָיוֹם. וּבוֹ תִנָּשֵׂא מַלְכוּתֶךָ. וְיִכּוֹן בְּחֶסֶד כִּסְאֶךָ. וְתֵשֵׁב עָלָיו בֶּאֱמֶת: אֱמֶת כִּי אַתָּה הוּא דַיָּן יְמוֹכִיחַ וְיוֹדֵעַ וָעֵד. וְכוֹתֵב וְחוֹתֵם וְסוֹפֵר וּמוֹנֶה. וְתִזְכּוֹר כָּל־הַנִּשְׁכָּחוֹת. וְכָל־בָּאֵי עוֹלָם תַּעֲבִיר לְפָנֶיךָ כִּבְנֵי מָרוֹן. כְּבַקָּרַת רוֹעֶה עֶדְרוֹ. מַעֲבִיר צֹאנוֹ תַּחַת שִׁבְטוֹ. כֵּן תַּעֲבִיר וְתִסְפּוֹר וְתִמְנֶה וְתִפְקוֹד נֶפֶשׁ כָּל חָי. וְתַחְתּוֹךְ קִצְבָה לְכָל בְּרִיָּה. וְתִכְתּוֹב אֶת גְּזַר דִּינָם:

Minister and Choir:

בַּמָּה יַעֲבֹרוּן. וְכַמָּה יִבָּרֵאוּן:

מִי יִחְיֶה וּמִי יָמוּת.   מִי בְקִצּוֹ וּמִי לֹא בְקִצּוֹ.

מִי בָאֵשׁ וּמִי בַמַּיִם.   מִי בַחֶרֶב וּמִי בָרָעָב.

מִי בָרַעַשׁ וּמִי בַמַּגֵּפָה.   מִי יָנוּחַ וּמִי יָנוּעַ.

מִי יִשָּׁקֵט וּמִי יִטָּרֵף.   מִי יִשָּׁלֵו וּמִי יִתְיַסָּר.

מִי יָרוּם וּמִי יִשָּׁפֵל.   מִי יֵעָשֵׁר וּמִי יֵעָנִי:

וּתְשׁוּבָה וּתְפִלָּה וּצְדָקָה מַעֲבִירִין אֶת רֹעַ הַגְּזֵרָה:

Minister:

Thou desirest not the death of the sinner, but that he turn from his evil path and live. Till the day of his death Thou waitest for him to receive him back in grace. Thou hast fashioned man, and knowest the inclinations of his heart. How weak is man! He comes from the dust and returns to the dust; must toil for his sustenance; passes away like withered grass, a vanishing shadow, a fleeting dream.

But Thou, O God, art eternal, Thou art King everlasting.

Organ Voluntary.

Minister:

(Congregation standing.)

LET us adore the ever-living God, and render praise unto Him, who spread out the heavens and founded the earth, whose glory is revealed in the heavens above us and whose greatness is manifest throughout the world: He is our God, and there is none else.

Choir and Congregation:

We bow the head and bend the knee and magnify the King of kings, the Holy One, the Ever-blest.

Minister:

Thus it is written, Know ye this day, and take ye to heart that the Eternal, He is God; in the heavens above and on the earth beneath, there is none else.

(Congregation sitting.)

DAY OF ATONEMENT.

Minister:

כִּי לֹא תַחְפּוֹץ בְּמוֹת הַמֵּת . כִּי אִם בְּשׁוּבוֹ
מִדַּרְכּוֹ וְחָיָה . וְעַד יוֹם מוֹתוֹ תְּחַכֶּה לּוֹ . אִם יָשׁוּב
מִיָּד תְּקַבְּלוֹ : אֱמֶת כִּי אַתָּה הוּא יוֹצְרָם . וְאַתָּה
יוֹדֵעַ יִצְרָם . כִּי הֵם בָּשָׂר וָדָם : אָדָם יְסוֹדוֹ
מֵעָפָר וְסוֹפוֹ לֶעָפָר . בְּנַפְשׁוֹ יָבִיא לַחְמוֹ . מָשׁוּל
כֶּחָצִיר יָבֵשׁ . וּכְצֵל עוֹבֵר . וְכַחֲלוֹם יָעוּף :

וְאַתָּה הוּא מֶלֶךְ אֵל חַי וְקַיָּם :

Organ Voluntary.

Minister:
(Congregation standing.)

עָלֵינוּ לְשַׁבֵּחַ לַאֲדוֹן הַכֹּל . לָתֵת גְּדֻלָּה לְיוֹצֵר
בְּרֵאשִׁית . שֶׁהוּא נוֹטֶה שָׁמַיִם וְיוֹסֵד אָרֶץ . וּמוֹשַׁב
יְקָרוֹ בַּשָּׁמַיִם מִמַּעַל . וּשְׁכִינַת עֻזּוֹ בְּגָבְהֵי מְרוֹמִים .
הוּא אֱלֹהֵינוּ אֵין עוֹד :

Choir and Congregation:

וַאֲנַחְנוּ כּוֹרְעִים וּמִשְׁתַּחֲוִים וּמוֹדִים
לִפְנֵי מֶלֶךְ מַלְכֵי הַמְּלָכִים . הַקָּדוֹשׁ בָּרוּךְ הוּא :

Minister:

אֱמֶת מַלְכֵּנוּ אֶפֶס זוּלָתוֹ . כַּכָּתוּב בְּתוֹרָתוֹ .
וְיָדַעְתָּ הַיּוֹם וַהֲשֵׁבֹתָ אֶל לְבָבֶךָ . כִּי יְיָ הוּא
הָאֱלֹהִים בַּשָּׁמַיִם מִמַּעַל וְעַל הָאָרֶץ מִתַּחַת אֵין
עוֹד :

(Congregation sitting.)

Minister:

GOD is the source of our strength. He redeems man from the degradation of sin; He has implanted in us a part of His own spirit, that we may recognize Him and follow the vestiges of His wisdom, His goodness and His holiness, and thus become a true image of Him, the all-just and merciful Father. He has appointed Israel to carry the knowledge of Him, the only One, and the assurance of His all-sustaining love through all ages and to all nations.

Gathered here on this most sacred of days, we look back upon the path in which God has led our fathers. When spiritual darkness covered the earth, He kindled the light of truth in the midst of His people. On Zion's height rose His sanctuary, the only one dedicated to Him. To His altar Israel brought the offerings of joy and gratitude, the sacrifices of contrition and repentance, the incense of fervent devotion and holy resolves. Upon that holy hill of Zion was planted the tree of spiritual life, whose fruit has nourished and enlightened the souls of men. Zion fell, the Temple sank into ruins. Centuries have since rolled by. Generations have come and passed away; kingdoms have risen and fallen; yet do we to-day look back with reverence to that sacred spot on Palestine's soil, remembering that from Zion went forth the law, and the word of God from Jerusalem.

Since those days numberless trials and vicissitudes have passed over us. The light of God's truth has increased in purity and power, and its influence is felt in every sphere of human life. Yet, the same divine spirit that animated our fathers, still dwells in our midst; our hearts are stirred by the same emotions, quickened by the same hopes, filled with the same longings, and uplifted by the same inspirations which once guided and encouraged them. And on this most sacred of days, the faithful of Israel, wherever dispersed, appear before His throne of mercy to offer their sacrifice of atonement and reconciliation, with the same contrite and repentant spirit as did our fathers of old. We proclaim the same divine truths, which, notwithstanding the changes of time, have remained our heritage, and which no power of temptation or persecution and tyranny could destroy. For His providence has preserved and sustained us amid our struggles in behalf of His truth, against darkness, superstition and error. May, then, the memory of the past teach us the lesson of duty to remain faithful to ourselves and to our mission.

We remember to-day the solemn ceremonies of atonement in the Temple of old, when the high-priest of Israel, arrayed in the garments of his holy office, entered the sanctuary to plead for God's forgiveness in behalf of the people. He first implored pardon for himself and his household. Though guardian of the sanctuary, and set apart for its holy service, he deemed himself not free from human imperfections and failings, for there is no man so righteous that doeth good and sinneth not.

O God, may we recognize in the office of the

ancient high-priest the lesson of our own mission. May the teachers appointed to lead and instruct the people, be ever watchful of their conduct. May they be mindful of their sacred office, and strive to live worthy of it. May the spirit of truth and peace pervade their teachings and practices. Grant them wisdom and strength to proclaim Thy word with earnestness and love, and awaken in the hearts of Thy people the spirit of hope and zeal for Thy cause. And so, too, may these reminiscences imbue every Israelite with the spirit of purity and truth, that his every act and aspiration may be worthy of the name he bears, and every Jewish home become the sanctuary of love and peace, of righteousness and truth. And knowing our own sins and imperfections, we approach Thee, O Father, craving Thy forgiveness. With sincere contrition and heartfelt repentance we pray in the words of the ancient high-priest:

Minister and Congregation, the Choir responding:

O Lord, pardon the sins, iniquities and transgressions which Thy people, the house of Israel, have committed, as it is said: On this day the Lord will grant you atonement from all your sins; before God you shall be pure.

אָנָּא יְיָ . כַּפֶּר נָא . לַחֲטָאִים . וְלַעֲוֹנוֹת . וְלַפְּשָׁעִים . שֶׁחָטָאתִי . וְשֶׁעָוִיתִי . וְשֶׁפָּשַׁעְתִּי לְפָנֶיךָ . אֲנִי וּבֵיתִי : כַּכָּתוּב . כִּי בַיּוֹם הַזֶּה יְכַפֵּר עֲלֵיכֶם לְטַהֵר אֶתְכֶם מִכֹּל חַטֹּאתֵיכֶם לִפְנֵי יְיָ תִּטְהָרוּ :

Minister:

WHEN the high-priest had made atonement for himself and his household, he offered the sacrifice of atonement in behalf of the whole congregation of Israel. Then he entered the holy of holies, where he made expiation for the sins of the people.

Even so may this day all Israel be reconciled to Thee, that all the erring may be led back, that those estranged from the heritage of their fathers may be restored, that those who have grown cold and indifferent may be quickened with new zeal, so that the house of Israel may again be one community, united in the bonds of hope and faith and devotion to Thy service. As it is promised: Yet now hear, O Jacob, my servant; and Israel, whom I have chosen: Thus saith the Lord that made thee: Fear not, O Jacob, my servant; and thou, Jeshurun, whom I have chosen. For I will pour water upon the thirsty land, and floods upon the dry ground; I will pour my spirit upon thy children, and my blessing upon thine offspring; and they shall spring up as among the grass, as willows by the watercourses. One shall say, I am the Lord's; and another shall call himself by the name of Jacob; and another shall subscribe with his hand unto the Lord, and surname himself by the name of Israel.

And so we pray again in the words of the high-priest:

AFTERNOON SERVICE FOR THE

Minister and Congregation, the Choir responding:

O Lord, pardon the sins, iniquities and transgressions which thy people, the house of Israel, have committed, as it is said: On this day the Lord will grant you atonement, purifying you from all your sins; before God you shall be pure.

אָנָּא יְיָ. כַּפֶּר נָא. לַחֲטָאִים. וְלַעֲוֹנוֹת. וְלַפְּשָׁעִים. שֶׁחָטְאוּ. וְשֶׁעָווּ. וְשֶׁפָּשְׁעוּ. לְפָנֶיךָ עַמְּךָ בֵּית־יִשְׂרָאֵל: כַּכָּתוּב. כִּי בַיּוֹם הַזֶּה יְכַפֵּר עֲלֵיכֶם לְטַהֵר אֶתְכֶם מִכֹּל חַטֹּאתֵיכֶם לִפְנֵי יְיָ תִּטְהָרוּ:

Organ Voluntary.

Minister:

And when the priests and the people who stood in the court, heard the ineffable name uttered by the high-priest, solemnly and reverently, they fell on their knees and worshiped, praising the name and the glory of the kingdom of the everlasting God. And in the same words of praise we render homage to Thee to-day and exclaim: Praised be the name, the glory and the majesty of God forever.

Choir and Congregation:

בָּרוּךְ שֵׁם כְּבוֹד מַלְכוּתוֹ לְעוֹלָם וָעֶד:

Minister:

AND now, O Lord, our God, throughout the habitations of man, Thy people, Israel, stands this day before Thee to worship Thee and to beseech Thy mercy and Thy pardon. Still is Israel imbued with the prophetic spirit that renders it a servant unto all humanity. Still we uplift Thy banner, awaiting the blessed time when the Almighty, who revealed himself to our fathers on Sinai, shall be proclaimed God by all the children of men. Then, not for ourselves alone, but for all upon whose souls Thy divine image is stamped, do we implore Thy divine assistance. O let Thy message of peace and pardon reach unto the furthermost bounds of the earth!

When Solomon dedicated the temple on Zion's hill, he prayed: Moreover concerning a stranger, that is not of Thy people Israel, but cometh out of a far country for Thy name's sake, for strangers shall hear of Thy great name and of Thy strong hand, and of Thine outstretched arm; when he shall come and pray toward this house: Hear Thou in heaven, Thy dwelling-place, and do according to all that the stranger calleth to Thee for; that all people of the earth may know Thy name, to fear Thee, as do Thy people Israel; and that they may know that this house, which I have builded, is called by Thy name."

In the same spirit we pray for all mankind. Grant that wherever a heart sighs in anguish under the load of guilt, wherever a soul yearns to return to Thee, it may feel the influence of Thy pardoning love and mercy. May superstition, falsehood and malice everywhere vanish. May Thine all-redeeming love be revealed to those who still grope in the darkness of ignorance and error, and the knowledge of Thy truth shed its rays into deluded minds and clouded hearts. May Thy house become a house of prayer for all nations.

We pray that the time may come when strife shall no more set nation against nation; when every one shall sit in peace beneath his own vine and fig tree and none shall disturb them; when swords shall be beaten into plow-shares, and spears into pruning hooks; when nation shall not lift sword against nation, and they shall learn war no more.

Then shall Thy kingdom be established on earth and upon all the nations shall rest the spirit of the Lord, even the spirit of wisdom and understanding, the spirit of counsel and might, the spirit of knowledge and fear of the Lord.

God will reign forever, thy God, O Zion, from generation to generation. Hallelujah.

Choir:

יִמְלֹךְ יְיָ לְעוֹלָם אֱלֹהַיִךְ צִיּוֹן לְדֹר וָדֹר הַלְלוּיָהּ:

DAY OF ATONEMENT.

Alternate Reading for Minister and Congregation:

(Psalm li.)

BE gracious unto me, O God! according to Thy loving-kindness; according to the greatness of Thy mercy, blot out my transgressions!

Wash me thoroughly from my iniquity, and cleanse me from my sin!

For I acknowledge my transgressions, and my sin is ever before me.

Against Thee, Thee only, have I sinned, and in Thy sight have I done evil;

So that Thou art just in Thy sentence, and righteous in Thy judgment.

Behold! Thou desirest truth in the heart; so teach me wisdom in my inmost soul!

Hide Thy face from my sins, and blot out all my iniquities!

Create within me a clean heart, O God! renew within me a steadfast spirit!

Cast me not away from Thy presence, and take not Thy holy spirit from me!

Restore to me the joy of Thy protection, and strengthen me with a willing spirit!

Then will I teach Thy ways to transgressors, and sinners will be converted to Thee.

O Lord! open Thou my lips, that my mouth may show forth Thy praise!

For Thou desirest not sacrifice, else would I give it; Thou delightest not in burnt-offerings.

Choir:

The sacrifice which God loveth is a broken spirit, a broken and contrite heart, O God, Thou wilt not despise.

Minister:

THOU demandest not sacrifice, O Lord, but love with the whole heart and soul. Thou hast taught us, through Thy prophets, what is good and what Thou requirest of us: to do justly, to love mercy and to walk humbly with Thee; to plead the cause of the widow and the orphan; to love and protect the stranger; to feed the hungry; to break the bonds of wickedness; to free the oppressed, and not to hide ourselves from our own flesh. By such offering shall we bear witness of Thee and glorify Thee throughout the world, and to this end alone hast Thou sent us to all parts of the earth.

For many centuries the children of Israel mourned over their exile from their ancient home, and the loss of the altar of atonement and the ministering priest. Especially on this day our fathers recalled with deep sorrow the solemn rites of atonement and lamented over the fall of the sanctuary of Zion and its continuous desolation in such strains as these: "Happy the eyes that saw the high-priest in his sacred vestment, as he stood, clad in the snow-white robe of purity and honor, as he poured forth the seven-fold sprinkling of the atoning blood. Happy the eyes that saw the chief of the sons of Aaron holding up his hands for blessing, like the proud cedar of Lebanon compassed by palm-trees round about. He was as the morning star risen out of the dark night, and as the sun casting his splendor upon the temple of the most High, like a golden censer spreading rich perfume near and far, and as the cypress tree which reacheth high up toward the sky. Happy the ears that heard the thousand-voiced song of the Levites, accompanying the sounds of the trumpets, the many-stringed harp and the flute, in sweet and soul-stirring melodies, echoing the praise of the Most High."

Choir:

My soul thirsteth for God, for the living God!
    When shall I come up and appear before God?
My tears have been my meat day and night, while
    they continually say to me, where is thy God?
When I remember these things, I pour out my soul
    within me. Why art thou cast down, O my
    soul, and why art thou disquieted in me?
Hope Thou in God, for I shall yet praise Him, who
    is the health of my countenance and my God.

Minister:

WHEN Thy glory departed from Zion, and the sacrifices ceased upon Thine altar, then was Israel banished from his patrimony and became a wanderer in foreign lands. In their grief and humiliation our fathers thought only of the sins that had provoked the Divine wrath and brought that terrible judgment upon them. Every day, but mostly on the Day of Atonement, they felt the bitterness of their exile from the holy land and the loss of the ordained means of atonement. But in course of time they learned to recall rather the promises of grace, which abound in God's word, than the threatenings of his anger; they began to understand better and even better the deep meaning of the teachings of the prophets, that all true atonement is perfected in the heart and when this returns to God in sincerity and with the firm resolve to do justly, to love mercy and to walk humbly with God, the loss of altar, sacrifice and priest need not make them doubt of their acceptance with God. Nay, it dawned upon them, like the rising of a new day, that their separation from their ancestral homes and their dispersion over the earth, far from being a punishment only, was in the hand of God a means of blessing to all mankind. Israel is to witness to the one true and living God and endeavor to unite all peoples into a covenant of peace, so that the word should be fulfilled in him: "In his stripes the world was healed, and in his bruises men found new strength, and through his chains the prisoners of error were set free."

Choir:

Shall I say unto God, my rock, why hast Thou forgotten me? When, with a sword in my bones, mine enemies reproach me, saying daily unto me: Where is Thy God?

Why art thou cast down, O my soul, and why art thou disquieted within me?

Hope thou in God, for I shall yet praise Him, who is the health of my countenance and my God.

Minister:

WE give thanks and praise to Thee, our guardian and redeemer. All the torrents of hatred, all the waves of persecution could not quench our love for Thee and Thy law. Not as an accursed sinner, but as a teacher of Thy truth did Israel wander through the centuries, to kindle everywhere the flame of a pure faith and lead the nations to a reconciliation with Thee, their common Father.

And behold, wherever there is a temple reared in Thine honor, there is the foundation-stone laid to the Jerusalem of the future; and wherever Thy name is invoked, there burn the flames of the true worship of Thee. Truly, not backward shall we turn our eyes, but forward, to the grand and promising future. Though we cherish and revere the spot on which once stood the cradle of our people, the land where Israel grew up a tender plant, and the knowledge of God rose like the morning-dawn, yet our longings and aspirations go forth toward a higher goal. The morning-dawn shall rise into a bright and radiant noonday. The tender sprout shall grow to a heaven-aspiring tree, a refuge to all the families of the earth. This is Thy gracious promise proclaimed by Thy prophets, and with unshaken faith we wait and hope for its fulfilment. Then shall a sanctuary be reared in which reconciliation and atonement shall be made by the seven-fold brightness of the sun of truth, that first arose on Sinai's mount. Amen.

ANTHEM.

(Psalm cxi.)

PRAISE ye the Lord! I will praise the Lord with my whole heart, in the assembly of the upright and in the congregation.

The works of the Lord are great; sought out of all that have pleasure in them.

His work is honorable and glorious, and His righteousness endureth forever.

He hath made His wonderful works to be remembered; the Lord is gracious and full of compassion.

He giveth food to them that fear Him; He will ever be mindful of His covenant.

He hath shown His people the power of His works, and that He may give them the heritage of the nations.

The work of His hands are truth and justice; all His commandments are sure;

They stand fast forever and ever, and are done in truth and justice.

He sent redemption unto His people; He hath commanded His covenant forever; holy and reverent is His name.

The fear of the Lord is the beginning of wisdom; a good understanding have all they that do His commandments.

His praise endureth forever.

DAY OF ATONEMENT.

ANTHEM:

(Psalm cxi.)

הַלְלוּיָהּ׃

אוֹדֶה יְהֹוָה בְּכָל־לֵבָב. בְּסוֹד יְשָׁרִים וְעֵדָה׃

גְּדֹלִים מַעֲשֵׂי יְהֹוָה. דְּרוּשִׁים לְכָל־חֶפְצֵיהֶם׃

הוֹד־וְהָדָר פָּעֳלוֹ. וְצִדְקָתוֹ עוֹמֶדֶת לָעַד׃

זֵכֶר עָשָׂה לְנִפְלְאֹתָיו. חַנּוּן וְרַחוּם יְהֹוָה׃

טֶרֶף נָתַן לִירֵאָיו. יִזְכֹּר לְעוֹלָם בְּרִיתוֹ׃

כֹּחַ מַעֲשָׂיו הִגִּיד לְעַמּוֹ. לָתֵת לָהֶם נַחֲלַת גּוֹיִם׃

מַעֲשֵׂי יָדָיו אֱמֶת וּמִשְׁפָּט. נֶאֱמָנִים כָּל־פִּקּוּדָיו׃

סְמוּכִים לָעַד לְעוֹלָם. עֲשׂוּיִם בֶּאֱמֶת וְיָשָׁר׃

פְּדוּת שָׁלַח לְעַמּוֹ. צִוָּה לְעוֹלָם בְּרִיתוֹ׃

קָדוֹשׁ וְנוֹרָא שְׁמוֹ׃ רֵאשִׁית חָכְמָה יִרְאַת יְיָ

שֵׂכֶל טוֹב לְכָל־עֹשֵׂיהֶם. תְּהִלָּתוֹ עוֹמֶדֶת לָעַד׃

For Alternate Reading or Chanting:

O FATHER, forgive us, for in our perversity have we strayed from Thee.

Pardon us, O our King, for we have greatly offended.

Lord of hosts, who dwellest above the spheres, Thou alone art God.

With infinite pity Thou callest Thine erring children to return unto Thee, saying:

Draw nigh unto me with words of repentance, seek ye me and ye shall live.

Thy words are true, Thy promises are sure, and relying on them we approach Thee.

Remember us unto life; be gracious unto us according to Thy mercy.

Thy mercy extendeth unto the wicked as to the good;

Thy hand is stretched out to receive the penitent.

Thou desirest not the death of the guilty, but that they may return and live.

King of mercy, glorified among the hosts of Thy servants, cleanse us from sin and guilt.

Forgive us our trespasses, though they be many; hear us, God of our fathers.

Open unto us the gates of forgiveness; may our penitence be acceptable unto Thee.

Bring us nigh unto Thee, O God of life, for we are poor and destitute without Thee.

DAY OF ATONEMENT. 243

For Alternate Reading or Chanting:

סְלַח לָנוּ אָבִינוּ ‧ כִּי בְּרוֹב אִוַּלְתֵּנוּ שָׁגִינוּ ‧ מְחַל לָנוּ מַלְכֵּנוּ ‧ כִּי רַבּוּ עֲוֹנֵינוּ:

יְיָ צְבָאוֹת יוֹשֵׁב הַכְּרוּבִים ‧ בְּטִיתָ שׁוּבוּ בָנִים שׁוֹבָבִים:

גְּשׁוּ אֵלַי בִּדְבָרִים עֲרֵבִים ‧ דִּרְשׁוּנִי וִחְיוּ יָמִים רַבִּים:

הֲלֹא דְבָרֶיךָ לְעוֹלָם נִצָּבִים ‧ וּבָם אָנוּ נִשְׁעָנִים וּנְקְרָבִים:

זָכְרֵנוּ לְחַיִּים טוֹבִים ‧ חָנֵּנוּ כַּחֲסָדֶיךָ הַמְרֻבִּים:

טוֹב אַתָּה לָרָעִים וְלַטּוֹבִים ‧ יְמִינְךָ פְּשׁוּטָה לְקַבֵּל שָׁבִים:

כִּי לֹא תַחְפֹּץ בְּמוֹת חַיָּבִים ‧ לָכֵן אָנוּ מַשְׁכִּימִים וּמַעֲרִיבִים:

מֶלֶךְ מְהֻלָּל בְּמַחֲנוֹת כְּרוּבִים ‧ נַקֵּנוּ מֵחֵטְא וּמֵחִיוּבִים:

סְלַח נָא פְּשָׁעֵינוּ הָרַבִּים ‧ עֲנֵנוּ לְמַעַן צוּרִים הַחֲצוּבִים:

פִּתְחֵי תְשׁוּבָה בַּל יְהוּ נִשְׁלָבִים ‧ צַעֲקוֹתֵינוּ יְהוּ נִקְשָׁבִים:

We approach Thee this day, both young and old, relying on Thine abundant mercies.

Yea, on Thine abundant mercies do we rely, and for Thy forgiveness do we hope.

Thou art the King who lovest righteousness and forgivest the iniquity of Thy servants.

Thou hast made a covenant with our fathers, and fulfillest Thy promise to the latest generation.

The way of Thy goodness Thou hast revealed unto Moses, and hast shown him the path of grace.

Thou hast made known to him the paths of Thy mercy, who art almighty, merciful and gracious, and governest the world in love.

Thou hast said: I will cause all my goodness to pass before thee, and will teach thee the name of the Lord.

And I shall be gracious to him who trusteth in my grace, merciful to him who relieth on my mercy.

O Lord, gracious and long-suffering, All-Merciful is Thy name.

Thou hast taught us the way of repentance.

In Thine abundant mercy remember this day the descendants of Thy beloved.

Turn unto us in Thine infinite compassion; for Thou alone art dispenser of mercy.

With prayer and supplication we appear before Thee; in humility we crave Thy forgiveness.

DAY OF ATONEMENT.

קָרְבְנוּ אֵלֶיךָ חוֹצֵב לְהָבִים ׃ רְאֵה עֲמִידָתֵנוּ דַלִּים וְרֵקִים׃

שַׁבְנוּ אֵלֶיךָ נְעָרִים וְשָׂבִים ׃ תְּמוּכִים עַל רַחֲמֶיךָ הָרַבִּים׃

כִּי עַל רַחֲמֶיךָ הָרַבִּים אָנוּ בְטוּחִים ׃ וְעַל צִדְקוֹתֶיךָ אָנוּ נִשְׁעָנִים׃

וְלִסְלִיחוֹתֶיךָ אָנוּ מְצַפִּים ׃ וְלִישׁוּעָתְךָ אָנוּ מְקַוִּים׃

אַתָּה הוּא יְיָ מֶלֶךְ אוֹהֵב צְדָקוֹת מִקֶּדֶם ׃ מַעֲבִיר עֲוֺנוֹת עַמּוֹ וּמֵסִיר חַטֹּאת יְרֵאָיו׃

כֹּרֵת בְּרִית לָרִאשׁוֹנִים ׃ וּמְקַיֵּם שְׁבוּעָה לָאַחֲרוֹנִים׃

אַתָּה הוּא שֶׁיָּרַדְתָּ בַּעֲנַן כְּבוֹדְךָ עַל הַר סִינַי ׃ וְהֶרְאֵיתָ דַּרְכֵי טוּבְךָ לְמֹשֶׁה עַבְדֶּךָ׃

אָרְחוֹת חֲסָדֶיךָ גִּלִּיתָ לּוֹ ׃ וְהוֹדַעְתּוֹ כִּי אַתָּה אֵל רַחוּם וְחַנּוּן׃

אֶרֶךְ אַפַּיִם וְרַב חֶסֶד וּמַרְבֶּה לְהֵיטִיב ׃ וּמַנְהִיג אֶת כָּל־הָעוֹלָם כֻּלּוֹ בְּמִדַּת הָרַחֲמִים׃

וְכֵן כָּתוּב וַיֹּאמֶר אֲנִי אַעֲבִיר כָּל־טוּבִי עַל־פָּנֶיךָ ׃ וְקָרָאתִי בְשֵׁם יְיָ לְפָנֶיךָ׃

וְחַנֹּתִי אֶת־אֲשֶׁר אָחֹן וְרִחַמְתִּי אֶת־אֲשֶׁר אֲרַחֵם׃

אֵל אֶרֶךְ אַפַּיִם אַתָּה ׃ וּבַעַל הָרַחֲמִים נִקְרֵאתָ ׃ וְדֶרֶךְ תְּשׁוּבָה הוֹרֵיתָ׃

Protect us under the shadow of Thy grace; remove our transgressions and sins.

Accept our prayers as on the day when Thou didst reveal Thy glory unto Thy servant Moses.

The Lord revealed Himself unto him and said:

The Lord, the Lord God, gracious and merciful, long-suffering and abundant in goodness and truth;

Keeping mercy unto a thousand generations, forgiving iniquity, transgression and sin.

Yea, Thou wilt forgive our sins and iniquities, and make us again Thine heritage.

Minister and Choir:

Thy way, O God, is patience and compassion, alike to the wicked and the good; this is Thy glory.

Instil Thy healing balm into the sorrowing heart; be merciful to those who are but dust and ashes.

Cast away our sins and be gracious to Thy handiwork.

In Thee alone do we trust; deal with us according to Thy righteousness.

Minister and Congregation:

O MY King, who givest salvation, keepest mercy unto thousands, and forgivest transgression and sin; pardon my sins and in Thy mercy be gracious unto me.

DAY OF ATONEMENT. 247

גְּדֻלַּת רַחֲמֶיךָ וַחֲסָדֶיךָ. תִּזְכּוֹר הַיּוֹם לְזֶרַע יְדִידֶיךָ:

הֵפֶן אֵלֵינוּ בְּרַחֲמִים. כִּי אַתָּה הוּא בַּעַל הָרַחֲמִים:

בְּתַחֲנוּן וּבִתְפִלָּה פָּנֶיךָ נְקַדֵּם. כְּהוֹדַעְתָּ לֶעָנָו מִקֶּדֶם:

וּבְצֵל כְּנָפֶיךָ נֶחֱסֶה וְנִתְלוֹנָן. כְּיוֹם וַיֵּרֶד יְיָ בֶּעָנָן:

תַּעֲבוֹר עַל פֶּשַׁע וְתִמְחֶה אָשָׁם. כְּיוֹם וַיִּתְיַצֵּב עִמּוֹ שָׁם:

תַּאֲזִין שַׁוְעָתֵנוּ וְתַקְשִׁיב מֶנּוּ מַאֲמָר. כְּיוֹם וַיִּקְרָא בְשֵׁם יְיָ. וְשָׁם נֶאֱמַר:

וַיַּעֲבֹר יְיָ עַל פָּנָיו וַיִּקְרָא:

יְיָ יְיָ אֵל רַחוּם וְחַנּוּן. אֶרֶךְ אַפַּיִם וְרַב חֶסֶד וֶאֱמֶת:

נֹצֵר חֶסֶד לָאֲלָפִים. נֹשֵׂא עָוֹן וָפֶשַׁע וְחַטָּאָה. וְסָלַחְתָּ לַעֲוֺנֵנוּ וּלְחַטָּאתֵנוּ וּנְחַלְתָּנוּ:

Minister and Choir:

דַּרְכְּךָ אֱלֹהֵינוּ לְהַאֲרִיךְ אַפֶּךָ. לָרָעִים וְלַטּוֹבִים. וְהִיא תְהִלָּתֶךָ:

תַּעֲלֶה אֲרוּכָה. לְעָלֶה נִדָּף. תְּנַחֵם עַל עָפָר וָאֵפֶר:

תַּשְׁלִיךְ חֲטָאֵינוּ. וְתָחוֹן בְּמַעֲשֶׂךָ. תִּרְאֶה כִּי אֵין אִישׁ. עֲשֵׂה עִמָּנוּ צְדָקָה:

Congregation:

O Lord, unto Thee I cry all this day.

This day may Thy grace heal our wounds, and forgive our backslidings; take from us the burden of our guilt, and accept us graciously.

Congregation:

Let us forsake the evil way, and **return unto** the Lord.

This day reveal unto us Thy saving power, O Lord. Turn unto us in Thine infinite love, and have compassion on us.

Congregation:

Like as a father pitieth his children, so the Lord pitieth them that fear Him.

This day inscribe us in the book of life, and blot out our misdeeds, for Thou hast graciously promised forgiveness and pardon.

Congregation:

Draw nigh unto us, for on Thee do we call.

We lift up our hearts unto Thee and speak of Thy greatness. With songs and praises we approach Thee and seek Thy grace.

Congregation:

Let Thy countenance shine upon **us, O God, and** teach us Thy truth.

DAY OF ATONEMENT.

Minister and Congregation:

מַלְכִּי מִקֶּדֶם פּוֹעֵל יְשׁוּעוֹת בְּקֶרֶב הֲמוֹנִי . נֹצֵר חֶסֶד לָאֲלָפִים וְנֹשֵׂא פְּשָׁעַי וַעֲוֹנִי . כַּסֵּה חֲטָאַי וּבְרַחֲמֶיךָ הָרַבִּים חָנֵּנִי יְיָ .

כִּי אֵלֶיךָ אֶקְרָא כָּל הַיּוֹם :

הַיּוֹם רַפֵּא מְשׁוּבוֹתֵינוּ . כִּי אָתָאנוּ לְךָ וְהִנֵּנוּ . שַׁבְנוּ אֵלֶיךָ אֱלֹהֵינוּ . וּבְחַסְדְּךָ חָנֵּנוּ . דֶּרֶךְ רֶשַׁע עָזַבְנוּ וְהִנֵּה אֵינֶנּוּ .

פֹּה עִמָּנוּ הַיּוֹם :

הַיּוֹם יִגְדַּל נָא כֹחַ יְיָ וְכַעֲוֹנוֹתֵינוּ אַל תִּגְמוֹל . כְּרַחֵם אָב עַל בָּנִים רַחֵם עָלֵינוּ וַחֲמוֹל . רַחֲמֶיךָ וַחֲסָדֶיךָ פְּנֵה אֵלֵינוּ כִּתְמוֹל שִׁלְשׁוֹם .

גַּם תְּמוֹל גַּם הַיּוֹם :

הַיּוֹם רִשְׁעֵנוּ תָסִיר וּבְסֵפֶר הַחַיִּים אוֹתָנוּ תָחוֹק . בְּיוֹם קָרְאֵנוּ אֵלֶיךָ קָרֵב אַל תַּעֲמוֹד מֵרָחוֹק סְלִיחָה וְכַפָּרָה שַׂמְתּוֹ לְחוֹק .

וּלְמִשְׁפָּט לְיִשְׂרָאֵל עַד הַיּוֹם :

הַיּוֹם כַּפָּיו יִפְרוֹשׂ אֵלֶיךָ וּגְבוּרוֹתֶיךָ יְמַלֵּל . בְּצֶדֶק

O God, our stay and support, Thy children knock at Thy door of grace. Open unto us, and extend Thy hand, for on Thee do we lean. May we hear Thy word of welcome:

Congregation:

Ye, who cleave unto the Lord, your God, shall live, all of you, this day.

CANTICLE.

WHO is like Thee, O God! Thou art mighty and glorious, Creator of heaven and earth.

Thou revealest secret things; Thou alone speakest righteousness.

Thou art surrounded with majesty, and besides Thee there is no God.

Thou rememberest Thy covenant and art gracious to the remnant of the people.

Thou art pure of eyes, and dwellest above the heavens.

Thou forgivest iniquity and art clothed in righteousness.

King of kings, Thou art most exalted; Thou supportest the fallen, and answerest the prayer of the oppressed.

Redeemer and deliverer, Thou rulest in omnipotence. Thou art nigh unto those who call upon Thee, most merciful and gracious.

Thou dwellest above the highest heavens, and supportest the virtuous. Who is like Thee, O God!

DAY OF ATONEMENT.

יֶחֱזֶה פָנֶיךָ וּבְשִׁירוֹ אוֹתְךָ יְהַלֵּל. עֲוֹנוֹ מוֹדֶה וְעוֹזֵב יְבַקֵּשׁ מְחִילָה וְיִתְפַּלֵּל:

בַּעֲדוֹ תָמִיד כָּל הַיּוֹם:

הַיּוֹם סָמוּךְ עִם אֲשֶׁר דְּלָתֶיךָ דוֹפְקִים. וְתִיקָךְ נָא נַפְשָׁם כִּי עָלֶיךָ מִתְרַפְּקִים. פְּרוֹשׂ יָדְךָ לָהֶם וְקַבְּלֵם וּבַשְּׂרֵם.

וְאַתֶּם הַדְּבֵקִים בַּיְיָ אֱלֹהֵיכֶם חַיִּים כֻּלְּכֶם הַיּוֹם:

CANTICLE.

אַדִּיר וְנָאוֹר בּוֹרֵא דּוֹק וָחֶלֶד. מִי אֵל כָּמוֹךָ:

גּוֹלֶה עֲמוּקוֹת דּוֹבֵר צְדָקוֹת. מִי אֵל כָּמוֹךָ:

הָדוּר בִּלְבוּשׁוֹ וְאֵין זוּלָתוֹ. מִי אֵל כָּמוֹךָ:

זוֹכֵר הַבְּרִית חוֹנֵן שְׁאֵרִית. מִי אֵל כָּמוֹךָ:

טְהוֹר עֵינַיִם יוֹשֵׁב שָׁמַיִם. מִי אֵל כָּמוֹךָ:

כּוֹבֵשׁ עֲוֹנוֹת לוֹבֵשׁ צְדָקוֹת. מִי אֵל כָּמוֹךָ:

מֶלֶךְ מְלָכִים נוֹרָא וְנִשְׂגָּב. מִי אֵל כָּמוֹךָ:

סוֹמֵךְ נוֹפְלִים עוֹנֶה עֲשׁוּקִים. מִי אֵל כָּמוֹךָ:

פּוֹדֶה וּמַצִּיל צֹעֶה בְּרָב כֹּחַ. מִי אֵל כָּמוֹךָ:

קָרוֹב לְקוֹרְאָיו רַחוּם וְחַנּוּן. מִי אֵל כָּמוֹךָ:

שׁוֹכֵן שְׁחָקִים תּוֹמֵךְ תְּמִימִים. מִי אֵל כָּמוֹךָ:

Minister:

WHO is like Thee, O God, who pardonest iniquity and forgivest transgression to the remnant of Thy heritage? Thou retainest not Thine anger forever, because Thou delightest in mercy. Thou wilt again have compassion on us. Thou wilt suppress our iniquities; yea, Thou wilt cast all our sins into the depths of the sea. Thou wilt show faithfulness unto Jacob, and mercy unto Abraham, which Thou hast promised unto our ancestors in the days of old.

This day mayest Thou strengthen us!

Choir:—Amen.

This day mayest Thou bless us!

Choir:—Amen.

This day mayest Thou exalt us!

Choir:—Amen.

This day mayest Thou seek our good!

Choir:—Amen.

This day mayest Thou support us with Thy right hand!

Choir:—Amen.

DAY OF ATONEMENT.

Minister:

מִי אֵל כָּמוֹךָ נֹשֵׂא עָוֹן וְעֹבֵר עַל פֶּשַׁע לִשְׁאֵרִית נַחֲלָתוֹ · לֹא הֶחֱזִיק לָעַד אַפּוֹ · כִּי חָפֵץ חֶסֶד הוּא: יָשׁוּב יְרַחֲמֵנוּ · יִכְבּוֹשׁ עֲוֹנוֹתֵינוּ · וְתַשְׁלִיךְ בִּמְצֹלוֹת יָם כָּל חַטֹּאתָם: תִּתֵּן אֱמֶת לְיַעֲקֹב חֶסֶד לְאַבְרָהָם · אֲשֶׁר נִשְׁבַּעְתָּ לַאֲבֹתֵינוּ מִימֵי קֶדֶם:

Choir.	Minister:
אָמֵן:	הַיּוֹם תְּאַמְּצֵנוּ ·
אָמֵן:	הַיּוֹם תְּבָרְכֵנוּ ·
אָמֵן:	הַיּוֹם תְּגַדְּלֵנוּ ·
אָמֵן:	הַיּוֹם תִּדְרְשֵׁנוּ לְטוֹבָה ·
אָמֵן:	הַיּוֹם תִּשְׁמַע שַׁוְעָתֵנוּ ·
אָמֵן:	הַיּוֹם תִּתְמְכֵנוּ בִּימִין צִדְקֶךָ ·

SELECTIONS FROM THE SCRIPTURES.

(To be read as time will permit.)

I.

(From Deuteronomy.)

ALL the commandments which I command thee this day shall ye observe to do, that ye may live, and multiply, and go in and possess the land which the Lord sware unto your fathers. And thou shalt remember all the way which the Lord, thy God, led thee these forty years in the wilderness, to humble thee, and to prove thee, to know what was in thine heart, whether thou wouldst keep His commandments, or no. And He humbled thee, and suffered thee to hunger, and fed thee with manna which thou knewest not, neither did thy fathers know; that He might make thee know that man doth not live by bread only, but by every word that proceedeth out of the mouth of the Lord. Thy raiment waxed not old upon thee, neither did thy foot swell, these forty years. Thou shalt also consider in thy heart, that, as a man chasteneth his son, so the Lord, thy God, chasteneth thee. Therefore thou shalt keep the commandments of the Lord, thy God, to walk in His ways and to fear Him. For the Lord, thy God, bringeth thee into a good land, a land of brooks of water, of fountains and depths that spring out of valleys and hills; a land of wheat and barley and vines and pomegranates; a land of oil-olive and honey; a land wherein thou shalt eat bread without scarceness; thou shalt not lack anything in it; a land whose stones are iron, and out of whose hills thou mayest dig brass. When thou hast eaten and art full, then thou shalt bless the Lord, thy God, for the good land which He hath given thee. Beware that thou forget not the Lord, thy God, in not keeping His commandments and His judgments and His statutes, which I command thee this day: Lest when thou hast eaten and art full, and hast built goodly houses, and dwelt therein; and when thy herds and thy flocks multiply, and thy silver and thy gold is multiplied, and all that thou hast is multiplied: Then thine heart be lifted up, and thou forget the Lord, thy God, who brought thee forth out of the land of Egypt, from the house of bondage; who led thee through that great and terrible wilderness, wherein were fiery serpents and scorpions and drought, where there was no water; who brought thee forth water out of the rock of flint; who fed thee in the wilderness with manna, which thy fathers knew not, that He might humble thee, and that He might prove thee, to do thee good at thy latter end; and thou say in thine heart, my power and the might of mine hand hath gotten me this wealth. But thou shalt remember the Lord thy God; for it is He that giveth thee power to get wealth, that He may establish His covenant which He sware unto thy fathers, as it is this day. And it shall be, if you do at all forget the Lord, your God, and walk after other gods, and serve them, and worship them, I testify against you this day that ye shall surely perish, as the nations which the Lord destroyeth before your face, so shall ye perish; because ye would not be obedient unto the voice of the Lord, your God.

II.

(From Deuteronomy.)

NO man shall take the nether or upper millstone to pledge: for he taketh a man's life to pledge. If a man be found stealing any of his brethren of the children of Israel, and maketh merchandise of him, or selleth him, then that thief shall die; and thou shalt put evil away from among you. When thou dost lend thy brother anything, thou shalt not go into his house to fetch his pledge. Thou shalt stand abroad, and the man to whom thou dost lend shall bring out the pledge abroad to thee. And if the man be poor, thou shalt not sleep with his pledge; if it be his raiment, thou shalt deliver him the pledge again when the sun goeth down, that he may sleep in his own raiment, and bless thee; and it shall be righteousness to thee before the Lord, thy God. Thou shalt not oppress a hired servant that is poor and needy, whether he be of thy brethren, or of thy strangers that are in thy land within the gates. At his day shalt thou give him his hire, neither shall the sun go down upon it; lest he cry out against thee to the Lord, and it be sin to thee. Thou shalt not pervert the judgment of the stranger nor of the fatherless; nor take a widow's raiment to pledge; when thou cuttest down thy harvest in thy field, and hast forgot a sheaf in the field, thou shalt not go again to fetch it. When thou beatest thine olive tree, thou shalt not go over the boughs again to gather. When thou gatherest the grapes of thy vineyard, thou shalt not glean it afterward; all this shall be for the stranger, for the fatherless, and for the widow. And thou shalt remember that thou wast a bondsman in the land of Egypt; therefore I command thee to do this thing.

III.

(From Deuteronomy.)

WHEN thou hast come to the land of thine inheritance thou shalt take of the first of all the fruit of the earth and go to the place which the Lord, thy God, shall choose for His name and to the priest that shall be in those days and say: I profess this day to God that I am come to the country which was promised to our fathers, and I have brought the first-fruits of the land, a thanksgiving to the Lord. And thou shalt rejoice in all the good things which the Lord hath given thee and to thy house, thou, the Levite and the stranger that is among you. When thou hast made an end of tithing all the tithes of thine increase the third year, which is the year of tithing, and hast given it to the Levite, the stranger, the fatherless, and the widow, that they may eat within thy gates, and be filled; thou shalt say before the Lord, thy God: I have brought away the hallowed things out of my house, and also have given them to the Levite, to the stranger, to the fatherless and to the widow, according to all Thy commandments; I have not transgressed, neither have I forgotten them; I have not eaten thereof in my mourning, neither have I taken away aught thereof for any unclean use, but I have hearkened to Thy voice and done according to all that Thou hast commanded me. Look down from Thy holy habitation, from heaven, and bless Israel, and the land which Thou hast given us, as Thou hast promised to our fathers, a land that floweth with milk and honey.

IV.

(From Isaiah.)

NOW will I sing to my well-beloved a song of my beloved, touching his vineyard. My well-beloved had a vineyard in a very fruitful hill; and he fenced it, and gathered out the stones thereof, and planted it with the choicest vine, and built a tower in the midst of it, and also made a wine-press therein; and he looked that it should bring forth grapes, and it brought forth wild grapes. And now, O inhabitants of Jerusalem and men of Judah, judge, I pray you, betwixt me and my vineyard. What could have been done more to my vineyard, that I have not done in it? Wherefore, when I looked that it should bring forth grapes, brought it forth wild grapes? And now go to; I will tell you what I will do to my vineyard: I will take away the hedge thereof, and it shall be eaten up; and break down the wall thereof, and it shall be trodden down; and I will lay it waste; it shall not be pruned, nor digged; but there shall come up briers and thorns. I will also command the clouds that they rain no rain upon it. For the vineyard of the Lord of hosts is the house of Israel, and the men of Judah His pleasant plant; and He looked for judgment, but behold oppression; for righteousness, but behold an outcry. Woe unto them that join house to house, that lay field to field, till there be none left, that they may be placed as if alone in the midst of the earth! Of a truth, many houses shall be desolate, even great and fair ones, without inhabitant. Yea, ten acres of vineyard shall yield the measure of one bath, and the seed of a chomer shall yield an ephah measure.

Woe unto them that rise up early in the morning, that they may follow strong drink; that continue until night, till wine inflame them! And the harp and the viol, the tabret and the pipe and wine are in their feasts; but they regard not the work of the Lord, neither do they consider the operation of His hands. Therefore, my people go into captivity because they have no knowledge; and their honorable men are famished, and their multitude dried up with thirst.

Woe unto them that draw iniquity with cords of vanity, and sin as it were with a cart rope; that say, Let Him make speed, and hasten His work, that we may see it; and let the counsel of the Holy One of Israel draw nigh and come, that we may know it.

Woe unto them that call evil good, and good evil; that put darkness for light, and light for darkness; that put bitter for sweet, and sweet for bitter!

Woe unto them that are wise in their own eyes, and prudent in their own sight!

Woe unto them that are mighty to drink wine, and men of strength to mingle strong drink, and justify the wicked for reward, and take away the righteousness of the righteous from him! Therefore, as the fire devoureth the stubble, and the flame consumeth the chaff, so their root shall be as rottenness, and their blossom shall go up as dust: because they have cast away the law of the Lord of hosts and despised the word of the Holy One of Israel.

V.

(From Isaiah.)

IN the year that King Uzziah died I saw the Lord sitting upon a throne, high and lifted up, and His train filled the temple. Above it stood the seraphim: each one had six wings; with twain he covered his face, and with twain he covered his feet, and with twain he did fly. And one cried unto another, and said: Holy, holy, holy, is the Lord of hosts; the whole earth is full of His glory. And the posts of the door moved at the voice of him that cried, and the house was filled with smoke. Then said I: Woe is me! for I am undone; because I am a man of unclean lips, and I dwell in the midst of a people of unclean lips: for mine eyes have seen the King, the Lord of hosts. Then flew one of the seraphim unto me, having a live coal in his hand, which he had taken with the tongs from off the altar. And he laid it upon my mouth, and said: Lo, this hath touched thy lips; and thine iniquity is taken away, and thy sin purged. Also I heard the voice of the Lord, saying, Whom shall I send, and who will go for us? Then said I, Here am I; send me. And He said: Go and tell this people, Hear ye indeed, but understand not; and see ye indeed, but perceive not. Thou wilt make the heart of this people obtuse, and their ears heavy, and shut their eyes; they see not with their eyes, and hear not with their ears, and understand not with their hearts, and are not turned again and healed. Then said I, Lord, how long? And He answered: Until the cities be wasted, without inhabitant, and the houses, without man, and the land be utterly desolate. And the Lord have removed men far away, and there be a great forsaking in the midst of the land. But yet, in it shall be a tenth, and it shall return, and shall be healed.

VI.

(From Isaiah.)

ARISE, shine, for thy light is coming and the glory of the Lord shall appear upon thee. Behold, when darkness shall cover the earth and thick darkness the peoples, upon thee shall arise the Lord and His glory shall be seen upon thee. Nations shall come to thy light and kings to the brightness of thy rising. Lift up thine eyes round about and see; they all gather themselves together, thy sons shall come from afar and thy daughters shall be carried in the arms. Violence shall no more be heard in the land, nor wasting seen, nor destruction in thy borders; thou shalt call thy walls, salvation, and thy gate, praise. All thy people shall be called righteous, the branch of my planting, the work of my hands, that I may be glorified.

The spirit of the Lord God is upon me; because the Lord hath anointed me to preach good tidings unto the meek; He hath sent me to bind up the broken-hearted, to proclaim liberty to the captives and the opening of the prison to those that are bound; to proclaim an acceptable time of the Lord and the day of recompense of our God and to comfort all mourners, to give them garlands for ashes, the oil of joy for mourning, the robes of praise for the spirit of heaviness; they shall be called, trees of righteousness, the planting of the Lord, that He may be glorified. Their children shall be known among the gentiles and their offspring among peoples; all that see them shall acknowledge that they are children whom the Lord hath blessed. And thou wilt say: I will greatly rejoice in the Lord; my soul shall be joyful in God; for He hath clothed me with the garments of salvation; He hath covered me with the robe of righteousness, as a bridegroom decketh himself with ornaments and as a bride adorneth herself with her jewels. For as the earth bringeth forth her bud and as the garden causeth the things that are sown in it to spring forth, so the Lord God will cause to spring forth righteousness and praise before all nations.

VII.

(From Isaiah.)

SEEK ye the Lord while He may be found, call ye upon Him while He is near. Let the wicked forsake his way, and the unrighteous man his thoughts; and let him return to the Lord, and He will have mercy upon him; and to our God, for He will abundantly pardon. For my thoughts are not your thoughts, neither are my ways your ways, saith the Lord, but as the heavens are higher than the earth, so are my ways higher than your ways, and my thoughts than your thoughts. For as the rain cometh down, and the snow from heaven, and returneth not thither, but watereth the earth, and maketh it bring forth and bud, that it may give seed to the sower, and bread to the eater, so shall my word be that goeth forth from out of my mouth; it shall not return unto me void, but it shall accomplish that which I please, and it shall prosper in the thing whereto I send it. Thus saith the High and Lofty One that inhabiteth eternity, whose name is holy: I dwell in the high and holy place, with him also that is of a contrite spirit, to revive the humble, and to revive the heart of the meek. For I will not contend forever, neither will I be always wroth; since the spirit shall fail before me, and the souls which I have made. I have seen his ways, and will heal him; I will lead him, and restore comforts unto him and to his mourners. I create the fruit of the lips: Peace, peace to him that is afar off, and to him that is near, saith the Lord; yea, I will heal him.

But the wicked are like the troubled sea, when it cannot rest, whose waters cast up mire and dirt and slime. There is no peace, saith my God, to the wicked.

VIII.

(From Jeremiah.)

NOW these are the words of the letter that Jeremiah, the prophet, sent from Jerusalem to the residue of the elders which were carried away captives, and to the priests and to the prophets and to all the people whom Nebuchadnezzar had carried away captive from Jerusalem to Babylon. Thus saith the Lord God: Build ye houses and dwell in them, and plant gardens and eat the fruit thereof; take ye wives and beget sons and daughters and take wives for your sons and give your daughters to husbands, that ye may be increased there and not diminished. And, moreover, seek the welfare of the city whither I have caused you to be carried away captives and pray ye to the Lord for the city, for in the peace thereof shall ye have peace. Let not your prophets and diviners that are in your midst deceive you, neither hearken to their dreams; not until after seventy years are accomplished at Babylon will I visit you and fulfil my good word towards you in causing you to return to this place. For I know the thoughts that I think towards you; they are thoughts of peace and not of evil, to give you the end which you hope for. Then shall you call upon me, and ye shall go and pray to me and I will hearken unto you. Ye shall seek me and ye shall find me, for **ye will** seek me with your whole heart. I will turn your captivity and gather you from all the nations and all the places whither you were driven and bring you to your land to dwell in. Behold, the days come, saith the Lord, that I will make a new covenant with the house of Israel and with the home of Judah. I will put my law in their inward parts and write it in their hearts and will be their God and they shall be my people. And no more shall a man teach his neighbor and a man his brother: know the Lord, for they shall all know me, from the least of them unto the greatest of them; and I will forgive their iniquity and remember their sins no more. Again there shall be heard in the cities of Judah and in the streets of Jerusalem the voice of joy and the voice of gladness, the voice of the bridegroom and the voice of the bride, the voice of those that will sing:

Praise the Lord of hosts, for He is good, for His mercy endureth forever.

IX.

(From Ezekiel.)

THE hand of the Lord was upon me and I was carried out in the spirit and set down in the midst of the valley which was full of bones; and He caused me to pass by them round about and behold, there were very many in the open valley and they were very dry. And He said to me: Son of man: Can these bones live? And I whispered: O Lord God, thou knowest. Again He said to me: Prophesy over these bones and say to them: O ye dry bones, hear the word of the Lord: Behold, I will cause spirit to enter into you and ye shall live; and I will lay sinews upon you and cover you with skin and put breath in you and ye shall live. So I prophesied as I was commanded; and there was a thundering noise and an earthquake; and the bones came together, bone to its bone. And I beheld and lo! there were sinews upon them and flesh came up and skin covered them above; but there was no breath in them. Then He said to me: Prophesy to the breath and say: Come from the four winds, O breath! and breathe upon the slain that they may live. So I prophesied as He commanded me and the breath came into them, and they lived and stood upon their feet, an exceeding great army. Then He said to me: Son of man, these bones are the whole house of Israel. Behold, they say: Our bones are dried, our hope is lost, we were clean cut off. Therefore prophesy and say to them: Thus saith the Lord God: Behold, I will open your graves of captivity and cause you to come out of them, O my people. I will bring you again into the land of Israel, and ye shall know that I am the Lord, when I have opened your graves and caused you to come up out of them; and I will put my spirit into you and ye shall live; and I shall place you in your own land and ye shall acknowledge that I, the Lord, have spoken and performed it.

X.

(From Malachi.)

A SON honoreth his father, and a servant his master; if then I be a father, where is my honor? and if I be a master, where is my fear? saith the Lord of hosts to you, O priests, that despise my name. And ye shall know that I have sent this commandment to you, that my covenant might be with the house of Levi, saith the Lord of hosts. My covenant was with him, of life and of peace; I gave them to him for the fear wherewith he feared me. The law of truth was in his mouth, and iniquity was not found in his lips; he walked with me in peace and equity, and did turn many from iniquity. For the priest's lips should keep knowledge and they should seek the Law at his mouth: for he is the messenger of the Lord of hosts. But ye are departed out of the way; ye have caused many to stumble at the Law; ye have corrupted the covenant of Levi, saith the Lord of hosts. Therefore have I also made you contemptible and base before all the people, according as ye have not kept my ways, but have been partial in the Law. Have we not all One father? hath not One God created us? why do we deal treacherously, every man against his brother, by profaning the covenant of our fathers? Remember ye the law of Moses, my servant, which I commanded unto him in Horeb for all Israel, with the statutes and the judgments. Behold, I will send you Elijah, the prophet, before the coming of the great and dreadful day of the Lord; and he shall turn the heart of the fathers to the children, and the heart of the children to their fathers.

XI.

(From Ecclesiastes.)

IT is better to hear the rebuke of the wise, than for a man to hear the song of fools. For as the crackling of thorns under a pot, so is the laughter of the fool: this also is vanity. Surely oppression maketh a wise man mad; and a bribe destroyeth understanding. Better is the end of a thing than the beginning thereof, and the patient in spirit is better than the proud in spirit. Be not hasty in thy spirit to be angry, for anger resteth in the bosom of fools. Say not thou, What 'is the cause that the former days were better than these? for thou dost not inquire wisely concerning this. Wisdom is good with an inheritance; and by it there is profit to them that see the sun. For wisdom is a defense, but the excellence of knowledge is that wisdom giveth life to them that have it. Consider the work of God: for who can make that straight, which He hath made crooked? In the day of prosperity be joyful, but in the day of adversity consider: God hath set the one day over against the other in the end that man leaves nothing after him. Wisdom strengtheneth the wise more than ten mighty men which are in a city. There is not a just man upon earth, that doeth good always, and sinneth never. Also take no heed unto all words that are spoken, lest thou hear thy servant curse thee; oftentimes also thine own heart knoweth that thou thyself likewise hast cursed others. That which is far off, and exceedingly deep, who can find it out? Lo, this only have I found, that God hath made man simple but they have sought out many inventions.

XII.

(From Proverbs.)

MY son, hear the corrections of thy father and forsake not the teachings of thy mother; they are a chaplet of grace to thy head and an ornament around thy neck. Whoso despiseth his father or his mother, his lamp shall go out in the blackest darkness. The eye that mocketh at the father and despiseth the mother, the ravens of the valley shall pick it out, the young vultures shall eat it. Train a child the way it shall go; even when he is old he shall not depart from it. Foolishness is bound up in the heart of a child, the rod of correction will drive it from him. A just man that walketh in his integrity, blessed are his children after him. A servant that dealeth wisely shall have rule over a son that dealeth shamefully; he shall have part in the inheritance of the brethren. He that is greedy of gain troubleth his own house. The blessing of the Lord, it maketh rich and no sorrow is added therewith. The curse of God is in the house of the wicked, but He blesseth the habitation of the poor man. Better is a dinner of herbs where love is, than a stalled ox and hatred therewith. Though the righteous man fall seven times he will rise again; the memory of the just is for blessing. Say not: I will do evil to him as he hath done to me; I will render to a man according to his works. If thine enemy be hungry, give him bread to eat; if he be thirsty, give him water to drink; for thou shalt heap coals of fire upon his head and the Lord shall recompense thee. Faithful are the wounds of a friend, but the kisses of an enemy are treacherous. As coals are to hot embers and wood is to fire, so is a contentious man to strife. For lack of wood the fire goeth out and where there is no whisperer, contention ceaseth. Hatred stireth up strife, but love covereth a multitude of sins to forgive them. Strive not with a man without cause and have no quarrel with any one that hath done thee no wrong. Desire not evil against thy neighbor, seeing he dwelleth securely with thee.

XIII.

(From Proverbs.)

WITHHOLD not good from him who stands in need thereof when it is in the power of thy hand to do it; say not: go and come again and to-morrow I will give thee, when thou hast it now by thee. The man of a bountiful eye is blessed, for he giveth of his bread to the poor. Whoso stoppeth his ear to the cry of the poor, he also shall cry, but shall not be heard. Rob not the poor because he is poor, neither crush the afflicted in the gate; for the Lord will plead their cause and despoil those that despoil them. Deliver those that are carried away unto death and those that are tottering to be slain, see that thou keep back. If thou sayest: Behold, we know not this man, doth not He that weigheth the heart consider it and shall not He render to every man according to his works? The rich and the poor meet together, the Lord is the maker of both. He that is glad at his neighbor's calamity shall not go unpunished. Whoso oppresseth the poor reproacheth his Maker; but he that hath mercy on the needy honoreth Him. The righteous regardeth the life of his beast, but the wicked man is cruel and without compassion. Remove not an ancient landmark and enter not the field of the fatherless to take it from them; their protector is strong and He shall plead their cause against thee. Open thy mouth to judge righteously and minister judgment to the poor and the needy. The merciful man doeth good to his own soul, but he that is cruel troubleth his own flesh. There is that scattereth and increaseth yet more and there is that withholdeth but it leadeth only to want.

Selections from the Apocrypha.

XIV.

(From Sirach.)

THE greater thou art, the more thou must humble thyself, then shalt thou find favor before the Lord. My son, make not the needy eyes to wait long, neither provoke a man in his distress. Add not more trouble to a heart that is vexed; reject not the supplication of the afflicted, neither turn away thy face from a poor man. Honor thy father with thy whole heart and forget not the sorrows of thy mother;

how canst thou recompense them the things they have done for thee? Kindle not the coals of a sinner lest thou be burnt with the flame of his fire. Why is earth and ashes proud? when a man is dead he shall inherit worms. As the judge of the people is himself so are his officers, and what manner of man the ruler of the city is, such are all they that dwell therein. Who will justify him that sinneth against his own soul and who will honor him that dishonoreth his own life? Blame not before thou hast examined the truth; understand first and then rebuke. Judge no one blessed before his death. Say, not it is through the Lord I fell away; for thou oughtest not to do the things that he hateth. He that buildeth his house with other men's money is like one that gathereth himself stones for his own tomb. The heart of fools is their mouth, but the mouth of the wise is in their hearts. Oh, how comely a thing is judgment for gray hairs and for old men to know counsel! Much experience is the crown of old men and the fear of God is their glory. Whether a man be rich or poor, if he have a good heart toward the Lord, he shall at all times rejoice with a cheerful countenance. Be not as a lion in thy house nor frantic among thy servants.

XV.

(From Sirach.)

WHATSOEVER is brought upon thee take cheerfully and be patient when thou art brought to a low estate. For gold is tried in fire and acceptable

DAY OF ATONEMENT. 273

men in adversity. They that fear God will prepare their hearts and humble their souls in His sight, saying: We will fall into His hands and not into the hands of men; for as His majesty is, so is His mercy. Seek not out the things that are too hard for thee, neither search the things that are above thy strength; but that which is commanded thee, think thereupon with reverence; for it is not needful to thee to see things with thine own eyes that are in secret. Be not curious in unnecessary matters, for more things are shown unto thee than men understand. Deliver him that suffereth wrong from the hand of the oppressor, and be not faint-hearted when thou sittest in judgment; observe the opportunity and beware of evil, and be never ashamed when it concerneth the soul; for there is a shame that bringeth sin and there is a shame which is glory and grace. Accept no person's authority against thy soul and let no respect of any person cause thee to fall. Refrain not to speak when there is occasion to do good, and hide not thy wisdom; for by speech wisdom shall be known and learning by the word of the tongue. In no wise speak against the truth; but be ashamed of the error of thine ignorance. Be not hasty in thy tongue, whilst thou art slack and remiss in thy deeds. Say not: Who shall control me for my works? I have sinned and what harm hath happened to me? For, though the Lord is long suffering, yet will He in no wise let thee go unpunished. But neither do thou add sin upon sin and say: His mercy is great, He will be pacified for the multitude of my sins; for mercy and wrath both come from Him and His displeasure rests upon sinners. Let thy life be sincere; be swift to hear the words of the wise and learn from them to give all thine answers with patience. Honor and shame is in the speech and the tongue of man often causeth his fall. Be not known as a whisperer of slander and lie not in wait against thy neighbor with thy tongue.

XVI.

(From Sirach.)

THE beginning of pride is when one departeth from God and his heart is turned away from his Maker. Pride is not made for man nor furious anger for them that are born of woman. Whether a man be rich and of high station, or poor and lowly, their glory is in the fear of the Lord. Great men and judges and potentates shall be honored; yet is there none of them greater than he that feareth the Lord. Forgive thy neighbor the hurt that he hath done unto thee, so shall thy sins also be forgiven when thou prayest. One man beareth hatred against the other, and doth he seek pardon for himself from the Lord? He showeth no mercy to a man who is like himself and doth he ask forgiveness of his own sins? If he that is but flesh, nourish hatred, who will entreat for pardon of his sins? Remember the commandments not to bear malice to thy neighbor; abstain from strife and thou shalt diminish thine own sins. A sinful man disquieteth friends and maketh debate amongst them that are at peace. Have thou patience with a man in poor estate and delay not to show him mercy. There is no riches above a sound body and no joy above the joy of the heart. He that taketh away his neighbor's living slayeth him and he that defraudeth the laborer of his hire is a shedder of blood. He that washeth himself after the touching of a dead body, if he touch it again, what availeth his washing? So is it with a man that fasteth for his sins and goeth again and doeth the same—will his prayer be heard? or what doth his humbling profit him? He that keepeth the law bringeth offerings enough; he that taketh heed to the commandments, a peace offering; he that requiteth a good turn, offereth fine flour; he that giveth alms sacrificeth praise-offering; to forsake unrighteousness is a propitiation. In all thy gifts show a cheerful countenance and dedicate thy tithes with gladness. Fear not the sentence of death; remember them that have been before thee and that come after thee; this is the sentence of the Lord over all flesh. Work thy work betimes and in His time He will give thee thy reward.

XVII.

(From the Wisdom of Solomon.)

LOVE righteousness; think of God with a pure heart and seek Him with simplicity of mind, for He will reveal Himself to those that do not distrust Him. Into a malicious soul wisdom will not enter nor dwell in a body that is subject to sin. Beware of murmuring which availeth naught; refrain thy tongue from backbiting. There is no word so secret that it shall go for naught. If a man love righteousness, the fruit of his wisdom are virtues, for she teacheth Temperance and Prudence, Justice and Fortitude which are such things as nothing more profitable can man have in life. Thou, O God, hast mercy upon all and forbearest with the sins of men that they shall amend. Thou lovest all things that are and abhorrest nothing which Thou hast made; for never wouldst Thou have created anything, if thou hadst hated it. Thou sparest all, for they are Thine, Thou lover of souls! Thou hast taught Thy people that the just man should be merciful and hast made Thy children to be of good hope because Thou hast created repentance for sins! Our life here is not a pastime and our time here not a market for gain, as some think that they must be getting every way though it be by evil means. All the earth calleth upon truth and the heaven blesseth her. All kings shake and tremble at her and with her is no unrighteousness. She endureth and is always strong, and liveth and conquereth forevermore. With her there is no accepting of persons or bribes. She is the strength, the dominion, the power and the majesty of all ages. Blessed be the God of truth!

READING OF THE SCRIPTURE.

Minister:

(Isaiah lx.)

ARISE, shine, for thy light is come and the glory of God is risen upon thee. For behold, darkness shall cover the earth, and gross darkness the nations, but upon thee shall the Lord arise, and His glory shall be revealed unto thee. Nations shall come to thy light, and kingdoms to the brightness that riseth upon thee. Violence shall no more be heard in thy land, wasting or destruction within thy borders; thou shalt call thy walls salvation, thy gates praise, the people shall be all righteous, the branch of my planting, the work of my hands, that I may be glorified.

Choir:

No one is like unto Thee, O God, and no work can be compared unto Thy work. Thy kingdom is an everlasting kingdom, and Thy truth endureth for ever. Thou art King eternal. Thou hast reigned and shalt reign for evermore. The Lord will give strength unto His people, the Lord will bless His people with peace.

אֵין כָּמוֹךָ בָאֱלֹהִים יְיָ׃
וְאֵין כְּמַעֲשֶׂיךָ: מַלְכוּתְךָ
מַלְכוּת כָּל־עוֹלָמִים
וּמֶמְשַׁלְתְּךָ בְּכָל־דּוֹר
וָדֹר: יְיָ מֶלֶךְ ‧ יְיָ מָלָךְ ‧
יְיָ יִמְלֹךְ לְעוֹלָם וָעֶד: יְיָ
עֹז לְעַמּוֹ יִתֵּן ‧ יְיָ יְבָרֵךְ
אֶת־עַמּוֹ בַשָּׁלוֹם׃

(Minister takes the Scroll from the Ark, and turning to the congregation says:)

The Torah which God gave through Moses is the heritage of the house of Israel. Come ye and let us walk in the light of the Lord, that we may receive the spirit of wisdom and understanding, the spirit of counsel and strength, the spirit of knowledge and the fear of God.

Minister and Congregation:

Hear, O Israel, the Lord, our God, the Lord is One.

(Congregation sitting.)

Choir:

Thine, O Lord, is the greatness and the power, the glory, and the victory, and the majesty; for all that is in the heavens and in the earth is Thine, Thine is dominion, and Thou art exalted above all.

(Before reading from the Torah.)

Minister:

Blessed be Thou, O Lord, our God, Ruler of the world, who hast called Israel from amongst the nations and given him Thy Law. Praise be to Thee, O God, Giver of the Law.

(Exodus xxxiii, 12 to xxxiv, 10.)

AND Moses said unto the Lord, See, Thou sayest unto me: Bring up this people; and Thou hast not let me know whom Thou wilt send with me.

DAY OF ATONEMENT.

(Minister takes the Scroll from the Ark, and turning to the congregation says:)

תּוֹרָה צִוָּה לָנוּ מֹשֶׁה. מוֹרָשָׁה קְהִלַּת יַעֲקֹב:
בֵּית יַעֲקֹב לְכוּ וְנֵלְכָה בְּאוֹר יְהֹוָה:

Minister and Congregation:

שְׁמַע יִשְׂרָאֵל יְהֹוָה אֱלֹהֵינוּ יְהֹוָה אֶחָד:

(Congregation sitting.)

Choir:

לְךָ יְיָ הַגְּדֻלָּה וְהַגְּבוּרָה. וְהַתִּפְאֶרֶת וְהַנֵּצַח וְהַהוֹד
כִּי כֹל בַּשָּׁמַיִם וּבָאָרֶץ. לְךָ יְיָ הַמַּמְלָכָה. וְהַמִּתְנַשֵּׂא
לְכֹל לְרֹאשׁ:

(Before reading from the Torah.)

Minister:

בָּרוּךְ אַתָּה יְיָ אֱלֹהֵינוּ מֶלֶךְ הָעוֹלָם. אֲשֶׁר בָּחַר
בָּנוּ מִכָּל־הָעַמִּים וְנָתַן לָנוּ אֶת־תּוֹרָתוֹ. בָּרוּךְ
אַתָּה יְיָ נוֹתֵן הַתּוֹרָה:

שמות ל״ג

וַיֹּאמֶר מֹשֶׁה אֶל־יְהֹוָה רְאֵה אַתָּה אֹמֵר אֵלַי
הַעַל אֶת־הָעָם הַזֶּה וְאַתָּה לֹא הוֹדַעְתַּנִי אֵת אֲשֶׁר
תִּשְׁלַח עִמִּי. וְאַתָּה אָמַרְתָּ יְדַעְתִּיךָ בְשֵׁם וְגַם
מָצָאתָ חֵן בְּעֵינָי: וְעַתָּה אִם־נָא מָצָאתִי חֵן בְּעֵינֶיךָ
הוֹדִעֵנִי נָא אֶת־דְּרָכֶךָ וְאֵדָעֲךָ לְמַעַן אֶמְצָא־חֵן

Yet Thou hast said, I know thee by name, and thou hast also found grace in my sight. Now, therefore, I pray Thee, if I have found grace in Thy sight, show me now Thy way, that I may know Thee, that I may find grace in Thy sight; and consider that this nation is Thy people. And He said: My presence shall go with thee, and I will give thee rest. And he said unto Him: If Thy presence go not with me, carry us not up hence; for wherein shall it be known here that I and Thy people have found grace in Thy sight? Is it not in that Thou goest with us? So shall we be distinguished, I and Thy people, from all the people that are upon the face of the earth. And the Lord said unto Moses, I will do this thing also that thou hast spoken: for thou hast found grace in my sight, and I know thee by name. And he said, I beseech Thee, show me Thy glory. And God said, I will make all my goodness pass before thee, and I will proclaim the name of the Lord before thee; and will be gracious to whom I will be gracious, and will show mercy on whom I will show mercy.

And He said, thou canst not see my face, for there shall no man see me and live. And the Lord said unto Moses: Hew thee two tables of stone like unto the first: and I will write upon these tables the words that were in the first tables, which thou brakest. And be ready in the morning, and come up in the morning unto the Mount Sinai, and present thyself there to me in the top of the mount. And no man shall come up with thee, neither let any

בְּעֵינֶיךָ וּרְאֵה כִּי עַמְּךָ הַגּוֹי הַזֶּה: וַיֹּאמַר פָּנַי יֵלֵכוּ
וַהֲנִחֹתִי לָךְ: וַיֹּאמֶר אֵלָיו אִם־אֵין פָּנֶיךָ הֹלְכִים
אַל־תַּעֲלֵנוּ מִזֶּה: וּבַמֶּה יִוָּדַע אֵפוֹא כִּי־מָצָאתִי
חֵן בְּעֵינֶיךָ אֲנִי וְעַמֶּךָ הֲלוֹא בְּלֶכְתְּךָ עִמָּנוּ וְנִפְלֵינוּ
אֲנִי וְעַמְּךָ מִכָּל־הָעָם אֲשֶׁר עַל־פְּנֵי הָאֲדָמָה:

וַיֹּאמֶר יְהוָֹה אֶל־מֹשֶׁה גַּם אֶת־הַדָּבָר הַזֶּה אֲשֶׁר
דִּבַּרְתָּ אֶעֱשֶׂה כִּי־מָצָאתָ חֵן בְּעֵינַי וָאֵדָעֲךָ בְּשֵׁם:
וַיֹּאמַר הַרְאֵנִי נָא אֶת־כְּבֹדֶךָ: וַיֹּאמֶר אֲנִי אַעֲבִיר
כָּל־טוּבִי עַל־פָּנֶיךָ וְקָרָאתִי בְשֵׁם יְהוָֹה לְפָנֶיךָ
וְחַנֹּתִי אֶת־אֲשֶׁר אָחֹן וְרִחַמְתִּי אֶת־אֲשֶׁר אֲרַחֵם:
וַיֹּאמֶר לֹא תוּכַל לִרְאֹת אֶת־פָּנָי כִּי לֹא יִרְאַנִי
הָאָדָם וָחָי: וַיֹּאמֶר יְהוָֹה הִנֵּה מָקוֹם אִתִּי וְנִצַּבְתָּ
עַל־הַצּוּר: וְהָיָה בַּעֲבֹר כְּבֹדִי וְשַׂמְתִּיךָ בְּנִקְרַת
הַצּוּר וְשַׂכֹּתִי כַפִּי עָלֶיךָ עַד־עָבְרִי: וַהֲסִרֹתִי אֶת־
כַּפִּי וְרָאִיתָ אֶת־אֲחֹרָי וּפָנַי לֹא יֵרָאוּ:

וַיֹּאמֶר יְהוָֹה אֶל מֹשֶׁה פְּסָל־לְךָ שְׁנֵי־לֻחֹת אֲבָנִים
כָּרִאשֹׁנִים וְכָתַבְתִּי עַל־הַלֻּחֹת אֶת־הַדְּבָרִים אֲשֶׁר
הָיוּ עַל־הַלֻּחֹת הָרִאשֹׁנִים אֲשֶׁר שִׁבַּרְתָּ: וֶהְיֵה
נָכוֹן לַבֹּקֶר וְעָלִיתָ בַבֹּקֶר אֶל־הַר סִינַי וְנִצַּבְתָּ לִי
שָׁם עַל־רֹאשׁ הָהָר: וְאִישׁ לֹא־יַעֲלֶה עִמָּךְ וְגַם־
אִישׁ אַל־יֵרָא בְּכָל־הָהָר גַּם־הַצֹּאן וְהַבָּקָר אַל־
יִרְעוּ אֶל־מוּל הָהָר הַהוּא: וַיִּפְסֹל שְׁנֵי לֻחֹת אֲבָנִים

man be seen throughout all the mount; neither let the flocks nor herds feed before that mount. And he hewed two tables of stone like unto the first, and Moses rose up early in the morning, and went up unto Mount Sinai, as the Lord had commanded him, and he took in his hands the two tables of stone. And the Lord descended in the cloud, and stood with him there, and proclaimed the name of the Lord. And the Lord passed by before him and proclaimed, The Lord, the Lord God, merciful and gracious, long-suffering, and abundant in goodness and truth; keeping mercy for thousands, forgiving iniquity and transgression and sin, and that will by no means clear the guilty; visiting the iniquity of the fathers upon the children and upon the children's children, unto the third and the fourth generation. And Moses made haste and bowed his head toward the earth, and worshiped. And he said, if now I have found grace in Thy sight, O Lord, let my Lord, I pray Thee, go among us; for it is a stiff-necked people; and pardon our iniquity and our sin, and take us for Thine inheritance.

(After Reading from the Torah.)

Praise be to Thee, O Eternal, our God, Ruler of the universe, who hast given us a law of truth and implanted eternal life within us. Praise be to Thee, O God, Giver of the Law. Amen.

DAY OF ATONEMENT. 283

בָּרִאשֹׁנִים וַיַּשְׁכֵּם מֹשֶׁה בַבֹּקֶר וַיַּעַל אֶל־הַר סִינַי
כַּאֲשֶׁר צִוָּה יְהֹוָה אֹתוֹ וַיִּקַּח בְּיָדוֹ שְׁנֵי לֻחֹת אֲבָנִים:
וַיֵּרֶד יְהֹוָה בֶּעָנָן וַיִּתְיַצֵּב עִמּוֹ שָׁם וַיִּקְרָא בְשֵׁם יְהֹוָה:
וַיַּעֲבֹר יְהֹוָה עַל־פָּנָיו וַיִּקְרָא יְהֹוָה יְהֹוָה אֵל רַחוּם
וְחַנּוּן אֶרֶךְ אַפַּיִם וְרַב־חֶסֶד וֶאֱמֶת: נֹצֵר חֶסֶד
לָאֲלָפִים נֹשֵׂא עָוֹן וָפֶשַׁע וְחַטָּאָה וְנַקֵּה לֹא יְנַקֶּה
פֹּקֵד עֲוֹן אָבוֹת עַל־בָּנִים וְעַל־בְּנֵי בָנִים עַל־
שִׁלֵּשִׁים וְעַל־רִבֵּעִים: וַיְמַהֵר מֹשֶׁה וַיִּקֹּד אַרְצָה
וַיִּשְׁתָּחוּ: וַיֹּאמֶר אִם־נָא מָצָאתִי חֵן בְּעֵינֶיךָ אֲדֹנָי
יֵלֶךְ־נָא אֲדֹנָי בְּקִרְבֵּנוּ כִּי עַם־קְשֵׁה עֹרֶף הוּא
וְסָלַחְתָּ לַעֲוֹנֵנוּ וּלְחַטָּאתֵנוּ וּנְחַלְתָּנוּ: וַיֹּאמֶר הִנֵּה
אָנֹכִי כֹּרֵת בְּרִית נֶגֶד כָּל־עַמְּךָ אֶעֱשֶׂה נִפְלָאֹת
אֲשֶׁר לֹא־נִבְרְאוּ בְכָל־הָאָרֶץ וּבְכָל־הַגּוֹיִם וְרָאָה
כָל־הָעָם אֲשֶׁר־אַתָּה בְקִרְבּוֹ אֶת־מַעֲשֵׂה יְהֹוָה כִּי
נוֹרָא הוּא אֲשֶׁר אֲנִי עֹשֶׂה עִמָּךְ:

(After reading from the Torah.)

בָּרוּךְ אַתָּה יְיָ אֱלֹהֵינוּ מֶלֶךְ הָעוֹלָם. אֲשֶׁר נָתַן
לָנוּ תּוֹרַת אֱמֶת וְחַיֵּי עוֹלָם נָטַע בְּתוֹכֵנוּ.
בָּרוּךְ אַתָּה יְיָ נוֹתֵן הַתּוֹרָה:

Reading of Haphtharah:

(Jonah iii.)

THE word of the Lord came to Jonah the second time, saying: Arise, go to Niniveh, that great city, and proclaim to her the words which I shall speak to thee. And Jonah arose and went to Niniveh, according to the word of the Lord. Now Niniveh was through God a great city, three days' journey in extent. And Jonah began to enter into the city a day's journey, and he cried out and said, Yet forty days and Niniveh shall be overthrown. And the men of Niniveh believed God, and proclaimed a fast, and put on sackcloth, from the greatest of them even to the least of them. And when the matter came to the king of Niniveh, he arose from his throne, and put off his mantle, and covered himself with sackcloth, and sat in ashes. And he caused it to be proclaimed and published through Niniveh, by the decree of the king and his nobles, saying, Let neither man nor beast, herd nor flock, taste anything; let them not feed nor drink water, but let man and beast be covered with sackcloth, and cry mightily to God. Yea, let them turn every one from his evil way, and from the violence that is in their hands. Who can tell, if God will turn and repent, and turn away from His fierce anger, that we perish not? And God saw their works that they turned from their evil ways; and God repented of the evil which He had said that He would do to them, and He did it not. But this displeased Jonah exceedingly and he was very angry. And he prayed to the Lord and said: Ah! O Lord, was not this what I said, when I was yet in mine own country? Therefore I made haste to flee to Tarshish. For I knew that Thou art a gracious and merciful God, slow to anger and abundant in mercy, and that Thou repentest of a threatened evil. And now, O Lord, take, I pray Thee, my life from me! for it is better for me to die than to live. And the Lord said, Is it right that thou shouldst be angry? Now Jonah had gone out of the city, and had sat on the east side of the city, and had made himself a booth there, and he sat under it in the shade, till he should see what would become of the city. And the Lord appointed a gourd; and it grew up over Jonah to be a shadow over his head, to deliver him from his distress. And Jonah was exceedingly glad of the gourd. But God appointed a worm, when the morning rose the next day and it smote the gourd so that it withered. And when the sun arose God appointed a sultry east wind; and the sun beat upon the head of Jonah, and he was faint and he asked himself for death, and said, It is better for me to die than to live. And God said to Jonah, Is it right that thou shouldst be angry for the gourd? And he said, It is right that I should be angry, even unto death. And the Lord said, Thou hast pity on the gourd for which thou hast not labored, and which thou madest not to grow, which grew up in a night and perished in a night; and should not I spare Niniveh, the great city, wherein are more than a hundred and twenty thousand persons that cannot discern between their right hand and their left hand, and also much cattle?

Minister:

BRETHREN:—This Day of Atonement is given us to reconcile us with God, to restore peace with our fellow-beings and with ourselves, wherever discontent and selfishness mar the harmony of our lives. For all we are and all we call our own comes from God's hand. To His goodness we owe our life and our success, our health and happiness; and of all the good of the earth which He has placed at our command, we are but the stewards appointed by Him, wisely to dispose of it for the benefit of all His creatures. Rich or poor, strong or weak, wise or simple, He has knit us all together by bonds of sympathy and tender compassion, so that we may form one loving brotherhood, one household of goodness before our heavenly Father. The knowledge of this saving truth was fostered in Israel through the Sabbath, which was given as a day of redemption from the yoke of servitude; that the laborer might on that day also be free as his master. So likewise the law proclaimed Sabbatical release on every seventh year to each who bore the burden of distress, of slavery and of debt in Israel. But most solemnly did the Day of Atonement echo the law of equal justice to all, when in each Jubilee year it sent forth the trumpet call of liberty and of human brotherhood to all the oppressed in the land, restoring every inhabitant to his patrimony, thereby proclaiming that God is the Lord of the earth, the owner of the land and the proprietor and dispenser of its produce, and that all men are His vassals, His tenants and stewards. For the heavens and the earth are His, and we are but day-laborers, strangers and sojourners before Him. Therefore would God on this Sabbath of Sabbaths have restitution made for every wrong done in the management of human affairs and have all who were enfeebled and bruised in life's severe battle restored to their patrimony, their liberty and social independence. As a veritable time of atonement and reconciliation this day was designated to reconcile each human being to his own destiny and restore peace to every heart and home.

Choir:

For He satisfieth the longing heart and filleth the hungry with good. Oh, that men would praise the Lord for His goodness and for His kindness to the children of men.

Minister:

AGAIN, brethren, the Omnipotent finds no delight in the proud and mighty whose arm crushes the feeble and who call their successful strength their God. His mercy goeth forth to the humble whose cry He hears when they are afflicted and when their voices rise up to His throne. Neither sacrifice of rams and of rivers of oil, nor fasting and castigation of the body are sufficient in themselves to cleanse the soul from sin and to relieve the conscience from its burden of guilt. But these are the true means of grace: Let justice run as water and righteousness as a mighty stream. Show compassion, every man to his brother, oppress not the widow, the fatherless, the stranger nor the poor, and devise no evil against your brother in your heart. Speak ye every man the truth to his neighbor and execute the judgment of truth and peace in your gates! This, brethren, is the true fast in which God delights, for it will be turned into a feast of joy to all flesh. Grant, then, O Lord, that in the true contrition of heart and humbleness of spirit we may from this day hearken to the admonition of this Sabbath of Sabbaths and faithfully discharge our obligations to the needy and distressed. Incline our hearts to pity, that we may readily succor the poor and the shelterless and in true sympathy render the cause of every unfortunate being in our midst our own concern, and thus become a father to the fatherless, eyes to the blind and arms to the helpless. Let none in this community of Israel, under the beneficent sway of this free land, neglect his duty to aid and promote the institutions of benevolence and education in our midst according to the extent of his power. Bestow Thy blessing, O merciful Father, upon all those who lend their lives and energies to the sacred work of charity and love, to the maintenance of our religious institutions and our communal affairs, and grant Thy favor and grace **to all those who serve** Thee in truth and faithfulness.

Choir:—Amen.

DAY OF ATONEMENT.

Returning of the Scroll.

Minister:

O magnify the Lord with me and let us exalt His name together.

יְהַלְלוּ אֶת־שֵׁם יְיָ כִּי נִשְׂגָּב שְׁמוֹ לְבַדּוֹ:

Choir:

His glory is in the earth and in the heavens. He is the strength of all His servants, the praise of them that truly love Him. The hope of Israel whom He brought nigh to himself, Hallelujah.

הוֹדוֹ עַל אֶרֶץ וְשָׁמָיִם: וַיָּרֶם קֶרֶן לְעַמּוֹ תְּהִלָּה לְכָל חֲסִידָיו לִבְנֵי יִשְׂרָאֵל עַם קְרֹבוֹ הַלְלוּיָהּ:

Minister:

The law of the Lord is perfect, restoring the soul; the testimonies of the Lord are faithful, making wise the simple. The precepts of the Lord are plain, rejoicing the heart; the fear of the Lord is pure, enduring forever. Behold, a good doctrine has been given to you: forsake it not.

תּוֹרַת יְיָ תְּמִימָה. מְשִׁיבַת נֶפֶשׁ. עֵדוּת יְיָ נֶאֱמָנָה. מַחְכִּימַת פֶּתִי: פִּקּוּדֵי יְיָ יְשָׁרִים מְשַׂמְּחֵי לֵב. יִרְאַת יְיָ טְהוֹרָה. עוֹמֶדֶת לָעַד: כִּי לֶקַח טוֹב נָתַתִּי לָכֶם תּוֹרָתִי אַל תַּעֲזֹבוּ:

Choir:

(Psalm xl.)

| It is a tree of life to them that lay hold of it and the supporters thereof are happy. Its ways are ways of pleasantness and all its paths are peace. | עֵץ־חַיִּים הִיא לַמַּחֲזִיקִים בָּהּ וְתוֹמְכֶיהָ מְאֻשָּׁר׃ דְּרָכֶיהָ דַרְכֵי נֹעַם וְכָל־נְתִיבוֹתֶיהָ שָׁלוֹם׃ |

HYMN.

TO Thee we give ourselves to-day;
    Forgetful of the world outside,
We tarry in Thy house, O God,
    From eventide to eventide.

From Thine all-searching righteous eye
    Our deepest heart can nothing hide;
It crieth up to Thee for peace
    From eventide to eventide.

Who could endure, shouldst Thou, O God.
    As we deserve, for ever chide,
We, therefore, seek Thy pardoning grace
    From eventide to eventide.

O may we lay to heart how swift
    The years of life do onward glide;
So learn to live that we may see
    Thy light at our life's eventide.

Memorial Service.

ANTHEM.

O Lord! what is man, that Thou takest knowledge of him; or the son of man, that thou makest account of him! Man is like unto vanity; his days are as a shadow that passeth away. In the morning he flourisheth, and groweth up; in the evening he is cut down, and withereth. Thou turnest man to contrition, and sayest: Return, ye children of men! O that they were wise, that they would consider their latter end! For when man dieth, he shall carry nothing away; his glory shall not descend after him. Mark the perfect man, and behold the upright;	יְיָ מָה־אָדָם וַתֵּדָעֵהוּ בֶּן־אֱנוֹשׁ וַתְּחַשְּׁבֵהוּ: אָדָם לַהֶבֶל דָּמָה . יָמָיו כְּצֵל עוֹבֵר: בַּבֹּקֶר יָצִיץ וְחָלָף . לָעֶרֶב יְמוֹלֵל יָבֵשׁ: תָּשֵׁב אֱנוֹשׁ עַד־דַּכָּא . וַתֹּאמֶר שׁוּבוּ בְנֵי־אָדָם: לוּ חָכְמוּ יַשְׂכִּילוּ זֹאת . יָבִינוּ לְאַחֲרִיתָם: כִּי לֹא בְמוֹתוֹ יִקַּח הַכֹּל . לֹא־יֵרֵד אַחֲרָיו כְּבוֹדוֹ: שְׁמָר־תָּם וּרְאֵה יָשָׁר .

for the end of that man is peace. The Lord redeemeth the soul of His servants; and none of them that trust in Him shall be condemned.

כִּי־אַחֲרִית לְאִישׁ שָׁלוֹם׃ פֹּדֶה יְיָ נֶפֶשׁ עֲבָדָיו. וְלֹא יֶאְשְׁמוּ כָּל־־הַחֹסִים בּוֹ׃

Alternate Reading for Minister and Congregation:

LORD, Thou hast been our refuge in all generations. Before the mountains were brought forth, or ever Thou hadst formed the earth and the world;

Even from everlasting to everlasting Thou art God.

Thou turnest man to dust, and sayest, return ye children of men.

A thousand years in Thy sight are as yesterday when it is past, and as a watch in the night.

Thou carriest men away as with a flood, they are as a sleep.

In the morning they are like grass which groweth up.

In the morning it groweth up and flourisheth, in the evening it is cut down and withereth.

The days of our years are threescore and ten, and if by reason of strength they be fourscore years;

Yet is their pride but labor and sorrow; for it is soon cut off, and we fly away.

Teach us so to number our days, that we may apply our hearts to wisdom.

O satisfy us early with Thy mercy, that we may rejoice and be glad all our days.

Make us glad according to the days wherein we have been afflicted, and the years wherein we have seen evil.

Let Thy work appear unto Thy servants and Thy glory unto their children.

And let the favor of the Lord, our God, be upon us, and establish Thou the work of our hands; yea, the work of our hands, establish Thou it.

Man is of few days and full of trouble.

He cometh up like a flower and withereth, like a shadow he fleeth and stayeth not.

What man is he that liveth and shall not die, that can save his life from the power of the grave?

For man's days are ordained; the number of his months is with God, in whose hand is the soul of every living being, and the spirit of all flesh.

Lord, make me to know my end, and the measure of my days, that I may know how frail I am.

The Lord redeemeth the soul of His servants, and none that trust in Him will He forsake.

Thou wilt show me the path of life, and wilt lead me in the way everlasting.

In Thy presence is fulness of joy, at Thy right hand are pleasures for evermore.

Therefore, the sons of man seek refuge under the shadow of Thy wings.

They shall be satisfied with the abundance of Thy house.

Thou wilt cause them to drink of the full stream of Thy blessings.

For with Thee is the fountain of life; in Thy light shall we see light.

Minister:

O LORD, God of the spirits of all flesh, who dispenseth life and takest it away, who lowerest to the grave and leadest th soul unto eternal life: Thou hast appointed this Day of Atonement, that we may sanctify our lives on earth, and prepare ourselves for death and the life eternal. Thou hast hallowed this day as a Sabbath of the soul, so that, disengaged from worldly thoughts and interests, we may rise to thoughts of eternal life, and taste of the bliss which awaits the sanctified and the pure.

Man is feeble and perishable; his best laid plans and purposes are subject to disappointment and failure. Scarcely ushered into life, he begins his pilgrimage to the sepulchre. Through trial and suffering he hastens to the darkness of the grave. Thousands moisten their morsel of bread with tears and the sweat of ceaseless toil, till their fondest hopes vanish in death. Passions burn in the human breast and beguile to pleasure and to sinfulness. But the delight ends with the enjoyment, sin consumes the marrow of life; indulgence dwarfs the best impulses of the soul. Success and disappointment, pleasure and pain, mark the pathway of our earthly pilgrimage. Human life is a continual struggle against forces without and passions within. Man prevails, only to succumb, he fails, only to renew the combat the next moment.

Choir:

Oh, what is man, the child of dust? What is man, O Lord?

THE eye is never satisfied with seeing; endless are the desires of the heart. No mortal has ever had enough of riches, honor and wisdom, when death ended his career. Man devises new schemes on the grave of a thousand disappointed hopes. Like Moses on Mount Nebo, he beholds the promised land from afar, but into it he is denied an entrance. Discontent abides in the palace and in the hut, rankling alike in the breast of prince and pauper. Death finally terminates the combat, and grief and joy, success and failure, are all ended. Like a child falling asleep over his toys, man relinquishes his grasp on earthly possessions only when death overtakes him. The master and the servant, the rich and the poor, the strong and the feeble, the wise and the simple, all are equal in death; the grave levels all distinctions and makes the whole world kin.

Choir:

Oh, what is man, the child of dust? What is man, O Lord?

Minister:

WE are strangers before Thee, O God, and sojourners as were our fathers; like shadows our days vanish on earth. But the speedy flight of our life, and the gloom of the grave should not afright us, but teach us wisdom. It ought to encourage us to put our trust in Thee, who wilt not suffer Thy children to see destruction. For the dust only returns to the dust; the spirit is implanted by Thee, and returns to Thee, its ever-living source. And they who walk here in the light of Thy countenance and sow good seed though in weeping, go home to Thee laden with sheaves. They who sow but wind may tremble at the whirlwind which they must reap. He who toils but for vain things and boasts of his might, must dread the grave. He trusts in his house, it stands not; he lays hold of it, it endures not. Though he joins house to house and adds field to field, his place denies him as soon as he is vanished, saying: I have not seen Thee.

O, that we might die the death of the righteous and our end be like theirs. Suffer us not to pass away in our sins, O Judge of life and death Teach us to number our days, to improve the few hours ere they vanish. Grant to us all, the small and the great, the young and the old, strength and understanding, that we may not delay to remove from our midst all that is displeasing in Thy sight, thus to become reconciled to Thee. Help us, O God, in our endeavors that each may faithfully discharge his duty toward his family, toward his country and mankind.

Silent Devotion.

(Psalm xxiii.)

THE Lord is my shepherd: I shall not want. He maketh me lie down in green pastures; He leadeth me beside the still waters. He reviveth my soul; He leadeth me in paths of safety, for His name's sake. Even though I walk through the valley of the shadow of death I fear no evil, for Thou art with me; Thy rod and Thy staff, they comfort me. Thou preparest a table before me in the presence of mine enemies. Thou anointest my head with oil; my cup runneth over. Surely goodness and mercy shall follow me all the days of my life, and I shall dwell in the house of the Lord for ever.

HYMN.

WHY art thou cast down, **my soul,**
    Why disquieted in me?
Feel'st thou not the Father **nigh,**
    Him whose heart contains **us all?**
Lives no God for thee on high,
    Loving while His judgments **fall?**
        Look above!
        God is love!
Why art thou cast down, my **soul?**
        To the skies
        Turn thine eyes;
Every tear on earth that flows,
God the world's great Ruler knows.

Why art thou cast down, my soul?
Why disquieted in me?
>Was thy head in sorrow bending
'Neath the dreaded reaper's blight,
When thy loved ones were descending
In the darkness of death's night?
Have no fear!
God is near!
Be consoled, my soul, in God,
Tears take flight,
For in light
Walk thy dead on Heaven's shore,
Blessed, blessed, evermore!

Why art thou cast down, my soul?
Why disquieted in me?
Ever shall thy dead be living—
From the darkness of the tomb
God, thy Father, mercy-giving,
Takes them to his heavenly home.
Wilt thou trust
God, the Just?
Soul, my soul, be strong in God.
God's with thee
Eternally!
Then thy hopes shall be fulfilled
And thy heart's pain shall be stilled.

MEDITATION.

FORGET thine anguish,
  Vexed heart again!
Why shouldst thou languish
With earthly pain?
The husk shall slumber,
Bedded in clay,
Silent and sombre,
Oblivion's prey!
But, Spirit immortal,
Thou at Death's portal,
Tremblest with fear.
If He caress thee,
Curse thee or bless thee,
Thou must draw near,
From Him the worth of **thy works to hear**

Why full of terror,
Compassed with error,
Trouble thy heart,
For thy mortal part?
The soul flies home—
The corpse is dumb;
Of all thou didst have,
Follows naught to the grave.
Thou fliest thy nest,
Swift as a bird to thy place **of rest.**
What avail grief and fasting,
Where nothing is lasting?
Pomp, domination,
Become tribulation.

In a health-giving draught;
A death-dealing shaft.
Wealth—an illusion,
Power—a lie,
Over all, dissolution
Creeps silent and sly.
Unto others remain
The goods thou didst gain
With infinite pain.

Life is a vine-branch;
A vintager, Death.
He threatens and lowers
More near with each breath.
Then hasten, arise!
Seek God, O my soul!
For time quickly flies,
Still far is the goal.
Vain heart praying dumbly,
Learn to prize humbly,
The meanest of fare.
Forget all thy sorrow,
Behold, Death is there!

Dove-like lamenting,
Be full of repenting,
Lift vision supernal,
To raptures eternal.
On ev'ry occasion
Seek lasting salvation.
Pour thy heart out in weeping
While others are sleeping.

Pray to Him when all's still,
Performing His will;
And so shall the angel of peace **be thy guide**
On thy homeward journey
To the garden of delight.

Minister:

ALMIGHTY Father, Thy word of peace warns us of the supreme hour which will call us to the realm of eternal rest and gather us to our fathers, to all the unnumbered generations that have gone before us. And thus we remember, before thee, to-day, all dear and beloved ones that have already reached the goal whither we are tending. In this solemn hour we think of the time when they still walked on earth, and lived among us in love and tenderness, bestowing protection and blessing. They are near us, though many years have passed over their graves.

Alternate Reading for Minister and Congregation:

LET us call to remembrance the great and good, through whom the Lord hath wrought great glory.

Those who were leaders of the people by their judgment, giving counsel by their understanding and foresight.

Wise and eloquent in their teachings, and through knowledge and might fit helpers of the people.

MEMORIAL SERVICE.

All these were honored in their generation, and were the glory of their times.

There be some who have left a name behind them; whose remembrance is as sweet honey in all mouths.

And there be some who have no memorial; who are perished as though they had never been.

But their righteousness has not been forgotten, and the glory of their work cannot be blotted out.

Choir:

I set the Lord before me at all times, since He is at my right hand, I shall not be moved. Therefore, my heart is glad, and my spirit rejoiceth; yea, my flesh dwelleth in security. For Thou wilt not give me up to destruction: nor wilt Thou suffer Thy holy one to see corruption. Thou wilt show me the path of life; in Thy presence is fulness of joy; at Thy right hand are pleasures forever more.

שִׁוִּיתִי יְיָ לְנֶגְדִּי תָמִיד.
כִּי מִימִינִי בַּל־אֶמּוֹט:
לָכֵן שָׂמַח לִבִּי וַיָּגֶל
כְּבוֹדִי. אַף בְּשָׂרִי יִשְׁכּוֹן
לָבֶטַח: כִּי לֹא תַעֲזֹב
נַפְשִׁי לִשְׁאוֹל. לֹא תִתֵּן
חֲסִידְךָ לִרְאוֹת שָׁחַת:
תּוֹדִיעֵנִי אֹרַח חַיִּים.
שֹׂבַע שְׂמָחוֹת אֶת־פָּנֶיךָ.
נְעִמוֹת בִּימִינְךָ נֶצַח:

Organ Voluntary.

Silent Devotion:

In Memory of the Father.

THY memory, dearly beloved father, this solemn hour fills my soul, revives in me all the holy sentiments of love and tenderness which thou hast lavished so richly on me, when thou didst live on earth. Thy image will live for ever in my soul, as my guiding star on the path of virtue; and when my pilgrimage on earth is ended and I shall arrive at the throne of mercy, may I be deemed worthy of thee in the presence of God. May our merciful Father reward thee the faithful kindness thou hast ever shown me; may He grant thee eternal peace! Amen.

In Memory of the Mother.

I REMEMBER thee in this solemn hour, dearly beloved mother. I remember the days when thou still didst dwell on earth, and thy tender love watched over me like a guardian angel. Thou hast gone from me, but the bond which unites our souls can never be severed; thy image truly lives within my heart. May the merciful Father reward thee the faithful kindness thou hast ever shown me; may He lift up the light of His countenance in mercy upon thee, and grant thee eternal peace! Amen.

In Memory of the Husband.

I REMEMBER thee in this solemn hour, Thou dearly beloved friend of my youth. I remember the happy days we lived together; I remember the tender affection, the self-denial which filled thy being while we still walked hand in hand the common path of our wedded life, and when thy love and fidelity were my comfort, and thy counsel and aid my support. Though death has summoned thee from my side, thine image still lives in my heart, is still an inspiration to me, and thy spirit continues to live in a higher existence. May God cover thee with the shadow of His grace, and give thee eternal joy in abundance! Amen.

In Memory of the Wife.

THY memory, dear partner of my life, now fills my soul, revives once more in me the love, the tenderness, the fidelity and self-denial which distinguished thy noble heart and sweetened the days of my life. I will cherish thy memory as long as I live and strive to become worthy of thee. Though death has summoned thee from my side, thine image still lives in my heart, is still an inspiration to me, and thy spirit continues to live in a higher existence. May God cover thee with the shadow of His grace, and give thee eternal joy in abundance! Amen.

In Memory of Children.

I REMEMBER thee in this solemn hour, my beloved child. I remember the days, when I still delighted in thy bloom, in thy bodily and mental growth, in beautiful hopes for thy future. The inscrutable will of God took thee early from me; He called thee to His abode; yet in my wounded heart the fond remembrance of thee can never be extinguished. But the Almighty is kind and just in all His ways; His holy name be praised forever.

His paternal love is my solace, my staff and support, and on it I rest my hope for thy eternal destiny. As a father pitieth his children, may He look with compassion upon thee, and cause thy portion ever to be a delightful one. Amen.

In Memory of Brothers, Sisters and Other Relatives.

I REMEMBER thee in this solemn hour, my beloved brother—sister—friend—I remember the days when we lived together in one happy family circle, and thy love and friendship were my delight and support. Now thou slumberest in the grave, but thy image has not vanished from me. I think of thee with gratitude and bless thy memory for all the kindness thou hast shown unto me. May God bless thee with everlasting joy, may He cover thee with the shadow of His grace, and give thee eternal peace! Amen.

Minister:

WE remember with sorrowing hearts those whom death has taken from our midst during the past year.

*　*　*　*　*　*　*　*

O God, send Thy heavenly comfort to them who are bowed down in mourning and affliction. May they rest their troubled hearts, find consolation in their faith in Thee, merciful Father, and may Thy love be with them and announce peace to those who are nigh, and to those who are departed! Amen.

(Congregation standing.)

(The mourners standing and speaking with the Minister.)

EXTOLLED and hallowed be the name of God throughout the world which He has created, and which He governs according to His righteous will. Just is He in all His ways, and wise are all His decrees. May His Kingdom come, and His will be done in all the earth.

Congregation:

Blessed be the Lord of life and righteous Judge forever more.

Minister:

To the departed whom we now remember, may peace and bliss be granted in the world of eternal life. There may they find grace and mercy before the Lord of heaven and earth. May their souls rejoice in that ineffable good which God has laid up for those that fear Him, and may their memory be a blessing unto those that cherish it.

Congregation:

Amen.

Minister:

May the Father of peace send peace to all troubled souls, and comfort all the bereaved among us.

MEMORIAL SERVICE.

(The mourners standing and speaking with the Minister.)

יִתְגַדַל וְיִתְקַדַּשׁ שְׁמֵהּ רַבָּא. בְּעָלְמָא דִי־בְרָא
כִרְעוּתֵהּ. וְיַמְלִיךְ מַלְכוּתֵהּ. בְּחַיֵּיכוֹן וּבְיוֹמֵיכוֹן וּבְחַיֵּי
דְכָל בֵּית יִשְׂרָאֵל. בַּעֲגָלָא וּבִזְמַן קָרִיב. וְאִמְרוּ
אָמֵן:

Congregation:

יְהֵא שְׁמֵהּ רַבָּא מְבָרַךְ. לְעָלַם וּלְעָלְמֵי עָלְמַיָּא.

Minister:

יִתְבָּרַךְ וְיִשְׁתַּבַּח וְיִתְפָּאַר וְיִתְרוֹמַם וְיִתְנַשֵּׂא
וְיִתְהַדָּר וְיִתְעַלֶּה וְיִתְהַלָּל שְׁמֵהּ דְּקוּדְשָׁא. בְּרִיךְ
הוּא. לְעֵלָּא מִן כָּל בִּרְכָתָא וְשִׁירָתָא. תֻּשְׁבְּחָתָא
וְנֶחָמָתָא. דַּאֲמִירָן בְּעָלְמָא. וְאִמְרוּ אָמֵן:

עַל יִשְׂרָאֵל וְעַל צַדִּיקַיָּא. וְעַל־כָּל־מַן דְּאִתְפְּטַר
מִן עָלְמָא הָדֵין כִּרְעוּתֵהּ דֶּאֱלָהָא. יְהֵא לְהוֹן שְׁלָמָא
רַבָּא וְחוּלְקָא־טָבָא לְחַיֵּי עָלְמָא דְּאָתֵי. וְחִסְדָּא
וְרַחֲמֵי מִן־קֳדָם מָרֵא שְׁמַיָּא וְאַרְעָא. וְאִמְרוּ אָמֵן:

יְהֵא שְׁלָמָא רַבָּא מִן־שְׁמַיָּא וְחַיִּים. עָלֵינוּ וְעַל־כָּל־
יִשְׂרָאֵל. וְאִמְרוּ אָמֵן:

עֹשֶׂה שָׁלוֹם בִּמְרוֹמָיו. הוּא **יַעֲשֶׂה שָׁלוֹם עָלֵינוּ**
וְעַל כָּל יִשְׂרָאֵל. וְאִמְרוּ אָמֵן:

Choir:

THY glory, Lord, surroundeth
    The souls of saintly mortals,
And angel's music soundeth
    From heaven's open portals,
To pious pilgrims greeting
At dawn of life's new morning.

All earthly bodies perish;
    The soul, the Father's image,
Defieth all corruption;
    Is like Himself, eternal;
Though orbs from skies may sever,
    The soul lives on forever.

Hallelujah!

Concluding Service for the Day of Atonement.

Minister and Congregation:

(Psalm xxxii.)

HAPPY is he whose transgression **is forgiven,** whose sin is pardoned.

Happy the man to whom the Lord imputeth not iniquity, and in whose spirit there is no guile.

While I kept silence, my bones were wasted, by reason of my groaning all the day long.

For day and night Thy hand was heavy upon me; my strength dried up, as in summer's drought.

At length I acknowledged to Thee my sin, and did not hide mine iniquity.

I said: I will confess my transgressions to the Lord; and Thou forgavest the iniquity of my sin.

Therefore shall every pious man pray to Thee, while Thou mayest be found.

Surely, the floods of great waters shall not come near him.

Thou art my hiding-place; Thou preservest me from trouble;

Thou compassest me about with songs of deliverance.

The wicked hath many sorrows; but he that trusteth in the Lord is encompassed with mercies.

Choir:

Rejoice in the Lord and be glad, ye righteous, shout for joy, all ye that are upright in heart!

Minister and Congregation:

(Psalm ciii.)

BLESS the Lord, O my soul, and all that is within me, bless His holy name.

Bless the Lord, O my soul, and forget not all His benefits;

Who forgiveth all thine iniquities; who healeth all thy diseases;

Who redeemeth thy life from the grave; who crowneth thee with loving-kindness and tender mercies;

Who satisfieth thine old age with good, so that thy youth is renewed like the eagle's.

The Lord executeth justice and equity for all the oppressed.

The Lord is merciful and kind, slow to anger and rich in mercy.

He hath not dealt with us according to our sins, nor requited us according to our iniquities.

The Lord will not always chide; neither will He keep His anger forever.

As high as are the heavens above the earth, so great is His mercy to them that fear Him.

As far as the east is from the west, so far hath He removed our transgressions from us.

Even as a father pitieth his children, so the Lord pitieth them that fear Him.

For He knoweth our frame, He remembereth that we are dust.

As for man, His days are as grass; as a flower of the field, so he flourisheth.

The wind passeth over it, and it is gone; and its place shall know it no more.

But the mercy of the Lord is from everlasting to everlasting unto them that fear Him;

And His righteousness to children's children;

To them that keep His covenant and remember His statutes to do them.

The Lord hath established His throne in the heavens, and His kingdom ruleth over all.

Bless the Lord, ye His angels, ye mighty ones who do His commands, hearkening to the voice of His word.

Bless the Lord, all ye His hosts; ye, His ministers, who do His pleasure.

Choir:

Bless the Lord, all His works, in all places of His dominion! Bless the Lord, O my soul!

Minister:

(Job xxii and xx.)

CAN man be profitable unto God? Hath the Almighty advantage because thou art righteous, or is it His gain that thy ways are perfect? Is it not on account of thy sins that He enters with thee into judgment? Is not God in heaven above? Yes, see the stars how high! But thou hast said: What knoweth God? Through thick darkness can He judge? Dost thou observe the way of old which wicked men have trodden? Who said to God: Depart from us; and what good can the Almighty do us? Knowest thou not this truth of old time, since ever man was placed upon the earth: The triumph of the wicked is short; the joy of the godless is but for a moment. Like a dream he fleeth and cannot be found; he is chased away like a vision of the night. The eye that saw him shall see him no more; neither shall his place behold him again. He shall not look upon flowing waters; much as he gained enjoyed he not; because his greed knoweth no rest, and naught was left that he would not devour. The heavens shall reveal his guilt, and the earth rise up against him; and he will be swept away in the day of God's judgment.

This is the lot of a wicked man, the heritage appointed him of God. Make peace with God and prosper; thereby shall thine increase be good. Receive the law from His mouth, and lay up His words in thy heart. If thou turn to the Almighty, thy face shall not be put to shame; if thou put away unrighteousness out of thy tents, then shalt thou be built up. Then shalt thou delight thyself in the Almighty, and lift thy face unto God. To Him shalt thou pray, and He shall hear thee. What thou decidest shall stand fast, and light shall shine upon thy ways. The humble person God shall save: He will deliver the man that is innocent.

(Job, xxv and xxvi, 5 to 12.)

DOMINION and fear are with God; He holdeth sway in the heights. Have His armies any number? And upon whom doth His light not arise? The shades tremble beneath, the waters and they that dwell therein. He stretcheth out the North upon chaos, and hangeth the earth upon nothing. He bindeth up the waters in His black clouds; and the cloud-web is not rent beneath them; He enshroudeth the face of His throne, and spreadeth His cloud upon it. On the waters He setteth a circle, at the confines of light and darkness. The pillars of heaven tremble, they are astonished at His rebuke. He stirreth up the sea by His power, and by His wisdom He pierceth the darkness; by His breath the heavens are bright. Lo, these are but the outskirts of His way; how small a whisper is heard thereof! For the thunder of His power who could understand?

(Job, xxviii.)

MAN maketh an end of darkness, searching out to the uttermost bounds, stones of darkness and of deep shadow. He breaketh a shaft where none sojourn; they are forgotten of them that pass; afar from men, they hang, they swing. Out of the earth there cometh bread; and underneath, it is twisted as by fire; a place of sapphires are its stones, and dust of gold is found there. It is a path no vulture knoweth, and the falcon's eye hath not seen it; the boldest beast hath not trodden it; the fierce lion hath not passed thereby. Man putteth his hand to the flinty rock; he overturneth the mountains by the roots. He cutteth out channels among the rocks; and his eye seeth all that is precious. He bindeth the streams that they weep not; and that which is hid, he bringeth to light.

But wisdom—where shall it be found? And where is the place of knowledge? Man knoweth not the price thereof; and it is not found in the land of the living. The deep saith: It is not in me; and the sea saith: I have it not. Treasure may not be given therefor, nor silver be weighed for its price. It cannot be valued with the gold of Ophir, with costly onyx, or sapphire. Coral or crystal cannot equal it; yea, the price of wisdom is greater than pearls. The topaz of Ethiopia doth not equal it; it may not be matched with purest gold. Wisdom— whence doth it come? and where is the home of knowledge which is hid from the eyes of all living, and concealed from the fowls of the air? Destruction and death have said: With our ears have we heard a rumor thereof.

God understandeth the way thereto, and He knoweth the home thereof. For He beholdeth the ends of the earth, and seeth all that is under the heavens; appointing to the winds their weight, and meting out the waters by measure; establishing for the rain a law, and a way for the bolt of the thunder. He hath seen and numbered it; He established it, yea, and searched it out. And to man He said:

> Behold, the fear of the Lord is wisdom;
> To refrain from evil is knowledge.

HYMN.

THE sun goes down, the shadows rise,
　The day of God is near its close;
The glowing orb now homeward flies
A gentle breeze foretells repose.
Lord, crown our work before the night:
In the eve let there be light.

While still in clouds the sun delays,
Let us soar up, soar up to heaven;
That love may shed its peaceful rays,
New hope unto our souls be given.
O may the parting hour be bright:
In the eve let there be light.

And when our sun of life retreats,
When evening shadows 'round us hover,
Our restless heart no longer beats,
And grave-ward sinks our earthly cover,
We shall behold a glorious sight,
In the eve there shall be light.

Minister:

PRAISE be unto Thee, O Eternal, our God, God of our fathers Abraham, Isaac and Jacob; the great, mighty, and most high God. Thou bestowest lovingkindness upon all Thy creatures; Thou rememberest the goodness of the fathers, and Thou sendest redemption to their descendants for the sake of Thy name.

Remember us unto life, O Sovereign, who ordainest life, and seal us in the book of life, for Thy sake, O God of life. Thou art our helper, our redeemer and protector. Praise be to Thee, O God, shield of Abraham.

Thou art omnipotent, O Lord, and mighty to save. In Thy kindness Thou sustainest the living, upholdest the falling, healest the sick, and settest the captives free. Thou wilt, of a surety, fulfil Thy promise of immortal life unto those who sleep in the dust. Who is like unto Thee, Almighty, Author of life and death, Thou who sendest salvation.

Who is like unto Thee, Father of mercies, who rememberest Thy children unto life eternal. Praise be to Thee, O God, who hast implanted within us immortal life.

SANCTIFICATION.

(Congregation standing.)

We hallow Thy name on earth, even as it is hallowed in heaven; and with the prophet say in humble adoration:

DAY OF ATONEMENT. 317

בָּרוּךְ אַתָּה יְיָ אֱלֹהֵינוּ וֵאלֹהֵי אֲבוֹתֵינוּ. אֱלֹהֵי אַבְרָהָם אֱלֹהֵי יִצְחָק וֵאלֹהֵי יַעֲקֹב. הָאֵל הַגָּדוֹל הַגִּבּוֹר וְהַנּוֹרָא. אֵל עֶלְיוֹן. גּוֹמֵל חֲסָדִים טוֹבִים. וְקֹנֵה הַכֹּל וְזוֹכֵר חַסְדֵי אָבוֹת. וּמֵבִיא גְאֻלָּה לִבְנֵי בְנֵיהֶם. לְמַעַן שְׁמוֹ בְּאַהֲבָה:

זָכְרֵנוּ לַחַיִּים. מֶלֶךְ חָפֵץ בַּחַיִּים. וְחָתְמֵנוּ בְּסֵפֶר הַחַיִּים. לְמַעַנְךָ אֱלֹהִים חַיִּים:

מֶלֶךְ עוֹזֵר וּמוֹשִׁיעַ וּמָגֵן. בָּרוּךְ אַתָּה יְיָ מָגֵן אַבְרָהָם:

אַתָּה גִבּוֹר לְעוֹלָם אֲדֹנָי. רַב לְהוֹשִׁיעַ. מְכַלְכֵּל חַיִּים בְּחֶסֶד. מְחַיֶּה הַכֹּל בְּרַחֲמִים רַבִּים. סוֹמֵךְ נוֹפְלִים וְרוֹפֵא חוֹלִים וּמַתִּיר אֲסוּרִים. וּמְקַיֵּם אֱמוּנָתוֹ לִישֵׁנֵי עָפָר. מִי כָמוֹךָ בַּעַל גְּבוּרוֹת. וּמִי דוֹמֶה לָּךְ. מֶלֶךְ מֵמִית וּמְחַיֶּה. וּמַצְמִיחַ יְשׁוּעָה:

מִי כָמוֹךָ אַב הָרַחֲמִים. זוֹכֵר יְצוּרָיו לַחַיִּים בְּרַחֲמִים: בָּרוּךְ אַתָּה יְיָ נֹטֵעַ בְּתוֹכֵנוּ חַיֵּי עוֹלָם:

(Congregation standing.)

נְקַדֵּשׁ אֶת שִׁמְךָ בָּעוֹלָם. כְּשֵׁם שֶׁמַּקְדִּישִׁים אוֹתוֹ בִּשְׁמֵי מָרוֹם. כַּכָּתוּב עַל־יַד נְבִיאֶךָ. וְקָרָא זֶה אֶל־זֶה וְאָמַר:

Choir and Congregation:

Holy, holy, holy is the Lord of hosts, the whole earth is full of His glory.

Minister:

God our strength, God our Lord, how excellent is Thy name in all the earth.

Choir and Congregation:

In all places of Thy dominion Thy name is praised and glorified.

Minister:

Our God is one; He is our Father; He is our King; He is our Helper; and in His mercy He will answer our petition in the sight of all the living.

Choir and Congregation:

God will reign forever, thy God, O Zion, from generation to generation.—Hallelujah!

(Congregation sitting.)

Minister:

Holy art Thou and awe-inspiring is Thy name. There is no God beside Thee. The Lord of hosts is exalted in judgment and the Holy One is sanctified through righteousness. Praise be to Thee, O God, who rulest in holiness.

Choir:—Amen.

DAY OF ATONEMENT.

Choir and Congregation:

קָדוֹשׁ קָדוֹשׁ קָדוֹשׁ יְיָ צְבָאוֹת. מְלֹא כָל־הָאָרֶץ כְּבוֹדוֹ:

Minister:

אַדִּיר אַדִּירֵנוּ יְיָ אֲדוֹנֵנוּ מָה־אַדִּיר שִׁמְךָ בְּכָל הָאָרֶץ:

Choir and Congregation:

בָּרוּךְ כְּבוֹד יְיָ מִמְּקוֹמוֹ:

Minister:

אֶחָד הוּא אֱלֹהֵינוּ. הוּא אָבִינוּ. הוּא מַלְכֵּנוּ. וְהוּא מוֹשִׁיעֵנוּ: וְהוּא יַשְׁמִיעֵנוּ בְּרַחֲמָיו לְעֵינֵי כָל־חָי:

Choir and Congregation:

יִמְלֹךְ יְיָ לְעוֹלָם אֱלֹהַיִךְ צִיּוֹן לְדֹר וָדֹר הַלְלוּיָהּ:

(Congregation sitting.)

Minister:

קָדוֹשׁ אַתָּה וְנוֹרָא שְׁמֶךָ. וְאֵין אֱלוֹהַּ מִבַּלְעָדֶיךָ. כַּכָּתוּב. וַיִּגְבַּהּ יְיָ צְבָאוֹת בַּמִּשְׁפָּט. וְהָאֵל הַקָּדוֹשׁ נִקְדָּשׁ בִּצְדָקָה. בָּרוּךְ אַתָּה יְיָ הַמֶּלֶךְ הַקָּדוֹשׁ:

Choir:—Amen.

Minister and Congregation:

THE Lord is King; He did **reign** and He will reign for ever and ever.

Before the heavens were spread out, or the earth was founded, the Lord did reign. Ere the bright lights shone forth, and the darkness fled, the Lord did reign. And when the earth shall decay, and the heavens be no more,

Congregation:

The Lord shall reign for ever and **ever.**

Before the soil teemed with life, or paths were trod, the Lord did reign. When man arose and subdued the earth, the Lord did reign. And when the earth shall turn to chaos again, and darkness will enshroud all,

Congregation:

The Lord will reign for ever and **ever.**

O GOD, mighty in deeds, grant us pardon at the time of the concluding prayer of this day.

Congregation:

May it please Thee, O Father, to hear our prayer.

They who are few in number, raise their eyes towards Thee, and with awe they supplicate Thee, at this time of the concluding prayer.

DAY OF ATONEMENT. 321

Minister and Congregation:

יְיָ מֶלֶךְ · יְיָ מָלָךְ · יְיָ יִמְלוֹךְ לְעוֹלָם וָעֶד:

בְּטֶרֶם שְׁחָקִים וַאֲרָקִים נִמְתָּחוּ . יְיָ מֶלֶךְ:

וְעַד־לֹא מְאוֹרוֹת זָרְחוּ . יְיָ מָלָךְ:

וְהָאָרֶץ כַּבֶּגֶד תִּבְלֶה · וְהַשָּׁמַיִם כֶּעָשָׁן נִמְלָחוּ .

יְיָ יִמְלוֹךְ לְעוֹלָם וָעֶד:

וְעַד־לֹא עָשָׂה אֶרֶץ וְחוּצוֹת . יְיָ מֶלֶךְ:

וּבַהֲכִינוֹ יְצוּרִים עֲלֵי אֲרָצוֹת . יְיָ מָלָךְ:

יַרְגִּיז אֶרֶץ מִמְּקוֹמָהּ · וְתַכַּס עֲמוּדֶיהָ פַּלָּצוּת .

יְיָ יִמְלוֹךְ לְעוֹלָם וָעֶד:

אֵל נוֹרָא עֲלִילָה:

אֵל נוֹרָא עֲלִילָה · הַמְצִיא לָנוּ מְחִילָה · בִּשְׁעַת
הַנְּעִילָה:

אֵל נוֹרָא עֲלִילָה:

מְתֵי מִסְפָּר קְרוּאִים · לְךָ עַיִן נוֹשְׂאִים · וּמְסַלְּדִים
בְּחִילָה · בִּשְׁעַת הַנְּעִילָה:

אֵל נוֹרָא עֲלִילָה:

Congregation:

May it please Thee, O Father, to hear our prayer.

The feelings of their heart they express before Thee. O efface their transgressions and guilt, and let them obtain forgiveness at this time of the concluding prayer.

Congregation:

May it please Thee, O Father, to hear our prayer.

Protect and deliver them from every calamity, and grant them joy at this time of the concluding prayer.

Congregation:

May it please Thee, O Father, to hear our prayer.

O God, mighty in deeds, grant us pardon at the time of the concluding prayer of this day.

Congregation:

May it please Thee, O Father, to hear our prayer.

At the close of this day of rest we humbly approach Thee; incline Thine ear to us, O Thou who dwellest on high.

Congregation:

Hearken to our entreaties and our supplications.

May the cry of those who fear Thee, come before Thy throne; grant their petitions and answer them.

DAY OF ATONEMENT. 323

שׁוֹפְכִים לְךָ נַפְשָׁם . מְחֵה נָא פִשְׁעָם . וְתַמְצִיאֵם
מְחִילָה . בִּשְׁעַת הַנְּעִילָה :

אֵל נוֹרָא עֲלִילָה :

זְכוֹר צִדְקַת אֲבִיהֶם . וְחַדֵּשׁ אֶת יְמֵיהֶם . כְּקֶדֶם
וּתְחִלָּה . בִּשְׁעַת הַנְּעִילָה :

אֵל נוֹרָא עֲלִילָה :

חֱיֵה לָהֶם לְסִתְרָה . וְחַלְּצֵם מִמְּאֵרָה . וְזָכְרֵם לְדוֹר
וּלְגִילָה . בִּשְׁעַת הַנְּעִילָה :

אֵל נוֹרָא עֲלִילָה :

אֵל נוֹרָא עֲלִילָה . הַמְצֵא לָנוּ מְחִילָה . בִּשְׁעַת
הַנְּעִילָה :

בְּמוֹצָאֵי מְנוּחָה . קִדַּמְנוּךָ תְּחִלָּה . הַט אָזְנְךָ
מִמָּרוֹם יוֹשֵׁב תְּהִלָּה .

לִשְׁמוֹעַ אֶל הָרִנָּה וְאֶל הַתְּפִלָּה :

Congregation:

O Thou who hearest prayer, on Thee we call.

Israel shall be saved by the Lord with an everlasting salvation. This day announce Thy help, O Most High.

Congregation:

O Thou who art full of compassion and mercy, answer us.

Shelter us, O Lord, under the wings of Thy mercy; Thou, who searchest the heart, strengthen us and teach us to find Thee.

Congregation:

O Lord, our strength, be attentive to our supplication.

Let us hear Thy word of pardon, O God, who art unsearchable; uphold us with Thy right hand and graciously accept us.

Congregation:

O Eternal, our God, be Thou our help.

We come unto Thee, O God, to seek forgiveness; dismiss us not empty from Thy presence, nor put us to shame.

Congregation:

Send us help from on high, for mercy and truth come from Thee.

DAY OF ATONEMENT.

אֶנְקַת מְסַלְדֶיךָ. תַּעַל לִפְנֵי כִסֵּא כְבוֹדֶךָ. מַלֵּא מִשְׁאֲלוֹת עַם מְיַחֲדֶיךָ.

שׁוֹמֵעַ תְּפִלַּת בָּאֵי עָדֶךָ:

יִשְׂרָאֵל נוֹשַׁע בַּיְיָ תְּשׁוּעַת עוֹלָמִים. גַּם הַיּוֹם יִוָּשְׁעוּ מִפִּיךָ שׁוֹכֵן מְרוֹמִים.

כִּי אַתָּה רַב סְלִיחוֹת וּבַעַל הָרַחֲמִים:

יַחֲבִיאֵנוּ צֵל יָדוֹ תַּחַת כַּנְפֵי הַשְּׁכִינָה. חוֹן יָחוֹן כִּי יִבְחוֹן לֵב עָקוֹב לַהֲכִינָה. קוּמָה נָא אֱלֹהֵינוּ עֲנֵה עָנִי נָא:

יְיָ לְשַׁוְעָתֵנוּ הַאֲזִינָה:

יַשְׁמִיעֵנוּ סָלָחְתִּי יוֹשֵׁב בְּסֵתֶר עֶלְיוֹן. בִּימִין יֵשַׁע לְהוֹשֵׁעַ עַם עָנִי וְאֶבְיוֹן. בְּשַׁוְּעֵנוּ אֵלֶיךָ נוֹרָאוֹת בְּצֶדֶק תַּעֲנֵנוּ.

יְיָ הֱיֵה עוֹזֵר לָנוּ:

אָתָאנוּ לְחַלּוֹת פָּנֶיךָ. כִּי חֶסֶד וֶאֱמֶת יְקַדְּמוּ פָנֶיךָ: נָא אַל תְּבִישֵׁנוּ. נָא אַל תְּשִׁיבֵנוּ רֵיקָם מִלְּפָנֶיךָ:

סְלַח לָנוּ. וּשְׁלַח לָנוּ יְשׁוּעָה וְרַחֲמִים מִמְּעוֹנֶךָ:

We come unto Thee, O God, to seek atonement; O, quicken us and be gracious unto us, when we call on Thee.

Congregation:

Send us help from Thy sanctuary, Thou who art our refuge in time of need.

Minister:

THOU puttest forth Thy hand unto him who is astray, and Thy right hand is outstretched to take back in love those who turn again unto Thee. Thou hast taught us, O Lord, to acknowledge all our sins before Thee, to the end that we may withhold our hands from unrighteousness. Receive our sincere repentance. Thou knowest, O Lord, that we are but dust and ashes; therefore, Thou art ready to forgive. What are we, and what is our life? What is our merit and what our righteousness? What is our power, what our strength? What can we say before Thee, O Lord, God of our fathers? Are not our heroes as naught before Thee, men of renown as though they had never been, the wise as though without knowledge, the intelligent as though without reason; for the sum of their deeds is vanity, the days of their life are as nothing before Thee.

Thou hast chosen mortal man to know and to reverence Thee. For, who dare say unto Thee, what doest Thou? And though man were righteous, of what advantage could he be to Thee? In Thy love Thou hast given us this Day of Atonement, to forgive and

DAY OF ATONEMENT. 327

אָתָאנוּ לְבַקֵּשׁ מִמְּךָ כַּפָּרָה. אָיוֹם וְנוֹרָא. מְשֻׂגָּב
לְעִתּוֹת בַּצָּרָה: תְּחַיֵּינוּ וּתְחָנֵּנוּ. וּבְשִׁמְךָ נִקְרָא:
סְלַח לָנוּ. וּשְׁלַח לָנוּ סְלִיחָה וְרַחֲמִים מִמְּעוֹנֶךָ:

Minister:

אַתָּה נוֹתֵן יָד לְפוֹשְׁעִים וִימִינְךָ פְּשׁוּטָה לְקַבֵּל
שָׁבִים וַתְּלַמְּדֵנוּ יְיָ אֱלֹהֵינוּ לְהִתְוַדּוֹת לְפָנֶיךָ עַל
כָּל עֲוֹנוֹתֵינוּ וּתְקַבְּלֵנוּ בִּתְשׁוּבָה שְׁלֵמָה לְפָנֶיךָ
לְמַעַן דְּבָרֶיךָ אֲשֶׁר אָמַרְתָּ: וְאַתָּה יוֹדֵעַ
שֶׁאַחֲרִיתֵנוּ רִמָּה וְתוֹלֵעָה לְפִיכָךְ הִרְבֵּית סְלִיחָתֵנוּ
מָה אָנוּ מֶה חַיֵּינוּ מֶה חַסְדֵּנוּ מַה צִּדְקֵנוּ מַה
יִּשְׁעֵנוּ מַה כֹּחֵנוּ מַה גְּבוּרָתֵנוּ וּמַה נֹּאמַר לְפָנֶיךָ
יְיָ אֱלֹהֵינוּ וֵאלֹהֵי אֲבוֹתֵינוּ הֲלֹא כָּל הַגִּבּוֹרִים
כְּאַיִן לְפָנֶיךָ וְאַנְשֵׁי הַשֵּׁם כְּלֹא הָיוּ וַחֲכָמִים כִּבְלִי
מַדָּע וּנְבוֹנִים כִּבְלִי הַשְׂכֵּל כִּי רוֹב מַעֲשֵׂיהֶם
תֹּהוּ וִימֵי חַיֵּיהֶם הֶבֶל לְפָנֶיךָ:

אַתָּה הִבְדַּלְתָּ אֱנוֹשׁ מֵרֹאשׁ. וַתַּכִּירֵהוּ לַעֲמוֹד
לְפָנֶיךָ. כִּי מִי יֹאמַר לְךָ מַה תִּפְעָל. וְאִם יִצְדַּק
מַה יִּתֶּן לָךְ: וַתִּתֶּן לָנוּ יְיָ אֱלֹהֵינוּ. בְּאַהֲבָה אֶת
יוֹם הַכִּפֻּרִים הַזֶּה. לִמְחִילָה וּסְלִיחָה עַל כָּל
עֲוֹנוֹתֵינוּ. לְמַעַן נֶחְדַּל מֵעֹשֶׁק יָדֵינוּ. וְנָשׁוּב אֵלֶיךָ
לַעֲשׂוֹת חֻקֵּי רְצוֹנְךָ בְּלֵבָב שָׁלֵם: וְאַתָּה בְּרַחֲמֶיךָ

pardon all our sins, that we may withdraw from unrighteousness and turn again to Thee to do Thy will with a perfect heart. Have pity upon us in Thy mercy, for it is not Thy desire that man should perish. Seek ye the Lord while He may be found, call ye upon Him while He is near; let the wicked forsake his ways, and the unrighteous man his evil thoughts, and let him return unto the Lord, who will have mercy upon him, and to our God, who will abundantly pardon. Yes, Thou art merciful and gracious, long-suffering and of infinite patience and faithfulness; Thou desirest only the repentance of the sinner, not his destruction, as the prophet has spoken: Say to them, As I live, saith God, the Lord, I desire not the death of the sinner, but that he should turn from his evil ways and live. Therefore, turn ye from your evil ways; wherefore will ye die, O house of Israel?

Pardon our transgressions, O God, on this Day of Atonement; remove our guilt, and blot out our iniquities, as Thou hast promised: I, even I, blot out thine iniquities for my sake, and thy sins will I remember no more. I have made thy sins to vanish, like a cloud, and thy transgressions, like a mist; return to me for I have redeemed thee. On this day shall ye be forgiven and cleansed from all your sins; before God ye shall be pure.

Praised be Thou, O God, who forgivest transgressions, King of the world, who sanctifiest Israel, and the Day of Atonement.

Choir:—Amen.

DAY OF ATONEMENT.

הָרַבִּים רַחֵם עָלֵינוּ. כִּי לֹא תַחְפּוֹץ בְּהַשְׁחָתַת
עוֹלָם. שֶׁנֶּאֱמַר דִּרְשׁוּ יְיָ בְּהִמָּצְאוֹ קְרָאֻהוּ בִּהְיוֹתוֹ
קָרוֹב: וְנֶאֱמַר יַעֲזֹב רָשָׁע דַּרְכּוֹ וְאִישׁ אָוֶן
מַחְשְׁבֹתָיו. וְיָשֹׁב אֶל יְיָ וִירַחֲמֵהוּ וְאֶל אֱלֹהֵינוּ כִּי
יַרְבֶּה לִסְלוֹחַ: וְאַתָּה אֱלוֹהַּ סְלִיחוֹת. חַנּוּן וְרַחוּם
אֶרֶךְ אַפַּיִם וְרַב חֶסֶד וֶאֱמֶת וּמַרְבֶּה לְהֵטִיב.
וְרוֹצֶה אַתָּה בִּתְשׁוּבַת רְשָׁעִים וְאֵין אַתָּה חָפֵץ
בְּמִיתָתָם. שֶׁנֶּאֱמַר אֱמֹר אֲלֵיהֶם חַי אָנִי
נְאֻם אֲדֹנָי יֱהוִֹה. אִם אֶחְפֹּץ בְּמוֹת הָרָשָׁע. כִּי
אִם בְּשׁוּב רָשָׁע מִדַּרְכּוֹ וְחָיָה: שׁוּבוּ שׁוּבוּ
מִדַּרְכֵיכֶם הָרָעִים. וְלָמָּה תָמוּתוּ בֵּית יִשְׂרָאֵל:
וְנֶאֱמַר. הֶחָפֹץ אֶחְפֹּץ מוֹת רָשָׁע. נְאֻם אֲדֹנָי
יֱהוִֹה. הֲלֹא בְּשׁוּבוֹ מִדְּרָכָיו וְחָיָה:

אֱלֹהֵינוּ וֵאלֹהֵי אֲבוֹתֵינוּ. מְחַל לַעֲוֹנוֹתֵינוּ בְּיוֹם
הַכִּפּוּרִים הַזֶּה. מְחֵה וְהַעֲבֵר פְּשָׁעֵינוּ וְחַטֹּאתֵינוּ
מִנֶּגֶד עֵינֶיךָ. כָּאָמוּר. אָנֹכִי אָנֹכִי הוּא מֹחֶה
פְשָׁעֶיךָ לְמַעֲנִי וְחַטֹּאתֶיךָ לֹא אֶזְכֹּר: וְנֶאֱמַר.
מָחִיתִי כָעָב פְּשָׁעֶיךָ. וְכֶעָנָן חַטֹּאתֶיךָ. שׁוּבָה אֵלַי
כִּי גְאַלְתִּיךָ: וְנֶאֱמַר. כִּי בַיּוֹם הַזֶּה יְכַפֵּר עֲלֵיכֶם
לְטַהֵר אֶתְכֶם מִכֹּל חַטֹּאתֵיכֶם. לִפְנֵי יְיָ תִּטְהָרוּ:

בָּרוּךְ אַתָּה יְיָ מֶלֶךְ מוֹחֵל וְסוֹלֵחַ לַעֲוֹנוֹתֵינוּ מֶלֶךְ
עַל כָּל הָאָרֶץ מְקַדֵּשׁ יִשְׂרָאֵל וְיוֹם הַכִּפּוּרִים:

Alternate Reading for Minister and Congregation:

SEEK ye the Lord while He may be found; call ye upon Him while He is near.

Let the wicked forsake his way, and the unrighteous man his thoughts;

Let him return unto the Lord, and He will have mercy upon him; and to our God, for He will abundantly pardon.

For my thoughts are not your thoughts, neither are your ways my ways, saith the Lord.

For as high as the heavens are above the earth, so are my ways higher than your ways, and my thoughts higher than your thoughts.

For, as the rain cometh down and the snow from heaven, and returneth not thither;

But watereth the earth, and maketh it bring forth and bud;

That it may give seed to the sower and bread to the eater:

So shall my word be that goeth forth out of my mouth; and it shall not return to me void;

But it shall accomplish that which I please, and it shall prosper in the thing whereto I sent it.

Israel shall be saved by the Lord with an everlasting salvation; ye shall not be put to shame nor confounded.

Light is sown for the righteous, and joy for the upright heart.

DAY OF ATONEMENT.

Minister and Congregation, then Choir:

Open unto us, O God, the gates of mercy, before the closing of the gates, ere the day is done. The day vanishes, the sun is setting; let us enter Thy gates.

פְּתַח לָנוּ שַׁעַר . בְּעֵת נְעִילַת שָׁעַר . כִּי פָנָה יוֹם : הַיּוֹם יִפְנֶה . הַשֶּׁמֶשׁ יָבֹא וְיִפְנֶה . נָבוֹאָה שְׁעָרֶיךָ :

Minister:

THE day is fading, the sun is setting; the silence and peace of night descend upon the earth. Vouchsafe rest, O Father of peace, unto our disquieted hearts; lift up the soul that is cast down. Turn, in Thine all-forgiving love, to Thy children that hope for Thy mercy; turn, O Father, to all fainting hearts, to all heavy-laden souls. Let this hour bring us the assurance that Thou hast forgiven, that we have found favor in Thy sight. O consecrate our hearts unto Thee, and make them Thy living altars, whereon shall burn the holy flame of devotion to Thee, O merciful God.

From Thy house, O kind Father, we are about to return to our homes, to seek the shelter which Thou hast prepared for us in the dear communion of our family life. Open unto us the gates of Thy love! O enter Thou with us into our home, that it may become Thy dwelling-place, Thy sanctuary, and that

Thy spirit abide within its walls. Then will our tent stand firm in the midst of all tempest and trials, be a grateful shade against heat, a shelter for all that is good, a bulwark against temptation.

And still another dwelling Thou hast destined for us, O Father of life, an eternal abode, the last resting place to which we shall all go after the brief day of life has closed. Open unto us the gate of Thy grace: unlock for us the portals of eternal peace when the gates of our earthly home shall close for ever behind us. Be Thou our guiding star on our homeward journey, that we may go hence in joy and dwell in peace. Let Thy light shine in the night of our death as the dawn of a new morning; that from our grave may sprout not the barren thistle, but the fragrant myrtle, a blessed memory redounding to Thy honor and glory.

This twilight hour reminds also of the even-tide when, according to Thy gracious promise, Thy light will arise over all the children of men, and Israel's spiritual descendants will be as numerous as the stars in heaven. Endow us, our Guardian, with strength and patience for our holy mission. Grant that all the children of Thy people may recognize the goal of our changeful career, so that they may exemplify by their zeal and love for mankind the truth of Israel's watchword: One humanity on earth, even as there is but One God in heaven. Enlighten all that call themselves by Thy name with the knowledge that the sanctuary of wood and stone which erst crowned Zion's hill, was but a gate, through which Israel should step out into the world, to reconcile all mankind unto Thee!

Thou alone, knowest when this work of atonement shall be completed; when the day shall dawn in which the light of Thy truth, brighter than that of the visible sun, shall encircle the whole earth. But, surely, that great day of universal reconciliation, so fervently prayed for, shall come, as surely as none of Thy words return empty, unless they have done that for which Thou didst send them. Then joy shall thrill all hearts, and from one end of the earth to the other shall echo the gladsome cry. Hear, O Israel, hear, all mankind, the Eternal, our God, the Eternal is One! Then myriads will make pilgrimage to Thy house, which shall be called a house of prayer for all nations, and from their lips shall sound in spiritual joy: Lord, open for us the gates of Thy truth, now when the gates of the old world are closing. Lift up your heads, O ye gates, and be ye lifted up, ye everlasting doors, for the King of glory shall come. Who is the King of glory? The Lord strong and mighty, the Lord of hosts, the Prince of peace.

Choir:

Lift up your heads, O ye gates, and be lifted up ye everlasting doors, for the King of glory shall come.

Who is the King of glory? The Lord of hosts— **He is the** King of glory. Selah!

LOOK down with compassion, O Lord, upon Israel, Thy servant, and in Thy love accept his worship offered Thee at all times. Praise be to Thee, O Lord, whom alone we will serve in reverence.

We gratefully acknowledge, O Lord, our God, that Thou art our creator and preserver, the rock of our life and the shield of our help. We render thanks unto Thee for our lives which are in Thy hands, for our souls which are ever in Thy keeping, for Thy wondrous providence and for Thy continuous goodness, which Thou bestowest upon us day by day. Truly, Thy mercies never fail and Thy loving-kindness never ceases. Therefore, in Thee do we forever put our trust.

OUR God, and God of our fathers, O may Thy blessing rest upon us, according to the gracious promise of Thy word, spoken through the priests of yore, ministering at Thy holy altar, saying:

May the Lord bless thee and keep thee.

Choir:—Amen.

May the Lord let his countenance shine upon thee and be gracious unto thee.

Choir:—Amen.

May the Lord lift up his countenance upon thee and give thee peace.

Choir:—Amen.

DAY OF ATONEMENT.

רְצֵה יְיָ אֱלֹהֵינוּ בְּעַמְּךָ יִשְׂרָאֵל. וּתְפִלָּתָם בְּאַהֲבָה תְקַבֵּל. וּתְהִי לְרָצוֹן תָּמִיד עֲבוֹדַת יִשְׂרָאֵל עַמֶּךָ. בָּרוּךְ אַתָּה יְיָ שֶׁאוֹתְךָ לְבַדְּךָ בְּיִרְאָה נַעֲבוֹד:

מוֹדִים אֲנַחְנוּ לָךְ. שָׁאַתָּה הוּא יְיָ אֱלֹהֵינוּ וֵאלֹהֵי אֲבוֹתֵינוּ לְעוֹלָם וָעֶד. צוּר חַיֵּינוּ מָגֵן יִשְׁעֵנוּ. אַתָּה הוּא לְדוֹר וָדוֹר. נוֹדֶה לְּךָ וּנְסַפֵּר תְּהִלָּתֶךָ. עַל חַיֵּינוּ הַמְּסוּרִים בְּיָדֶךָ. וְעַל נִשְׁמוֹתֵינוּ הַפְּקוּדוֹת לָךְ. וְעַל נִסֶּיךָ שֶׁבְּכָל־יוֹם עִמָּנוּ. וְעַל נִפְלְאוֹתֶיךָ שֶׁבְּכָל־עֵת. עֶרֶב וָבֹקֶר וְצָהֳרָיִם. הַטּוֹב כִּי לֹא־כָלוּ רַחֲמֶיךָ. וְהַמְרַחֵם כִּי לֹא־תַמּוּ חֲסָדֶיךָ. מֵעוֹלָם קִוִּינוּ לָךְ:

אֱלֹהֵינוּ וֵאלֹהֵי אֲבוֹתֵינוּ. בָּרְכֵנוּ בַּבְּרָכָה הַמְשֻׁלֶּשֶׁת הַכְּתוּבָה בַּתּוֹרָה:

יְבָרֶכְךָ יְיָ וְיִשְׁמְרֶךָ:

Choir:—Amen.

יָאֵר יְיָ פָּנָיו אֵלֶיךָ וִיחֻנֶּךָּ:

Choir:—Amen.

יִשָּׂא יְיָ פָּנָיו אֵלֶיךָ וְיָשֵׂם לְךָ שָׁלוֹם:

Choir:—Amen.

Minister:

(Before the open Ark.)

O LORD, whither shall I go before Thy spirit? or whither shall I flee from Thy presence? If I ascend into heaven, Thou art there, and if I lie down in the nether-world, behold, Thou art there. And if I take the wings of the morning and fly to the uttermost parts of the sea, even there shall Thy hand lead me, and Thy right hand hold me. And if I say: Surely the darkness shall cover me—even the night shall be light about me. Yea, darkness hideth not from Thee, but night shineth as day, darkness and light are alike unto Thee. I will praise Thee, O Lord, who hast made me wonderfully. Marvelous are Thy works, and that my soul knoweth right well.

When I consider Thy heavens, the work of Thy hands; when I think of the wonders of the universe, the countless hosts of stars which move with inconceivable speed through the immensities of space and time; when, soaring from sun to sun and from world to world, I endeavor to fathom the extent of Thy majesty, the end of Thy power, the source of Thy wisdom, O Infinite One, I am bewildered at the thought of Thy greatness. Before Thee all these myriads of worlds are but a breath of Thy spirit, and all these luminous orbs, sparks of Thy light. What is man that Thou hast given him to perceive Thy truth, and to follow Thy sublime thoughts! For what is the earth with all the beauty and richness of life, with its forests filled with song and melody, with its stupendous mountains, reared like pillars, with its roaring billows of the tempestuous sea; what the stars' majestic pageant and the brilliancy of their light, the mysteries of the boundless depths and heights of creation, hadst Thou not placed man at their very summit, to herald forth Thy grandeur and to voice the longing of all beings for Thee, O King of the Universe, Fountain of all goodness, Father of love. In man, the son of dust and the child of heaven, Thou hast blended the two worlds: perishable earth and the spirit that lasts forever, finite matter, fettered to time and space, and the infinite power which soars through eternity. Thou hast made him a little lower than angels, nay, Thou hast crowned him with dignity and honor, to excel the seraph that sings Thy praise forever. Yet Thou desirest that he should humble his pride and bow his head in reverential obedience to Thee, O sublime Master.

But alas, passions dazzle his eye, and rebellion fills his heart with discord; and when he ought to rise above earth's temptations to join the assembly of the righteous and glorify Thee by a life of goodness, then the serpent of sin allures him, and the appetites overpower him, and alas, his life is filled with gloom. Nature no longer sings for him her charming carols; on account of his sins the earth seems shrouded in darkness, and within him sounds the voice of self-reproach: Man, where art thou? How hast thou fallen, son of the Most High!

But Thy mercy, O Lord, is without end. Thou

desirest not the death of the sinner, **but that he** should turn to Thee and live. Wide open are **the** gates of Thy forgiveness to all who seek **with singleness** of heart their peace with Thee.

Trusting in Thy gracious promise we have come before Thee, O Father, pining under our guilt, and yearning after Thine altars of peace. Heavily burdened we entered Thy sanctuary, longing and panting for Thy forgiveness. Accused by the judge within our bosom, and drooping under the load of our misdeeds, we mournfully reflected on a life misspent and filled with regrets, on hopes blasted and opportunities neglected; for before us rose the mystery of the future, the unknown, yet certain end. O, how beautiful are Thy dwellings, Lord of hosts! Better one day spent in Thy courts than a thousand without. Poor we came, and rich we depart. And now at the fall of eve, light dawns within us; **the** burden that weighed us down is lifted; our hope and our trust are revived; the gloomy shadow which darkened our spirit is vanished; and through the passing cloud breaks with the last ray of the setting sun the divine image of forgiving peace. We have not prayed, in vain, for Thy mercy and help. We feel that we are new-born, that our will and our desires are purified. We know our fate to be in Thy hand, and whatever it be, we are reconciled. Our hearts are filled with joy; and yet, solemn tones vibrate through our soul, as though we were standing at the threshhold of eternity. O God, what is man, that Thou thinkest of him? What the son of earth that Thou art mindful of him! Where shall mortal man find words worthily to thank Thee? The only praise which we can offer Thee is in reverence to sink into the dust and to adore Thee!

(Congregation standing.)

Minister and Congregation:

וַאֲנַחְנוּ כּוֹרְעִים וּמִשְׁתַּחֲוִים וּמוֹדִים לִפְנֵי מֶלֶךְ מַלְכֵי הַמְּלָכִים הַקָּדוֹשׁ בָּרוּךְ הוּא:

We bow our head and bend our knee before the King of kings, the Holy-One, the Ever-blest.

שְׁמַע יִשְׂרָאֵל יְהֹוָה אֱלֹהֵינוּ יְהֹוָה אֶחָד:

Hear, O Israel, the Eternal is our God, the Eternal is One.

בָּרוּךְ שֵׁם כְּבוֹד מַלְכוּתוֹ לְעוֹלָם וָעֶד:

Praised be His glorious name for evermore

יְהֹוָה הוּא הָאֱלֹהִים:

The Eternal is our God.

(Congregation sitting.)

BENEDICTION.

Minister:

AND now we implore Thee once more, O Lord, our God, at the close of this day's service, in the words of the high-priest of yore:

Let the year upon which we have entered be for us. for Israel and for all mankind:

A year of blessing and of prosperity.

Choir:—Amen.

A year of salvation and comfort.

Choir:—Amen.

A year of peace and contentment, of joy and of spiritual welfare.

Choir:—Amen.

A year of virtue and of fear of God.

Choir:—Amen.

A year which finds the hearts of parents united with the hearts of the children.

Choir:—Amen.

A year of Thy pardon and favor. Amen.

Choir:

The Lord will give His angels charge over thee to guard thee on all thy ways.

The Lord will bless thy going out and thy coming in, from this time forth, even forever. Amen.